ROAD SERIES

ROAD SERIES | HUGO RACE

MELBOURNE, AUSTRALIA
www.transitlounge.com.au

First Published 2016
Transit Lounge Publishing

Cover images: Corrado Vasquez
Cover and book design: Peter Lo

Printed in China by Everbest

This project has been assisted by the Australian government through the Australia Council for the Arts, its arts funding and advisory body.

A cataloguing- entry is available from the
National Library of Australia: http://catalogue.nla.gov.au
ISBN: 978-0-9943958-0-1

For Ruben and Violetta,
Elaine and Alannah

There are two gates of Sleep:
one of which is said to be of horn,
through which an easy passage is given to true shades,
the other gleams with the whiteness of polished ivory,
but through it the Gods of the Dead
send false dreams to the world above ...

– Virgil, *The Aeneid*

CONTENTS

Consciousness is only the beginning of the road;
the ultimate destination is unknown.

The Crystal Blitz | Melbourne, 1981

I can see myself lying on the bed. I've been awake for days, I've lost track of time, I feel like I'm somebody else. I'm busy, busy pretending to forget who I used to be.

The music inside my skull – I can feel it in the background of everything I do, a galaxy of frequencies shaping my thoughts and electrifying my flesh and blood. The music drills into my nervous system, its bitter dissonance chemical-sour in the back of my throat while the world shrieks with mystery. Here in the red-light district by the bay, the safety catch is off. We are reinventing ourselves in a new image, something we've never seen before reflected in each others' eyes – but the light, the light is very deceptive.

The front door of the St Kilda house I'm sharing with two tearaway schoolgirls is never locked. People just seem to come and go at all hours. I pay them scant attention. There's a box of stale cornflakes, a few chipped cups and a bowl in the kitchen cupboard. Several chairs scavenged from the street sit on the scarred linoleum floor near a box of groceries my mum brought over. I didn't hear her voice, just watched her lips move, and I think she said my frame was gaunt, that I looked haggard and bone-thin; it was a while ago now, before I moved out. Not that I told her I was leaving – I just walked out one day and didn't come back.

I wear the same clothes all the time, adopted from Salvation Army thrift store racks: suits and shirts in various shades of black, old man's clothes, even better with holes, defying the insipid fashions of the suburban zombie world through which I move. My head is full of high-frequency distortion, like an untuned television seething static. Nothing seems worth explaining. I don't want to talk. Nothing offends me quite like a question.

Music is my obsession, delivered at volume high enough to drown out the background noise of everyday life. Joy Division's Ian Curtis hanged himself six months ago and some said it was because he was married. Married? That came as a shock. The three of us in this house all come from so-called broken homes where marriage went out of fashion around the same time as tie-dye, patchouli, marijuana and folk music.

Instead, the Lounge Lizards' no-wave jazz spins on the turntable; the guitar sounds like it's being angle-grinded into sawdust and iron filings. The Channel Nine all-night movie marathon broadcasts films until dawn, Orson Welles's *Touch of Evil* introduces me to Henry Mancini film noir orchestrations, the *Ipcress File* to John Barry's austere Cold War exotica. I'm never bored; I read books, history more than fiction, and watch TV all night long until the century begins to open up for me with its evil fairytales of concentration camps and napalm and nuclear stockpiles and empires lost. Bowie's 'Five Years' has echoed through this teenage brain long enough. Clearly, it's time to get dissonant. I write and record atonal songs on a beaten-up cassette recorder until, in an unslept trance, it's time to go to work.

The warehouse manager, on my case since they hired me a fortnight ago, lies in waiting in the men's room in the basement. He kicks in the cubicle door where I'm reading a music magazine and glowers at me.

Are you slacking off on the job? Grab your kit and get the fuck out before I go you, mate.

I'm stunned by his incursion and before I've had time to think it through, I open my mouth – Yes, okay, I'm slacking off, what'd you expect? Nobody could take this mindless job seriously.

Get lost, he barks, and don't ask for a bloody reference!

Apparently the bare minimum I did was not enough to humour the boss.

I find my mate Richard as I'm quickly making my exit and grab the guitar, a white Rickenbacker copy he's selling me because he needs the cash to see AC/DC at the Myer Music Bowl next week. The neck and the body are separated, spray-painted chop-shop white. And now I'm broke, can't get the dole because I've been fired, don't know how I'll afford to have the guitar glued and bolted back together. I carry the parts home, walking 10 kilometres down Punt Road to the Wellington Street house.

The girls I live with are in the kitchen with their catlike friends, daintily shooting speed. They laugh like strobe lights, speaking sweet nothings in shrill voices. Amphetamine swirls around this sunny vortex of nihilism like the Wizz Fizz sherbet powder they've exchanged for a more decadent high. The cats shit on the floor and in the dead of night you can hear the girls scrubbing the carpets in time to the beat of Cabaret Voltaire's 'Nag, Nag, Nag'.

They're getting ready for a party here this evening, safety-pinning kewpie doll heads to the lapels of their faded trench coats, tying ribbons in their hair. Who's coming? I ask. Wait and see, they reply. That means they don't know. More strangers, more chaos.

I go to warn Bill, the downstairs neighbour, of our plans for tonight. Bill manages an independent record store on Greville Street, one of only two stores in the city of Melbourne where you can hear the latest underground releases from Britain and the US. The records are vinyl imports, expensive and mysterious, and they arrive after a time delay of several months in shipping containers.

Bill plays new releases by Wire, Chrome, Pere Ubu, records he thinks I'll like. Upstairs, we have a small record collection of thirty-odd albums that spin relentlessly, day in and night out. The default album is Public Image's *Metal Box* – anarchic electric-guitar music, the sound of speed. Since Elvis Presley, guitars are where it's at. Not that this noise sounds like Elvis – it's the premeditated opposite – because it's 1981 and provocation is the new entertainment. Provocation and shock get you noticed: more gigs, maybe a record deal. We dig deep into the unbeautiful, looking for a piece of action and reaction we can brand our own.

The band, Dum Dum Fix, rehearse in my bedroom using decrepit, second-hand gear inherited from my brother's band after they split up. A pale, volatile girl with long dark hair I've been seeing is auditioning for lead vocals but she can't really sing. When she slips out of the room to fetch a drink, the bass player asks me, Are you serious? She's tone deaf. You'll have to get rid of her, or I'm warning you, I'll quit!

But she looks the part, I reply, all she really needs is more rehearsal.

We don't have time for this, he says.

Right then she strides back into the room and proposes we learn a Fairport Convention cover. At this, the rest of the band lose all patience, making snide folk-rock asides as they pointedly put down their instruments. The poor girl throws a tantrum and storms out of the room, smashing a snow dome against the wall as she goes. I feel bad for her but the feeling quickly fades as the band get back to work, kicking up their arrhythmic, atonal howl.

I take the microphone myself and scream the lyrics tonelessly, slashing on the beat-up Burns solid-body six-string electric I swapped for a few Clash vinyls and a flagon of Penfolds claret with a teenage alcoholic from down the road. I'm not sure we understood each other exactly because I hear he's talking sour grapes behind my back about the trade but the guitar is untuneable and anyway, I've got my eye on a cut-down Maton Firebird at the Chapel Street Pawnbrokers. A hundred and twenty dollars and it's mine – but a hundred and twenty dollars is a month's rent, and money is so very hard to come by. Somehow we need to make a name for ourselves, get the band some gigs, make some money and buy proper instruments.

Robin, my friend and musical partner since we met at school aged thirteen, writes neat musical score on a Hohner electric piano while I load the playback deck with another of the cassettes we use as abstract background noise. Everybody's waiting for us to count in the next song: the bass player in the corner stares intently at a coffee stain on the carpet, my sister's boyfriend perches on the desk by the bay windows licking the reed on the tenor saxophone strapped around his skinny neck. Suddenly the drummer puts down his sticks and stands up.

Got to go home, he says, there's a funeral.

We all stare at him blankly.

My uncle, he says, the burial, it's today.

The band look suitably awed but I'm not so easily put off.

Why didn't you tell us before?

I forgot!

How are we going to ever put this together if you just keep walking out whenever you feel like it?

I told you, I forgot about it. It's not my fault he's dead!

Incredulous, I can the rehearsal and walk up Chapel Street to the Hare Krishna soup kitchen, Gopals. Before I've even sat down to eat, a shaven-headed, orange-sheeted case manager starts chatting me up about religion and spirituality, and the free rice and vegetable goulash suddenly sticks in my throat; I realise I've been coming here too often. I've already had my share of God and the Bible at the boys' school I finished with last year, spending most of final term on suspension in my bedroom writing and listening to records by The Pop Group, Eno, Talking Heads.

Back home the apartment is full of people, most of them I've never seen before. They sit or sprawl on the floor, Gang of Four on the turntable, sharing rollie cigarettes and beer. The air is thick with tobacco and cat shit. I try to hide out in my room but some hippie kids have taken it over, holding hands in a circle. The bathroom is locked; I can hear people inside having sex, knocking things over, yelling at me to fuck off and die.

In the lounge room, a tall guy with glasses and a mouth full-lipped as a goldfish is busily engraving our vinyl records one by one with a metal geometric compass. Don't be angry, says his girlfriend, it's just that he's off medication. He's drawing sunbeams on the records because he loves music. He doesn't mean any harm.

I move the band rehearsals to a loft over a Chapel Street whitegoods store where two girls have a screen-printing set-up and a vacant room. The room, formerly a painter's studio, is splattered with violent colour, walls, floor and ceiling. The girls invite two rockabilly boys, Frank and Dave, to audition for our band on bass and drums. Our newly named band, Plays With Marionettes, catches spark with the big backbeat these new guys have brought with them. Brian, the saxophonist, and Robin, on keyboards, play blue note jazz melodies over the top of the rhythm section and a wild new sound emerges.

Robin draws complex musical charts on the walls in sign language for a song that changes time signature every sixty seconds. It's like snake handling. We drill it over and over again because this music is counterintuitive and the rest of us are untrained. I call the song 'Witchen Kopf' after a supernatural decapitation story told to me by a young ex-soldier from South Vietnam who my mother briefly took in as a boarder. Everybody thinks I'm joking but really I take myself far too seriously to kid around.

Chris Wyatt organises a recording session in the midnight-to-dawn downtime of a sound studio on Kings Way. We get high on the sheer novelty of recording technology as Wyatt plays with the tape machine, speeding it up and slowing it down, reversing the sounds to reflect the ghost-story narrative of the song. Soon it feels like the ghosts of this office tower block are toying with us – doors open and shut autonomously and strange babble echoes through the ambient microphones slung down the long office corridors we've been using as reverb chambers.

'Witchen Kopf' is picked up by the Au-Go-Go record label for a 7-inch single shared with People With Chairs Up Their Noses. It seems we have crossed the threshold to immortality, having actually made a record! Preparing to launch it, we rehearse intensively. A kilo of flathead from Prahran Market sunbakes on the window ledge of our studio, turning rotten, ready for use as part of a performance at a South Melbourne theatre next weekend. Magically, maggots have begun to appear. They increase in numbers until the moment in performance when I douse both fish and maggots in lighter fluid, firing up the whole mess with a metal Zippo. Uniformed security waving CO_2 canisters shut us down in minutes flat.

What was the point? they demand.

I don't answer, because there was no point. It was pointless – that was the point.

Word soon spreads. More shows are offered, like tonight's support for The Fall, out from England on their first Australian tour. Watching The Fall, I'm both challenged and inspired. They are so radically out of tune and authentically dangerous, pushing and shoving and taunting each other in the backstage. They seem the real thing to me – and us, well, there is work to be done. Our shows, featuring Robin dressed as a vampire girl, rotten fish and masses of spangled confetti, draw as much derision as applause. We are fumbling for originality, embracing the ridiculous in our search for the sublime.

I fall for a new girl several years older than me; Mary drives a hot little purple Torana and seems to know things that I don't. Moving my personal trash into her apartment down on Acland Street, a phantom junkie steals the renovated Rickenbacker from the street kerb while I'm not looking. I search the block and its shadowy alleys but all I see are the street girls and their creepy suburban stalkers, no sign of the guitar.

In this haze of sleepless nights and unknown pleasures, events are moving so fast there's no time to grasp anything beyond the immediate moment: there's no past and no future. All through the midnight hours I notice the traffic of other kids who've got no time for sleep visiting the speed dealer next door. The whole neighbourhood is wired.

A hot girl in a tight dress gives me the eye at a house party in a Richmond backstreet; when she bends over to rummage in her handbag for a compact or a packet of cigarettes or whatever else she hides in there that I shouldn't know about, I can't resist the urge to stare. Don't fuck with me, says my girlfriend, don't even think about messing with those girls or I'll kill you.

I'm so unnerved by her and them all I can do is flush guiltily and mumble, I wasn't looking at anything… Truth is, I don't know a lot about girls and like everything else in my life, I'm just making it up as I go along and trying to save face at the same time.

We find the money to buy the pawnshop Firebird for our next gig north of the river supporting Laughing Clowns at The Club. That night, after expenses and studio rent, the five of us in the band divide a one-dollar bill in torn fifths. Later, in the early hours of morning, we split a souvlaki in five on a Carlton street while kids driving by fling beer cans and insults from open windows.

In this remote and conservative city an emerging scene is pulsing with transgression and revolt, new bands appearing from nowhere at light speed with names like Whirlywirld, Dresden War Crimes, Shower Scene From Psycho, Primitive Calculators, all boarding a wave they've just started calling new wave.

We are oblivious, our reference is still punk – a case of whatever you're for, we're against it; whoever you are, we are not you. Rebels without a cause, rebels for fashion's sake – if not, what else does it mean to be young? Unconscious actions. Automatic desires. Everything is accident and discovery happening for the first time. Looking for something new, something to claim as my own leads me through strange backstreets of the soul and the city into the new codes of an underground scene where it's hard to know who to trust.

Down on Fitzroy Street, the packed foyer of the Crystal Ballroom is illuminated by the yellow glow of a dazzling chandelier, kids spilling down the stairs, the energy like a cage full of parakeets. The girls wear heavy kohl eyeliner and dress like wayward Catholic beauties, larger than life and strangely inscrutable. The boys mix up rockabilly and punk and suburbia. Some do drink and some do powders and some are utterly straight. Cigarettes are fundamental, the room is thick with them – more smoke, more mirrors to cover up our essential emptiness. Self-consciously we pirouette and pose, striking absurd attitudes we hope will shape new identities.

A boy with styled hair and clean clothes and his black-robed girlfriend strike up a conversation with me in the backstage after our set.

You guys are good, she says.

But two guitars, he says, are better than one. You know The Stooges? They invented rock music. Your band has potential but it's missing that rock element. I've got these mind-blowing new songs I'm working on, maybe we should get together and write?

It's Ed from The Marquises and he wants to play guitar with us. It seems the band might be expanding. I'm packing up my gear before the headliner goes on while we shout to be heard over all the noise; my ears are ringing with high frequency and my throat is dry, but we understand each other. I'll talk to you later, he says as the two of them disappear into the massing crowd.

The Birthday Party take the stage with a wall of noise – fuzz distortion, the sonic aroma of pure electricity eating itself. The bassist plays through three huge bass speakers lined up all in a row. It's the loudest thing I've heard since the Avalon air show, and with this kind of violent firepower the stage resembles a wrestling ring or a Grand Guignol circus, the singer standing in the middle as ringmaster, blowing smoke out both nostrils.

I talk to the band after the show and we get to know each other a little. It seems like doors are slamming open all down the line. Quickly, I'm being drawn into a new and secret society I never knew existed. The scene drags me down into a churning, whirling mass of sound behind which you can occasionally hear the snickering background bitching. There is a lot of acid talk about who is cooler than who. At eighteen, everything is really happening in the now – it is fresh, it is brutal and there's no time to see which direction everyone is running in. We're eggshell fragile, trying to act tough, growing thicker skins to protect our own egotistic absurdity.

We know almost nothing, yet think we know everything even when we really know that we don't – a kind of self-deceiving triplethink where tomorrow does not exist because tomorrow is always the day after now and so everything is justified: speeding all night, writing songs we think are masterpieces but in the cold comedown of morning all sound the same, running down chord changes in an orbit around E minor – the deepest, most open chord you can hit with two fingers, it floats through the scene like a cement graveyard angel come to life, all gothic overtones and tremolo arm harmonics.

Epochal bands from overseas start arriving in a continuous stream. We play for bigger crowds, supporting groups like Psychedelic Furs, New Order, Violent Femmes. I get a chance to demystify their approach from the side of stage – how they handle audiences, how they light stages, what kind of equipment they're using. We've thrown ourselves in the deep end, and this is a crash course in what it takes to be a touring band.

The Gun Club perform at Melbourne University and the atmosphere is weirdly volatile, something like the energetic tension of The Birthday Party – almost inexplicably violent. Our set is treated with downright hostility by the audience, beer cans and coins flying like shrapnel past my face. Even if it is only a show, when this music interacts with audience expectation there's a kind of psychic fission where music draws power from the verbal beyond, conveying the inexpressible, venting the collective mind.

We're building rapidly in this music scene and the sparks are fanned by community radio and fanzines. Interview requests arrive, band photographs are snapped and published. Becoming better-known and using publicity to build an audience bring unexpected problems in their wake – the attention proves hard to handle and my friends say I'm getting too full of myself, acting out of character, losing the plot.

An inquisitive green-eyed girl interviews me in the derelict Victorian house on Williams Road where the band now rehearses. I've been up all night, strung-out, and clean forgot about the interview appointment. Her questions are piercing and intense and her insistent curiosity about my most secret dark self is increasingly irksome. She produces a Polaroid camera from nowhere and I quickly recoil from the lens, telling her I don't want my photo taken.

What sort of girls do you like? she asks. Do you like sex? Do you even have sex?

I'm mute with confusion, so she changes tack.

What about recurring dreams, she says, what are your obsessions?

I'm a musician, I mumble, aren't we here to talk about music?

Oh, no one cares about music, she replies, music's just rubbish! I want to know about you! What is the point of your existence?

The point?

Yes, of your existence! What is the point of you?

My mind goes dark. I give her nothing. I can the interview.

The band tell me I'm rude and arrogant, and apologise to her for my punk behaviour while she takes photos of Edward, always ready to pose for a girl with a Polaroid. I storm out into the decaying kitchen, where my black mood and I talk together about these trendy Blitz girls sporting buffalo dresses and bows in their hair daring to waste my fucking time. I hear her leave and try to jolt everyone back into my E-minor force field against the world, but they ignore me. Faintly, I hear her crying on Williams Road and her boyfriend scathing her for being so uncool. Ignoring her sobs and Edward's glances of disappointment in me, I walk down the road to a phone box, drop a coin into the slot and call the dealer.

I can see there are cracks forming in me, in the music, in the worn and torn city streets, and a whole lot of chaos out there waiting to get in. I want to stretch open those apertures to the possible, to the beyond; I want to tear it all down and let havoc reign supreme. I don't want to know where I'm going, I don't want to have to think about what happens next. I don't want anyone to see me, I don't want to be seen through. I'm moving so fast, I blur. There's no time for questions, no time left to explain – because eighteen, it's a speeding bullet where the days dissolve like minutes and tomorrow never comes.

And the light, the light is very deceptive.

Codeine Linctus | Europe/USA, 1984

Last night's dose of Rohypnol, a parting gift from a weepy-eyed girlfriend in the car park at Melbourne airport, has long since worn off over the course of a thirty-hour flight. Battered suitcase at my feet, the foggy, alien English suburbs rewind across the semi-opaque windows of a train bound for central London. Following half-remembered instructions I change at Victoria for the underground, emerging from Queensway tube station into the chill, smoggy February air. I'm underdressed in a jacket and jeans, inadequate to address this city in winter, but I'm too excited to care – this is London after all, Mecca of the music world and the source of nearly everything I've been listening to over the last three years – punk, post-punk, new wave, the sounds of modernity.

I've joined a new band, Man or Myth, as a guitar player. We toured Australia together last summer. Sometimes their drummer, Mick, played drums for us in the Marionettes; at the same time, he taught me guitar lines for the Birthday Party songs we played in Man or Myth.

The singer, Nick, is already a charismatic underground star, six years older than me and possessed of a deadly sense of humour that keeps me on edge – at any given moment he might be taking the piss without me even knowing it. People unconsciously gravitate towards his powers of attraction and he has learnt to use this fact: a force to be reckoned with.

Deciphering a number scrawled in spidery handwriting on crumpled paper, I make the call from a red phone box on a dour high street prowled by black taxis and homeless panhandlers. Minutes later Nick rolls up in a tight green suit, dark rings under his eyes like he's been awake all night. It's good to see him. I've never been here before and know no one else in the city except for Mick.

We walk up to the bed and breakfast. The room is small with a single window, three beds and a bathroom. Almost immediately there's a knock on the door. The Indian landlady cranes her head inside the room and asks tentatively, Is this the other young man staying here? Can I have your documents, please? She disappears with my passport into the nether regions of the terrace.

We take a black cab to the record company offices on the west side. Gathered in the street out the front is a restless crowd of kids punked up in pancake foundation and eyeliner, hair teased high. They raise a cry when the cab pulls up but then realising we're not who they're waiting for, they drift away and regroup, inciting each other to greater heights of enthusiasm with snatches of Depeche Mode songs.

While I hang in the background, the singer negotiates a cash advance from a girl behind a desk. Rehearsals and per diems, she says, a few hundred quid should cover that.

My ears prick up – a few hundred quid? Currently I have at most two hundred dollars to my name. My Dad, bless him, gave me just enough money for a one-way ticket out of the country: Australia, he used to say, yes – but it's too boring! So a few hundred quid changes everything. We both sign something and bolt out the door through the *Night of the Living Dead* remake on Kensington Square Gardens.

Who are you? says a guy in an Alien Sex Fiend T-shirt.

Nobody, I reply, getting into another cab that weaves expertly through heavy traffic before dropping us outside a depressing tower block.

We visit a friendly couple on one of the lower floors. Children's toys are scattered about the dilapidated apartment. The man's just been, they say, lucky you gave us some warning.

The crushed brown rock evaporates on heated tinfoil, the chemical warmth embracing me like an old friend with no name and no face, just a vague, reassuring presence that smells like fermenting garbage.

Just about everyone I know is doing this shit, casual as lighting a cigarette.

We're recording in the Trident Studios in Soho where artists of the sixties and seventies taped sounds that defined rock music itself in times past that already feel to me like centuries ago. They were forces of history, and the rest of the band seem like this to me also, worldly and experienced in ways I'm only just beginning to grasp.

The songs, several of them begun the year before with a different crew, form fascinating shapes over a period of weeks only to be torn down again and restarted from scratch. There is great tension between the band members because the stakes are high – an epochal recording is sought and nothing less will do. The other guitarist, Blixa, a Nietzschean avatar from mythical Berlin, sets the agenda:

Don't play anything I've heard before, he booms, it must be original. Original! Do you know what that even means?

Now that the German has arrived on the scene, the recording

is marked with jagged intensity. Bass loops rumble through the studio for hours while we tinker with sounds. Guitar loops whistle all night long through a harsh, dry landscape decorated with long, epic lyrics drawn from Nick's cryptic notebooks. Mick and Barry play drums and bass; natural-born musicians, they move between different instruments, trying out different ideas, brutally discarding experiments that don't make the cut. Constructions of wood and metal appear in the studio to be used as percussion, speaker enclosures, vocal booths. No reverbs soften the impact or create artificial spaces; every detail is etched with naked clarity. It doesn't sound like anything I've heard before – we are traversing unknown territory.

Scathing comments and put-downs are the ordinary state of play between the three of us, Nick, Blixa and me, now cohabiting in the single hotel room where the atmosphere has become singularly weird. The landlady knocks on the door at odd hours to ask questions or call us to the telephone, strangers come and go, sometimes girls stay all night then vanish at dawn into the drizzling English haze. I start to freeze into a cold, dark space, fading fast until Sandy knocks at the door.

C'mon, she says, come out with me. We'll go up to the heath for a picnic.

But first she needs to make her pharmacy run. We take the tube to Camden to visit a sure-fire chemist. Sandy whips off her pink wig to reveal a short back and sides before entering the shop. I watch her through the windows chatting up the chemist before pointing to a bottle high on the shelf. After another five minutes' banter, the chemist sells her the bottle in a paper bag.

Now, she says, we have to wait awhile. She drums thin painted fingers on the sleeve of her trench coat. Well, I know a guy who lives around the corner, she says, we can drop by and see if he's home, he hardly ever leaves the house.

While her friend tidies up the house to the metallic throb of a Killing Joke record, Sandy inverts the bottle so that the noxious contents introduced to spike the codeine rise to the top. Anaemic English sunlight filters through curtains of pseudo-lace discoloured by time and nicotine. Sandy re-inverts the bottle and draws up the separated codeine with a syringe. A clock ticks and a bus passes, but to me time is standing still.

Sandy starts fixing her make-up in a cracked pocket mirror and when her eyeliner and lip gloss are right, tries on some different wigs to match. Between the narcotic and the make-up she turns into a whole new girl; her pretty features seem older, more sophisticated and relaxed. I just needed something before work tonight, she says, strangely elated and deadly cool.

The three of us sit on Hampstead Heath watching the sunset fade to grey, shivering slightly in the rising damp. I reach out and hold her hand.

Don't be silly, she says without even looking at me, I've got to go to work.

I don't ask what her job is, I've already read the signs.

I'm watching the video *Basket Case* in Jessamy's apartment. It's a horror film about mutation, cannibalism. Other people in the room are finding the gruesome content kind of funny, but I've been awake for days and can't really remember what I've been doing. In this jarred psychic state, the film is terrifying; it renders me mute, speaking to every individual dread in my psyche. That's me, I think: I'm a basket case too.

I decide to get out of town.

Early springtime English countryside hurtles past the train windows. Sprays of wildflowers ignite fields between rivers and lakes, rich bodies of water glistening in the alien European green. Where I come from, time moves slowly; dust and flies are always hanging in the air. Here there are birds and cottages and a sense of old-world order echoing sentimental books I read as a child. Nothing seems real.

The train pulls into Oxford and my old school friend Humphrey greets me on the platform with a welcoming smile. We played together in our first high school band not so long ago. I sleep in a house shared with a group of students; their talk is of philosophy, poetry, the theatre. I envy their certitude and confidence and humour, their ease in the world. The soft-focus countryside haunts me with its strange feelings of nostalgia for somewhere I never knew. But I can't stay here in this safe parallel world. I've run out of time and money. I say goodbye to Humph and board a London train that all-too-quickly penetrates the city's industrial fringe; the smog embraces me as one of its own, drawing me into its grey vortex before spitting me back out onto the streets of Soho.

The new album is rush-released. The turn around from mixdown to pressing is bewilderingly fast. No wonder there was so much pressure in the studio – a plan is running invisibly in the background and we are bound to it. We sit in pubs drinking warm English beer with publicists, shows are booked, photos taken, baited hooks dropped into the piranhic waters of the music press.

The singer and I wait for a train early one morning at a tube station, no one around, wind whistling gently from the tunnels.

What do you think, he says, of the band name the Bad Seeds?

Ed, the guitarist from the Marionettes, arrives in London with his girlfriend who has just received a compensation payout for a nasty car accident; cashed up, they move in to a nearby hotel. As Blixa is elsewhere and Barry's substituting on guitar, Ed plays bass for the band over the upcoming English dates. We share substances and boyish dreams – like the idea for a band called The Wreckery that we plan to form back in Melbourne in some distant future when all of this is over. Our heads are fixed in the clouds, feet way off the ground. Reality, after all, is just for people who can't handle drugs.

The Bad Seeds meet up for their first live-show rehearsals in a padded cell of a room in Kilburn, the dead acoustics making it hard to summon up the intensity of the studio recordings. The band argue about arrangements and tempos, business agreements and schedules. Tension is high but the machinery is already in motion and there's no going back.

The first show in London is under a pseudonym, The Cavemen; although it was only announced at the last minute, the Brixton Fridge is nearly sold out. Sparks of confrontation between demonic singer and rowdy audience ripple through the air as each winds up the other in a kind of psychic bullfight.

Nick chooses to experiment with this situation by opening the concert alone with a ten-minute piano and voice monologue. From the sidelines at the Manchester Hacienda, I watch him deliver the song in a spotlight while coins and catcalls rain down on the stage. Stepping out on cue, I discover all my effects pedals have been stolen. The jack cables curl pathetically on the floor near the microphone stand, spurned and cold. The audience, surge against the darkened stage as the rest of the band take up positions.

Flummoxed, I plug a guitar directly into the amp, turning all the knobs up to nine; it kicks and squeals with lacerating feedback as we launch into the drunken stagger of 'Mutiny in Heaven'. Nick shakes his fist and points at the sound mixer to the side of the stage. More voice, he yells, more fucking voice! His wild animation proves contagious and bodies start to move instinctively in a massed wave motion throughout the room. We lay down a dissonant rock drone while he spews stories of doom and damnation over the top, his melodramatic mayhem setting the night on fire.

These first shows rapidly turn into an ongoing tour as agents phone or fax dates in from across the UK and Europe. Mick works ceaselessly, vetting propositions and keeping tabs on expenses, making sure the band get paid. I draw money as advances just to survive: smokes, substances, tube tickets, Indian takeaway.

Days and nights merge together and I lose track of time as the industrialised landscapes blur along anonymous motorways – Birmingham, Sheffield, Leeds, Liverpool, Coventry, Leicester, Nottingham, Bristol, Brighton, Manchester again, Kingston upon Thames, London revisited.

The tour opens my mind as much as it scares the shit out of me and quickly I develop a taste for it, preferring to be in transit rather than staying still. It's a blast of adrenalised danger being onstage with this band and it's only just begun …

You can't not know this, says our Queensway landlady, you need to see this. She turns the television up in the timeless tedium of the basement breakfast room. I'm fully focused on her toast and strawberry jam, the first food I've eaten since I don't remember when but I humour her and watch the screen. The television report explains a whole new way to die horribly if you're gay or shoot drugs – a new pestilence they call AIDS.

Watch out, young man, she says, it's a dangerous world.

The scene cuts to striking coal miners at war with the English police under leaden grey skies – rain, pickets, misery. But it's not the only war going on out on the periphery of my awareness – the re-election of Reagan boosts the nuclear threat. Images flash by of Russian missile tests and Star Wars technologies, missile batteries orbiting the earth, new satellite systems: the future.

I pour out another cup of thick, cold English tea.

A letter arrives from my mother. Grandma has died in her sleep. She's been looked after in Mum's house these last three months. She was a great lady, serenely pragmatic right to the end. I wish I was there even though she has in fact signed out of this space-time and donated her body to medical research. I remember her explaining to me when I was much younger about the human soul and how death is only a transformation, not an ending, and suddenly I feel acutely homesick.

I change the thought pattern by scoring. Dope's alien warmth enfolds me in a comforting, unreal glove, like a Disney cartoon – my own private *Fantasia*. I wake up some time later in the dishwater-grey gloom of English morning and fail to recognise the room. Then I see the mess and clutter of spoons, glasses, papers and dirty clothes and it all comes back to me at once: I have to pack up my stuff – we're moving out of this haunted little bed and breakfast and onto a Belgium-bound ferry.

'Just be Good to Me', the latest US dance hit, plays on the jeep radio. Spring sunshine dazzles Dutch fields. The windmills spin. Vaguely I'm aware that the vehicle's cabin walls are lined with amphetamine. I assume this is privileged information – if the tour manager knew, I don't think he'd be along for the ride. And yet, Mick's the linchpin of the whole operation; without him, the tour and the band could well fall apart.

I'm in a swanky hotel room with a gram of crystal, watching the wallpaper pixilate while my guts churn. I'm not sure who I am now; all certainty is gone. I realise I can't keep doing this. It's making me paranoid. I think the rest of the band is out to get me.

I glance in a mirror and don't like what I see; maybe it's the unnatural tightness of my face or maybe I just need to update my look. Shirts are drying in the shower, socks in the sink. I open up the side seams in my old school trousers, tightening the leg, narrowing the ankle. Needle and thread, grinding my teeth. The phone rings. Down to reception, says Mick, we're leaving.

A band called The Smiths is headlining the festival tonight. They're the latest darlings of the English music press. A melee has broken out about who's supporting who. Egos spark, tempers flare. English music-business types swarm the backstage corridors of a huge discotheque barking in gangster dialect while a thousand people or more mill around on the dance floor under revolving lights.

Late in the night, still totally wired, we decide to visit a street in Amsterdam way off the tourist radar. A guy with knowing eyes leads us to a shooting gallery where the mood is electrically sour. Pushers pass the dope around in a kind of pass-the-parcel shell game to hide the fact they've switched the shit for some low-class substitute.

That's not the same shit, my friend says, this is a fucking rip-off. Let's go the cunts.

Behind us is a long corridor and a line of tombstone-eyed junkies with nothing much left to lose. The dealer pulls a knife on us like a snake recoiling to strike. I've got no skills in this area, happy just to forget the whole thing.

Let's fucking run for it, I hiss, and make a break for the only way out.

A scuffle erupts in the confusion and the knife glints and flashes and although everything appears to me to be in slow motion, we run the gauntlet at breakneck speed into the Amsterdam night, catching our breath in short, painful gasps below a jaundice-yellow streetlight. Clutching the stitch in his side, my mate looks me in the eye and unclenches his fist to reveal the silver-foiled shit therein – We got the real deal, he says and starts laughing.

The show in Hamburg is more hostile than anything we've experienced so far. Psychotic German fans goad the singer until he snaps and grabs a twist of coloured punk-rock hair, battering the taunter's surprised expression with a microphoned fist. Blood spatters on the stage monitors. I turn around to see if Mick is watching this and find his gaze fixed on the back of my head, boring holes into my brain with two laser-blue eyes.

Communist guards at the East German border examine the vehicle, eyeing our passports suspiciously. The autobahn degenerates into concrete slabs; the vehicle rattles like a cage. We stop at the only Mitropa roadhouse between the border and West Berlin for boiled bockwurst, crossing over the carriageway on a concrete footbridge framed by barbed wire. All around, the fields are brown and grey, wreathed in mist and trampled by dancing, sharp-eyed blackbirds.

The hotel is a high-rise near Potsdamer Platz, close by Hansa Tonstudio. The nearby wall is floodlit green by night. We play the Metropol on a double bill with Swans, a band from New York City even louder than us, heavier than anything I've ever heard.

It's my twenty-first birthday and I'm cutting loose. Having drunk half a bottle of Zubrowka vodka to celebrate, I'm helped through the stupor by a skinny cat with dark glasses and a fine line in psychobabble, cutting lines on the bar to medicate the alcohol overdose. The streets swim and shimmer before my eyes in the back of a stranger's car on the way to the Risiko bar as dawn breaks.

I find myself at a flea market ragpicking for souvenirs with a girl in a green leather jacket. I don't know her name or how we got here, but it doesn't matter. Maybe it's time for you to go, she says, do you know the way back?

She walks me to the hotel to meet the rest of the crew. Everybody appears to be in much the same psychotic state as me. Only Mick is showered, sober and organised. Grab your stuff, he says, it's a long drive back to the Netherlands and then there's the American tour.

New York is sweltering hot and overpoweringly huge. With the air-conditioning at the Algonquin Hotel on overdrive, I watch television and live off Hershey bars, scribbling lyrics for future songs in notebooks. Jessamy, who's signed on as our new tour manager, advances me twenty dollars and disappears into the city with the others. As dusk falls there's a knock at the door.

Jeffrey Lee is looking for somebody to take out to a jazz club and I'm the only one here. He barely knows me, but that doesn't impede his stream-of-consciousness monologue as we merge with the humid, neon-lit Manhattan night; maybe it even gives him more freedom to expand the rave.

Music is important, he says, it's important in our lives and that never changes no matter where or when. Jazz and punk rock, you know, it's just the same thing from different times. But when you bring that together, wow, that's future music… Now let's see, where do we go? There's always something happening somewhere in the Apple.

The club is a red-curtained, linoleum-floored dive on the razor's edge between squalor and luxury. There are maybe three other people here, parked at the bar. A black guy in a beret ducks out of the men's room, mounts the bandstand beside the bar and blows into a tenor saxophone.

Jesus Christ, you know who that is? Jeffrey grins, Pharoah Sanders! Righteous American legend! Can you believe you're even in the same room with this guy?

Wild freestyling torches the atmosphere. Horn, piano and double bass, Sanders's acoustic trio are dissonant, arrhythmic. Normally I can't stand jazz but this abstract noise is something else. Jeffrey yells in my ear about getting a trumpet and howling some raw freedom for himself in his band, The Gun Club. Blues and rock and roll is never enough, he says, there's so much more than that – there's got to be more than that.

The band tours in an American roadster up and down the east coast – Boston, Providence, Trenton, Baltimore, Philadelphia – playing in rock and roll clubs much smaller than the European venues to cool, compact audiences. Ringed by empty, decrepit post-industrial estates, cities like Pittsburg, Detroit and Washington appear as science-fiction visions. Fascinating and disenchanting in equal measure, the sheer scale of everything is overwhelming.

I'm at an afterparty somewhere in the suburbs of Chicago with a girl in a pillbox hat, Nathalie. She hasn't a good word for anyone in the room – They're all assholes, she says, smiling and waving to her friends. The kids do drugs in the parents' bedroom – a lawyer and his wife out of town on business – under the experienced supervision of a local dealer.

I'm so bored, says Nathalie, bored out of my brain.

Realising I'd just be one more disappointment in her life, I ask her to call a cab. Slumped exhausted in the back of the taxi, as dawn breaks over the great lake and its surrounding skyscrapers and condenses into a wall of searing light, I feel my brain turning with the planet, slowly erasing itself cell by cell.

The mood inside the band is turning sour. Maybe it's just tour fatigue but no one has any tolerance left to spare. We all know the songs too well by now, the concert set is always the same sequence. We barely speak. Passing through Columbus, San Francisco, Pasadena, Los Angeles, Kansas City, the tour accelerates towards its end in a blur of cities and celebrities and speed psychosis.

After the last show in Atlanta, I've got an early-morning flight to catch back to LA. With no time to sleep, I just stare out into the nightglow over the city, echoes of people and places and light and sound haunting my thoughts. Everyone else is crashed out in the hotel except for Jessamy. She calls a taxi and hugs me goodbye. The five of us in the band are all splintering off to different destinations, different fates.

The flight to LAX lands in blistering July heat. I stand frozen in the arrivals hall, staring at the forest of American flags sprouting on the strip in anticipation of Independence Day. Now that the schedule has stopped, I have no idea what to do. It feels like I've been dropped into an alien void and can't precisely remember how or why I got here. I fish a quarter from my pocket, walk over to a telephone box and drop a coin into the slot.

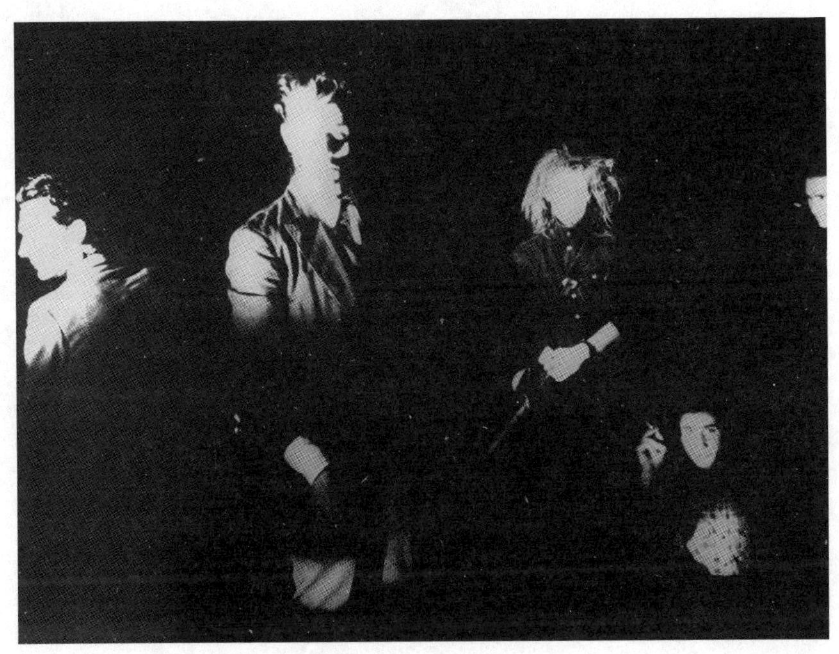

Ruling Energy | Australia, 1986

Sydney is baking in the fierce morning sunshine, all beaches and palm trees and open-neck sports shirts and soft-top sports cars, an antipodean Los Angeles where the giant Coke sign over Kings Cross glitters in the Pacific sun like corporate costume jewellery.

On Darlinghurst Road, clean-up crews hose down the footpaths after last night's routine bacchanalia while City Mission workers rouse the homeless sheltering under gaudy strip club awnings. I'm suffocating in a leather jacket and jeans, having stepped off the overnight bus at Central early this morning with thirty dollars in my pocket and a delirium of gum trees and headlights tattooed on my eyes.

You look like hell, says Richard, opening the door to a warehouse space swimming in dust and hot light. Come on in.

Richard spins records in some of the cooler Sydney clubs, drawing on a diverse record collection of cutting-edge import rarities to fill the floor.

Everybody's talking about Retribution on Saturday night, he says, it's going to be insane with you guys, the Deadly Hume, the Johnnies. When are the rest of the Wreckers getting here?

Hopefully tomorrow, if nothing goes wrong. I'm here doing press, mostly radio. The new manager, Paul, talked me into it.

Right, he replies, you've got to work the promo hard in this city, there's so much going on. You coming out tonight? I'm on the decks at Club 40.

Club 40 is a downtown hole in the wall with a red door guarded by moody Samoan bouncers. The mirror-balled dance floor and black granite walls faced with tall mirrors render the space infinite and void. Exotic Sydney club girls work behind the bar, their glamorous made-up faces wearing a vacant glare from sunset until dawn. It's exciting to be in the presence of these fast wild creatures and I'm fascinated and intimidated by them in equal measure. I take a dagger in the heart from a blue-eyed blonde called Laila who leads me on and puts me down with uncanny accuracy.

I wake up drenched in blinding sunlight, dreaming of Laila's taunts and barbs and the sadness in her eyes. Below the mezzanine, Rich and his angular, quick-witted housemate Dean are making coffee and cracking jokes, their voices hoarse and tired from the night before.

I wander across into the warehouse alcove where the vinyl albums are shelved in loose alphabetical order and put on a Hasil Adkins novelty song from 1957 – 'I Need Your Head (This Ain't No Rock 'N' Roll Show)' – psychotic hillbilly music from the shadow side of the fifties released the same year as Elvis's 'Jailhouse Rock'. Since the birth of rock music there's always been a musical underground of voices too weird to survive in plain view – I need your head, screams Hasil, and baby, I got room on my wall ...

If I have to clear a club at five in the morning, Rich yells out, I know this record will do it in minutes flat. Works every time!

Day fades into night as I fill virgin cassette tapes with songs by bands from around the world, looking for new directions in my own work. I've been writing songs on an open-tuned guitar more or less the same way I heard they did it back in the thirties, following echoes of the blues since I first heard Country

Joe's 'Crystal Blues' back as a sixties kid, the dust-soaked needle gouging into worn-out vinyl. All that dirt caked in the grooves made it sound like it was happening in a parallel dimension.

Dirt is important: mistakes and errors make music real to me. Compared to the old blues recordings, nothing sounds as good as it used to; modern technology has eliminated those physical artefacts that were part of the experience. I realise the blues is currently uncool, that it's considered old men's music, but to me the Delta blues sounds ancient and wise and charged with spiritual dimensions that defy analysis.

Wreckery songs are basically just two chords because pop songs use at least three, and somewhere I heard less is more. So far, we're getting away with it – feigned musical primitivism. But deep down I mistrust our growing popularity because it seems to me that to be popular, you have to be commercial rubbish, hence we lace everything we do with a little poison for the mainstream.

Link Wray's 'Strychnine' spins on the turntable at high volume, psyched surf-rock from the late fifties where everything in retrospect seems fresh and cool and dangerous. That's where we'd like to be, not in 1986, trying to make some waves in a provincial lagoon of haircut bands and manufactured pop. A cloud of radioactive hairspray masks the banality of a music scene driven by the carrot-and-stick politics of major labels. We're consciously trying to disengage from the contemporary aesthetic. We've got our own galaxy of inspired pretensions drawn from blues, punk, pulp fiction and the all-night movie marathons on TV.

Drinking tea until the break of dawn, or beer if we can afford it, we watch 1950s film noir like *Naked City*, *The Trap*, *Pickup on South Street* or *Kiss of Death*. Richard Widmark is a recurring presence through the small hours, and his urbane style can be cheaply replicated from suburban opportunity shops, right down to gaudy little details like tiepins, cufflinks and sleeve garters.

Our girlfriends fuss over the way we look, drawing on our faces with blunt eyeliner and violently teasing our hair with combs and spray; then they savage us with slaps and sarcasm when another girl looks our way. We suit up and boot up like sixties rebel rockers, all hair grease, faded pinstripes and pointy toes. The image doesn't really suit the pub rock circuit where we often play, but it does channel our influences onto the stage and sets us apart from the big hair and soft pastels of corporate pop.

All around us, musicians are rolling over to have their bellies scratched by the multinational robot claw, their youth and vision quickly digested and shat out by the music money machine. We want to be the backlash, not the client. This attitude is fragmenting as grey zones take hold, but it does infuse us with a certain righteous energy. You need conviction and ruthless determination to survive in this scene because the money is bad, the drives are long, the audiences small and the competition fierce. Without real conviction, no one lasts the distance.

'Retribution' is the brainchild of some savvy rock hustlers breaking the new wave into Sin City. The Paddington Town Hall is a maelstrom of noise and energy – the unexpectedly large crowd spills out onto the street, kids hang from balconies, the security guards are overwhelmed by the volume of people and sound. Spencer Jones and his Johnnies dress like rhinestone cowboys and play demonic country punk, mixing LSD with their beer. The Deadly Hume crank out a dissonant, eardrum-busting rock drone. Sweating camera crews are filming everything. Dealers haunt the backstage with their dilated pupils and incoherent chat. Even if your band isn't playing, you're hanging out. Suddenly it's our turn to get onstage.

Razor-sharp suited Charlie blows a massive baritone sax; Robin beats the drums with detached menace and precision; Barker plays a mean bass with his snarly punk attitude and Ed plays overdriven guitar and sings backup. The Wreckery really cut it when they're united, playing like a single organism with rhythm, humour and energy to burn. Although we think we've seen it all, it's our naivety that gives us the gall to carry it off. But that naivety won't last long: our first two records are sitting in the top ten on the national independent charts and the industry predators already have us in their sights.

We've been summoned to the Mushroom boardroom with its wall-to-wall gold records for a big meeting with Michael, godfather of Melbourne rock. His personal assistant greets us and delegates an executive assistant to serve us flutes of champagne while we wait until he sweeps into the room like a rock star, dictating a letter to a girl with glasses and a notepad.

You boys have to make a commitment, Michael says, firing up a huge joint in the filtered mid-afternoon glare. In partnership, there's nothing we can't achieve.

Then he rocks back in his leather chair and exhales a cloud of smoke that hangs in the air like the aftermath of a dynamited building. A telephone with multiple blinking lights sits beside him. It purrs and he picks it up and says, No more calls! I don't care if it's bloody Richard Branson!

Michael is very smart with piercing, no-bullshit blue eyes that pin you to the back of the chair while he communicates in bewildering industry-speak.

We'll scale up from the first to the second release, he says, but there's always an option to take it sideways or just straight up and down depending on if we go three or five years from the drop. You'll always be in charge, subject to the recommendations of our dedicated crew of specialists – but just think of them as fans with your best interests at heart. If it all works out we'll upgrade to a ten-year ten-album extension including 'best-ofs' with options of theatrical release and rebranding.

Slowly it dawns on me that under this agreement we lose control to their in-house record producers, publicists and designers.

So how do you blokes feel about that for a get-starter? he says and passes me the cigar-sized joint with an entrepreneurial flourish.

I give it a wary puff and shortly afterwards a strange kind of panic engulfs me; it seems Michael is mockingly staring me down through the dense pall of smoke. My head spins in a nonstop double take, instantly paranoid. This is the break? It feels more like the end: package tours, shopping mall gigs, industry barbecues, talk shows and trendy videos on network TV. And that's only if you make it! Chances are we'll wind up on the shelf, bound and gagged like little pin-struck voodoo dolls.

Meanwhile, Michael and our latest manager, Ritchie, have run away with the conversation. They're chatting amicably about exceptions, retentions and defaults while a chasm opens beneath my feet; spooked by certain soul death, I get to my feet and walk straight out of the room.

Barker chases me out, still wide-eyed and hopeful even as he watches the King of Pop crown slipping from his grasp.

What's got into your strides, mate, he asks, or do you actually enjoy shooting yourself in the foot? This is it! Michael's great! It's all happening! What's your problem? We're going to be stars! Live on *Countdown* every fucking Sunday night!

Giant Kylie posters stare down upon us from the Mushroom gallery of fame – 'I Should be So Lucky' – while the band's disappointed faces swim in front of my eyes. Where they saw a chance to go professional with the music, I saw a corporate alignment pact. Since the beginning I'd sworn to myself no sell-out, ever, and it wasn't going to change now.

Harry is silhouetted against a sunset through the kitchen window, wearing a three-day growth, a houndstooth jacket and corduroy jeans. He nods back and forth like an oracle, scratching his nose and laughing quietly to himself while I brew sweet strong tea.

I knew you wouldn't sign, he explains, I knew it! Because signing with them would have meant signing up to the whole deal – the half-time special at the Collingwood versus Collingwood grand fucking final, those prancing Russell Mulcahy video clips and endless nightmare pub gigs in the darkest drinking holes of regional Australia. It's a complete package, take it or leave it. You're either with them or against them, the elite machine or the revolution. What real choice do you have? This is the post-1984 world, mate, the society of the spectacle. And show business is political, it's only there to brainwash the masses! That's why they're cutting you cheques!

Harry is a few years older than me, a maverick political student at Melbourne Uni. He's my friend and mentor and visits me with obscurely interesting photocopied magazine articles and impenetrable books by European writers. Our girlfriends seem to have a little light for each other. They talk in high voices, nodding and agreeing enthusiastically about nothing in particular.

In the high-tech future, he continues, there'll be no distinction between corporations and government. We'll all be compelled to develop multiple identities just to stay ahead of the military–industrial complex. And even then, in the long run, they'll soon have your number logged in a computer observing everything you say and do. But I have a plan, mate … I'm going to India to live for a while, see how it feels to be part of the ancient world, just read and write and do pure dope, not the toxic shit you find around here on the streets, but the real thing. People can live way past a hundred years old on pure shit. It's actually good for you, good for your health and intelligence and for your soul. To hell with the machine, man, the masses can have it …

Just then we become aware of the girls standing in the doorway listening to our talk.

Just when are you coming back, Harry? asks Robyn, trying to keep a bright face on her fear.

Mary's coal-black eyes bore into me and she says, Right, well, so are you going too?

No, I reply, it's okay, I'm not going anywhere yet.

Harry doesn't answer, just strokes his beard and stares out the window into the night, laughing quietly at some joke no one else can hear but him.

The Queensland sun blazes down on my shabby winklepickers kicked off in the sand. Crows scream over the breaking surf from nearby trees. I've just woken up on a beach to the horror of small children building sand castles around me, their high-pitched screams drilling into my brain. I'm aware I may appear to them like a cartoon villain; a mother in terry-towelling shorts grabs her delinquent kid, telling it not to look at me. We're on the Gold Coast, pale, long-haired extraterrestrials in a doomscape of casinos, hotels, high-rise apartments and concrete shopping malls, the pungent stink of KFC and beached kelp floating on the breeze.

We're coasting in the slipstream of our Let Saigons Be Saigons Tour, playing an under-eighteens event in a vast, alcohol-dry suburban discotheque. It's mid-afternoon, an unlikely time of day for us to shine, but we're at the mercy of a Queensland booking agent working with Roger, our latest manager, high-powered and Sydney-based. We're just getting ready to go on when the fire alarms start ringing in the backstage and all the kids run screaming from the hall. Our sound mixer, Bill, stalks into the backstage, clenching and unclenching his fists with nervous agitation.

That's it, guys, he yells over the migraine-inducing war cry of the club security system, let's hit the road.

What the hell is going on? Charlie screams back.

Fire drill, says Bill.

Why?

I've got no fucking idea!

We still getting paid?

Bundled back into a Tarago reeking of dirty laundry and cigarette smoke, we drive through forty-degree heat into the swampy heart of Brisbane to play an inner-city pub that saw better times a hundred years ago. A wired Aboriginal man stalks the stage between us making shamanic hand gestures while kids bodyslam on the sodden pub floor and cops cruise by scoping the scene from blue-lighted panel vans. We load out at the end of the night through drunken, scuffling crowds, ambulance sirens in the distance, the damp Queensland heat informing and oppressing everything that moves.

Next day we're on the road to the inland town of Toowoomba with our tour roadie, Chappo, at the wheel. Behind us, the sun dips into the Pacific, the lights of paradise blasting through muslin clouds, parakeets hurling abuse from the shivering palms, the van windows wound open, warm air from the fetid, burping mangrove swamps blowing in my face. Huge insects gambol in the slipstream or splatter on the windshield; tribes of fruit bats wheel overhead powered by vast leathery wings.

When the wind-struck Aussie flags of the massive RSL club shimmy in our headlights, the feeling that we're rewinding time back to the age of dinosaurs is complete.

The lobby of the army club is saturated with symbols of Empire – battalion pennants and crests rampant between potted shrubs and rolls-of-honour and rows of poker machines lined up like little soldiers. A ghastly oil painting of the British Queen gazes down, her placid expression remote and alien. The bar is stacked with retired drinkers, freckled and pale as arctic snow. We're a long way out of our inner-city element in a place like this, and to me it all seems so very unreal. I collar Charlie and ask, Where the hell are we? Seriously, what is this bullshit patriotic carry-on all about?

Charlie, in an immaculately blue double-breasted suit draped over a dirty white singlet, looks at me perplexed. Watch your lip, he says, we're just going to get in and get out. Be nice, will you?

Chappo already has the stage set up – drums, guitars, microphones.

You on the speed? I ask him.

Don't like the vibe, he reckons, can't wait to leave.

I wander out to the bar, where the beginnings of what could be an audience are assembling, and order a vodka tonic. The guys next to me in their shorts, gumboots and wife-beaters are quiet and sullen and stare at my boots and one of them says something I can't quite catch. Next thing I'm arguing with the barman as it appears he wants me to pay for my drink. Indignant, I give him some back talk, at which point somebody knocks my vodka tonic off the bar then orders me another one. As I drink it down, the drone of conversation rises, the disco lights vibrate in enhanced technicolour, the room spins and weaves.

You're on, says Chappo, tapping me on the shoulder. The group snaps purposefully into action, kicking out a long introduction while my mind searches for the lyrics. Somehow, I'm drawing blank. I can't even remember what the song is called. The forgetting feels like agony – this can't just be the alcohol. And then it hits me – somebody spiked my drink! I look into the crowd and their faces grimace and contort like a horror movie and I get the feeling I'm about to be lynched onstage.

John Lee Hooker's 'Burning Hell' extends for an eternity while I mumble nonsense lyrics into the mic, watching Ed's fingers to follow the changes, only recognising the E minor us-against-the-world drone as the song draws to a close. I don't want this tune to stop, I won't recognise the next one, we'll just keep doing this, I tell myself, for an hour or so … Then Ed starts the next track, waiting for me to come in, which I don't – so he sings it himself. I press a shiny metal knob and the fuzz overdrive kicks in and I lean in to the amplifier, feeding back. Somewhere very far away, the band and the audience are moving in slow motion. Then as suddenly as the show started, it's all over, Chappo and Bill talking in monstrous, slowed-down voices as they clear the stage.

Some huge security guards in ludicrous khaki shorts and white socks are giving me the evil eye. I don't know why, maybe I said the wrong thing to the wrong person, maybe it was only a matter of time anyway but now they're closing in on me, empowered by their uniforms and steroids and ID badges.

C'mon, champ, says Charlie, pushing me towards the heavy RSL doors, I think you better make a run for it.

Out front, Chappo guns the engine, the others peering anxiously out of the windows. Fela Kuti's horn howls on the van stereo as the jungle streams past in fecund midnight green. My heart beats like a jackhammer.

What the hell happened back there? asks Robin.

I look at Ed who looks at Charlie who looks at Nick who looks back at me. Nobody says a word.

People come and go at the Burnley Hotel in Sydney's Kings Cross. We've been on the road for several weeks now and reality has gone soft around the edges. Someone has overdosed in one of the hotel's tiny haunted rooms and the night clerk is having a nervous breakdown, another ambulance outside reception and police on the way. Our girlfriends, flown up north to meet us for the last shows, stand around whispering to each other, plainly horrified. Sydney's humidity is wreaking havoc with their look: their long, teased hair hangs limply over the melting make-up on their lovely faces. Junkies stagger by, drawn to the flashing lights like disco divas to a mirror ball.

What's happening? a miniskirted transvestite asks me.

Somebody turned blue, I hear myself say.

Anyone you know? she whispers furtively.

I shake my head to answer no but as her eyes are closed, the response doesn't register. Instead, she breaks into a gap-tooth smile. Well, don't you worry, darling, they'll be alright – and if not, there's always another fish in the sea! Shit happens …

Then she pauses, chemically suspended in mid-sentence, a thin trail of drool hanging from her precision-painted lower lip.

Leanne quickly takes my arm and walks me on down Darlinghurst Road towards the taxi rank, the others following behind. It's the last night of the tour and we've failed to score, waiting for her connection until the last minute. Leanne's tall and reckless and scared of nothing except her dad, an eastern-suburbs lawyer known to incarcerate his daughter in rehabs and mental hospitals. Sick and despondent, she tries to cheer me up, faking a gun in her hands, *Avengers*-style. If I see a man I don't like, she says raising her voice, you watch, I'm going to just blow him away – boom! And what's he going to do about it? Nothing! Ha!

She screams so loud it rattles the metal-screened pawnshop windows and echoes across the street. Drive-by boys whoop with delight, yelling obscenities into the slipstream. Saturday night's insanity is gathering momentum. Suburban psychotics are cruising for bent kicks, spruikers barking their song of Sodom. Police in four-packs circle the beat, ignoring two unknowns beating each other up in an otherworldly slow-motion dance from the planet Mandrax.

Inside the Trade Union Club it's hard to see anything through the bodies and cigarette smoke. Rose Tattoo rumble over the sound system; the lighting is hell-red and low. Roger and Charlie stand in a corner whispering conspiratorially about business. I'm sick as a dog by now and just hoping the Greek will show up with some sleeping pills. Suddenly she's standing there with her boyfriend, both of them smiling weirdly, and I know the gods are smiling weirdly on me too – they've copped from their friend of a friend of Abe Saffron …

Something shifts in the atmosphere as the last few drops of adrenaline in my entire endocrine system start pushing the dopamine to my brain: the thought arrives in bold face with strobe lights – what a pleasure to be here in this crazy place with these exciting people in this incredible moment in time! The smile swells up from my deep unconsciousness into the fluorescent light of the backstage and consumes me whole as somebody shouts out of the stage door – You lot, get on in five.

Hitchhiking up to Port Macquarie, I find the rugged beauty of the coast and the hills feels strangely familiar, like déjà vu or a premonition. My brother and his girlfriend are living wild there in a comfortably rundown house near the beach. The sun burns like dripping wax, the water stings like jellyfish and salt sterilises the wounds. Nature strips me down to nothing but simple needs and deep relief.

We listen to old records and play campfire guitars and throw tarot by candlelight while the mosquitoes school around us and huntsmen spiders teleport through the shadows. The mornings and evenings are for the beach and the surf, and the heat of the afternoon for reading journalists like James Fenton and Ryszard Kapuscinski, front-line reporters covering secret wars in current conflict zones, dirty deals, black ops. It's inspiring, the idea of travelling this global horror show and writing it into truth.

Weeks of paradise blur at hyperspeed until the overnight bus pulls into Melbourne's Spencer Street one cold early morning. It's raining and the city feels sour and jaded, like the faint taste of vinegar and garbage in the back of my throat. It's so cold I pull down the blinds and will myself to go to bed and sleep, but I'm too wired. Coming home gets me thinking about how much time I've got left to live and what it might take to leave here for good.

We're in the green room at The Venue in St Kilda, drinking the rider and being roundly chastened by a hapless tour manager with a stammer and desperation in his eyes. Ed seems to be asleep on a couch by the window, his latest girlfriend passed out beside him, while Robin, blithely ignoring everyone and everything, practises paradiddles on a rubber pad. Tonight, The Wreckery are up first before Died Pretty and the industry scouts are out in force.

Sally, a Mushroom Records A&R person, corners me on a terrace overlooking the Esplanade and looks me straight in the eye.

Please, she says, Michael really wants to talk with you, about business. Come on, what have you got to lose?

It's too late, I reply, John's here from Citadel. Maybe we're going to go with them. I don't know. Talk to Anne, I think she's managing us now, but I'm really not sure.

Just talk to him, she pleads, he's a business genius, an ideas man, and he's got ideas for you. I mean, really, what have you got to lose?

I'm going away, so what's the point?

She hands me a card with numbers on it. Call me, she says.

But I'm already determined: Mick's Berlin postcard of a Boeing 747 is stuck up on my studio wall like the window to an alternative future.

Two nights at The Club in Collingwood sell out. A little ready money is finally coming into our hands but it seems the band is getting paranoid, suspicions circulate: Are all members being paid the same? Who's really in charge? We're not thinking straight; too many mind-bending substances and lost, late nights sour the first taste of success. Strange and disturbing incidents start to occur, to do with girlfriends, affairs, pawned guitars, disappearing equipment, bad debts, broken promises.

A darkness is gathering and won't be denied. Somewhere in the last year the band lost its naivety and the spell broke. There was a time when we were single-minded and solid as a machine; now we're in danger of parody. We've lost our sense of humour, we've lost the point, the plot.

Change is necessary, a shift to a different, more futurist direction. Experimenting with samplers and electronic sounds, my engineer mate Peter and I record metal on metal in a Richmond garage; the Greek garage mechanic picks up quickly on the idea, proposing various machines and metals for us to record and splice and feed into the PPG, a new-generation sampler we've just got our hands on.

The ghost-in-the-machine will one day soon supersede the idea of 'the band', Peter says, it's already happening. What this machine can do will soon change everything, just watch.

Robin is still my main musical partner and we work closely together, merging industrial sounds with The Wreckery's guitar-and-sax attack in a recording studio where two sixteen-track reel-to-reel recorders talking through a timecode keep losing synch. It's slow work in the windowless dark of this deadly boring warehouse studio, and after weeks of toil the strain is showing.

Let's sack the band, I propose to Robin, and create a new sound.

Maybe not a good idea, he replies deadpan, giving nothing away. But … we could bring in some extra players. At least that way I could get off the drums and concentrate on arrangements.

Let's do it, I enthuse, an expanded line-up!

The seeds of the band's autodestruction are already sown, just when success itself is in reach through television and the power of the cathode ray; we're featured on the emerging national music shows in studio concerts and with Alain Rodier's videos. The underground scene is joining the mainstream at the hip; free street magazines are circulating, advertisers putting their money down. Independent music is now big business, but I'm too perverse to look after my own interests.

Don't be a wanker, says Ed, it's all just a big fucking stupid game. Grab the money and run.

A week later friends drag us apart during a backstage altercation at the Ballroom, best friends beating up on each other but neither one really knowing why or wanting to back down. Undone by self-sabotage, the band is paralysed, finished.

Gradually the intense light and noise begin to fade until the days grow long and quiet and I get a high-pitched ringing in my ears followed by the eerie feeling that the implosion is totally my own fault.

Harry drops by with a torn supermarket bag stuffed with books. I've got something for you, he says absently, Roland

Barthes, the mathematics of need … his voice tapers off and he scratches his neck.

I just got to use your bathroom for a moment, is that alright?

Fifteen minutes later he ventures out with pupils so pinned he can barely see, moving around the room by touch, high as an extraterrestrial.

Yeah, mate, he says looking right through me, sorry. I'm giving up, any day now, maybe tomorrow … or the day after that. Sorry.

In the background, The Platters harmonise 'Smoke Gets in your Eyes' on a scarred vinyl scavenged from some op shop.

You know how it is, he says with an anguished smile, all red beard and yellow teeth. The problem is, a person can't be revolutionary and shoot dope at the same time because of the slave mentality dope demands … I ask myself – if dope isn't the ultimate capitalist creation, a product that compels users to continue with it and costs very little money to make, then what is? It's the perfect commodity … So that's why I've got to give it up, on principle. But first there's India, to taste the fruits, and then that's it, I swear. But you, he rounds on me, are wasting your time. What's actually keeping you here?

The needle skips on the last groove of *The Platters' Greatest Hits* with a repetitive arrhythmic thump. We listen to the locked stylus until it builds up enough grit on its diamond tip to abruptly skate back across the vinyl surface with a screech like car tyres braking on a wet road.

A little after midnight there's a knock on the front door. I can hear my girlfriend with her soft sleeping sounds in the next room, watching everything with her eyes wide shut. I slope down the hallway wondering who it could be dropping in so late, unannounced. As I slip the latch, the flyscreen swings open and the piggish metal nostrils of a sawn-off shotgun are shoved into my face.

Don't say a fucking word, you cunt, a hard voice barks at me from the darkness, don't you fucking look at me or talk to me, you get that, cunt-head? We're going for a little drive, so don't do anything stupid or I'll break you in two.

A powerful hand on the back of my neck drags me out of the house as the door clicks shut behind us. I'm paralysed with fear, words come with difficulty – Wait, I blurt out stupidly, I haven't got any keys!

The guy sharply slaps me once and I taste blood on my tongue and he says, Your girlfriend will let you in if you come home tonight – but that, you cunt, remains to be seen.

Time both slows down and speeds up. The stunted trees in the garden and the neighbouring Richmond houses seem mute and unfamiliar. Raw terror grips me. I glance around, trying to see his face in the darkness but he just belts me again. Don't fucking look at me, he says, just keep walking and do what you're bloody told.

He's got a mate behind the wheel of a rust-bucket Holden parked down the street. I can't see his face either. The back door swings happen and I'm shoved sprawling onto the torn bucket seat. The driver watches me silently in the rear-view mirror as the guy with the gun gets in the passenger side and sits there for a while saying nothing.

As the shock wears off, my brain starts working again and I open my mouth long enough to ask, What the hell is this all about?

Shotgun man, without even turning around, thumps me right between the eyes with brutal accuracy. A fist is all his hand seems to be, especially made for pummelling idiots like me. I hear his voice speaking in a distant, dreamlike kind of way – You know why I'm here, prick, he says in his flat Aussie drawl, you fucking know it so just have yourself a long hard think.

Time passes slowly in the loaded silence.

Haven't got all night, he says, people to see, debts to collect.

The driver fires up the engine, U-turns across the street with a screech of tyres and accelerates towards Swan Street. Shotgun man suddenly thumps the dashboard with his fist. I said I haven't got all fucking night, cunt!

He balances the sawn-off on his shoulder, pointing it at my face.

You know a girl called Fee, like Fee as in Fiona? Well, you've got a fucking fee to pay, mate, and it's not a bloody parking ticket!

I know who he's talking about: a doe-eyed biker-chick dope dealer I've been stringing along for a while, paying her extra attention to squeeze more gear from her on credit. I almost feel a strange sense of relief, knowing this is all a petty misunderstanding over a couple of hundred dollars.

Yeah, everybody knows Fee.

She's my girlfriend, you bogsplat, he says, I've just gotten out of fucking G-block and I'm not feeling very good about the world so you're just about to pay me eighteen hundred dollars or I beat you into dog meat, get it?

Eighteen hundred dollars? It's a fortune. And it's not even true. Just then I notice the door handles have been removed from inside the car.

But I'm not a bad bloke, he contends, in fact I'm quite the softy.

At which the driver starts sniggering and pulls over into the Victoria Street high-rise commission flats' car park. The scene we're in resembles a Crawfords television crime show and the thought makes me laugh with the shock and absurdity of it all.

He's a tough little bugger, says the driver.

Yeah, I guess he's not such a bad cunt after all, says shotgun man.

Under the hepatitic-yellow glow of the high-rise floodlights we talk in the car for an hour. I reassure him that I never touched his girlfriend and his attitude lightens a little more. He offers me a smoke and I very, very carefully explain that Fee's habit may just have gotten out of control while he was put away, for which reason she's exaggerating the debts of her clients.

Yeah, he says dropping the sawn-off on the floor by his feet, I knew there was something different about her. Women, mate, you can't trust 'em.

We settle on six hundred dollars. It seems a small price to pay for my health.

Arriving home, I immediately sense something's terribly wrong: the house is completely dark and I can hear girls crying. I stand in the hallway listening to their sobs and the ticking of the lounge-room clock, wishing none of this was real, then walk on a few steps and switch on the bedroom light. Mary and Robyn are sitting on the rumpled sheets and blankets hugging each other, their pretty faces all raw and swollen.

We all look at each other for a frozen eternal moment and suddenly I know without being told that Harry is dead. Robyn starts talking all in a rush and as she does the dawn light bleeds through the cracks under the window blinds and the city around us begins to stir – the throbbing engines of early commuters on Church Street, the rumbling of the first trams, an alarm-clock radio bleeding talkback from the house next door.

I can't focus on everything she's telling me, but I pick up the key points – India, an overdose on the train, corrupt police, bureaucratic problems with flying his body back home. All I can really think of is the question that haunts me still – was it an accident, or suicide? Nobody knows and they never will. It could have been random, it could have been anyone, but it wasn't, it was him, Harry, and it was the end of something innocent and the beginning of something else, damaged but a little wiser – the burning desire to get out of this place, this street, this country, and go somewhere I don't speak the language in a place I don't yet know exists: to just disappear.

It's the band's last concert, filming a scene for a movie that I agreed to act in for the sole reason of getting enough money to fly to London. The lame script features The Wreckery playing live at The Club on Smith Street. The cameras roll, the smoke gushes and the guitar riff to the song 'Ruling Energy' chatters its staccato rhythm.

Turning around to count the band in, I see Robin's still there but my old bandmates have been substituted by Chris Hughes, Rowland Howard and John Murphy. World-class players, but it all seems strangely pointless and phoney under the artificial movie-set lights, going through the motions, just doing it for the cash. Now the original line-up has dissolved, it's clear the combination of who we were was key to what made us a happening proposition in the first place. The problem, it hits me, is the fact that I'm still here even though the party has long since finished.

I cold turkey under the supervision of an elderly, cancer-riddled Scottish doctor in a Barkly Street clinic. Don't worry, lad, he tells me in his thick gentle brogue, you're young, you're strong, you don't need anything more than courage to walk away from all this – no treatments, no substitutes, none of that rubbish. I don't have long to live, but you've got the rest of your life to go, the rest of your life! If I could, I'd do it all over again, don't you see? It's a gift, a gift to be alive, you just trust me, lad, mark my words! Then the hacking cough overwhelms him, his eyes glistening wet through his glasses.

I'm at the airport with Mary and my mum, picking up our tickets from the Air Thai office. The film production changed our flights so they could reshoot. The clerk hands me the coupons and I realise with mounting concern they've substituted my original return tickets for one-way flights. The girls' faces fall.

So how are we getting home again? Mary asks.

Yes, says Mum, how will you get back home?

I try to appear confident, on top of the situation, but secretly I'm awhirl with confusion. It's too late to change anything, I reply, we're leaving. I'll work it out. We'll be okay.

Now I'm staring out the porthole window from seat 23D as the aircraft taxis out to the runway, wondering if Mary knows that I need more time, that nothing is ever going to be enough, remembering everything that's happened in alternating waves of exhilaration and devastation. Beside me, she carefully shuffles the wads of flight tickets and documents, her long black hair out falling across her face so I can't see what she's thinking. I reach out to touch her hand and she shudders gently and pulls away. Are you cold? I ask. Silently she answers no.

Suddenly the fuselage shudders in the backdraught as its wheels leave the ground. Bracing myself against the seat, I watch Melbourne's vast suburban sprawl shrink into my unwanted past as the 747 swiftly gains altitude and disappears into the clouds.

Breaking the Ice | Berlin, 1989

In the six a.m. dawn light I'm awake again. Our room is furnished with hard rubbish scavenged in the summer – a trestle table, some chairs, an old couch, a colour-coded map of Europe tacked to the wall. On the windowsill there's the ghetto blaster cassette-radio combo I've been carrying around these last six months. The BBC World Service whispers through its small Japanese speakers, reporting demonstrations in East Germany, street fighting in the cities of Romania. There is movement in the Soviet satellites, pressure from the masses for greater freedom and the right to emigrate to the West.

The grey Old World museum that is Europe shows signs of splitting at the seams.

Berliner humour is dark. The city lives under a cloud, a nuclear future hazy with fallout from the recent Chernobyl reactor meltdown. Sardonic mutation jokes circulate on a wave of speculation about the radioactivity of supermarket foods. Nobody drinks the water unfiltered. A certain bluntness of speech, a disregard for conventional niceties sharpens the subtext of even the most trivial encounters and transactions. These are Cold War times; the Wall has been standing since before any of us was born and there is no reason yet to think it will ever fall, not with thirty thousand nuclear warheads deployed around it.

Andreas, the son of our landlord, points at a map to show me how the Wall cuts through the city like a jagged scar.

My new friend John, whom I met on my first night here when I played a solo concert in a Schoeneberg bar, speaks an almost perfect English he learnt from his Canadian mother. John and his girlfriend Ursula have invited us to stay in their converted doctor's surgery, sharing the rent.

Millions of brainwashed people waiting to get into West Berlin, John says, a prole invasion hungry for the fruits of capitalist materialism! But don't worry, the Wall is impenetrable, there's no way it will ever come down. Only a full-scale war could trigger it.

Ursula, tough and pretty, rolls her eyes, *Mann!* It's just a wall, you know, big deal. It's not there because it looks good. Everybody needs it or I don't know, she laughs, they kill each other? It's always been there. You get used to it.

No one questions the presence of the Wall; it is absolute.

But you never know, John says, nobody knows. Things change, *ja*?

Sometimes I sleep in Andreas's bombproof bunker underneath the internal courtyard. Old war photos ripped from books cover the walls – Wehrmacht soldiers crouching in doorways or behind tanks, throwing grenades, loading their guns, cooking a stew on an open fire, rotting in the rubble, unsung heroes of the fall of Berlin, fighting for the dark side, frozen in time.

Andreas has reinforced the inside of the front door with a sheet of some special metal for shooting practice, its dull sheen peppered with missile impacts like the surface of the moon. He says he can defend himself if they come over the Wall, that he'd rather die on his feet than live on his knees, that the scarred facade of the house is still riddled with mementos from the street fights of '45, and the battle for Germany isn't over yet – *Wir sind bereits!* We are ready …

The penny *groschens,* dank and crusty, are stacked up on the rush-matted floor beside the mattress. I'm kneeling down in the half-light, rolling them into military-brown Deutschebank wrappers. Grubby bar tips and supermarket change, rubbed so thin by time's grimy fingers you can barely read the year of minting. I stuff a heavy gloveful, ten marks' worth, deep into the pockets of an old leather greatcoat then step out into the drizzling sleet.

It's already night-dark at four in the afternoon; the streetlights saturate the iced mud and dog turds on the footpath with a strange yellow glow. Cold air blasts out of the stairwell to the underground. I hop a ride on a spray-can-tagged U-Bahn carriage through the tunnelled viscera of West Berlin for a couple of stations then walk up towards Potsdamer Platz. Black marketeers work here in the shadow of the Wall, hustling for West German currency.

Cigarettes with names like Dixie Filtertips or Westpoint, coined in some boardroom in Ukraine or Anatolia using a dated copy of *Vanity Fair* for reference, are splayed across a pair of upended Schultheiss beer crates. I tap a carton of Harvard filter tips and the vendor holds up five fingers. I lay four tubes of rolled pennies down and he pulls a face before whipping the money away with a rag-and-bone man's deft touch.

I light one up, choking on the stale chemical taste as he grins at me with brown, broken teeth, then hurry away towards the club, running late as usual.

The floor of the Ex'n'Pop glistens under a dirty film of melted snow studded with cigarette butts and broken glass. Tony Joe White on the stereo, bar flies drinking beer and vodka shots, the air thick with smoke. The small room is filling up and the sight and sound of the boisterous crowd make me nervous.

Mann, says Giselle rolling her eyes, too many people out of their heads, it's not safe in the little girls' room! You come with me, *ja*?

I'm waiting by the door when she calls me inside her cubicle, drumming her high heels with glee. Maybe it's our lucky day, she says – in the foam and crud on the floor lies a paper origami bird some careless girl let fall.

I quit that shit, I tell her.

Oh just this once won't hurt you, she replies with a wounded expression. *Mensch,* this is Berlin!

Skilfully she empties the contents onto the cistern lid, cutting lines with the blunt edge of a comb while I keep the door pressed shut. The kick is nasty and the rush comes fast in foaming chemical waves. Giselle whispers something in my ear that makes no sense and when I turn around she's gone. I light another Harvard, its predecessor burning into the plastic cistern lid, and step back into the room and the noise and the light. The room is filling up and the sight and sound of the boisterous crowd make me nervous.

My friend David, six feet of barely restrained aggression and twitchy unpredictability, is pacing up and down near the stage, working himself into a state. David's come to Berlin to avoid a warrant out for him back home due to an altercation in a nightclub and is now working with me as my manager.

Where've you been, man? Your first set started half an hour ago!

I feel slightly unreal, ready for nothing and everything, the taste of an unknown substance clinging to my tonsils like the memory of a bad dream.

Can you get me a drink? I ask him while tuning the three battered guitars we bought in London into open chords.

Sure, he snaps back, I'll get you one, but remember, I don't drink. You know what I mean? I quit. Because big things are in motion. Like, I've got to introduce you to this guy from Hamburg, works in German TV. He's very interested in you, right? And that's why I don't drink. I don't want to fuck up, get it? Not like Hippie Johnny. I've done twelve steps and I'm not stepping back again, you know what I'm saying?

I plug the little sampler into the guitar amp and check the cables and step up behind the microphone. A stage light shines directly into my eyes and I can't see anything except silhouettes in the haze. I'm singing into a void, singing Robert Johnson, Elvis, Mike Bloomfield, John Hammond, Jr, some originals. People clap and shout incomprehensible German slang between songs over the racket from the kicker tables in the back. Drinks are cheap and everybody in the room is hammered.

A row of Jaegermeisters is lined up along the lip of the stage beside the microphone stand. I finish something Marilyn Monroe used to sing and reach down for a shot. Heat burns my fingers, warm blood drips from my hand; there's smashed glass glinting back at me from down there in the dark. I realise I'm wounded but somehow the lines Giselle cut render the pain abstract, as if this is all happening to someone else. I flash on Nazi soldiers mainlining their military speed as they walk home from defeat in Russia in temperatures cold enough to freeze saliva.

Ursula's voice raised in habitual fury blasts every other thought from my head. *Mann, echt! Blueder idioten! Unglaublich!*

John and his twin brother Berndt, against her advice, have invested in building their own recording studio in the basement with capital from a shady business contact. And now the financier wants his money back and the twins don't have it. They sit in the kitchen rolling hashish and tobacco and blowing out thick clouds of black smoke, arguing solutions over tall cups of strong coffee and making obscure phone calls.

It doesn't matter anyway, says Ursula, absolute conviction glaring from her sky-blue eyes, because there's no point. This is all useless, you're kidding yourselves. You're just a couple of stupid kids, anyway. I could scream. *Mann!*

Ursula grew up in Bavaria in a military town flanked by a nuclear power station and a US base and never wants to go back there again.

I hate the place, she says, crossing her legs and smoothing down her tight black skirt. They're all assholes. Berlin is okay, because Berlin is not Germany!

The phone rings and she picks it up, *Hallo?*

Ursula listens to the caller with gathering impatience. Her face flushes with blood as the rage lodged deep within her whips itself up again. The pain and fury in Ursula are a combustible cocktail that keeps people around her in a state of permanent alert. She is sweet but dangerous, and never afraid to speak her mind.

Fick dich! she yells, slamming the phone down again.

Caya, Ursula's full-grown Doberman bitch, barks in the hall, loud as gunfire. The shattering sound grows in intensity, morphing into a keening howl.

Halts maul, mann! she says. Johnny, can't you make her stop?

The Doberman staggers into the room and writhes on its back, paws in the air, moaning in tongues, eyes staring wildly.

Scheisse! Something's wrong! she shrills.

Suddenly Ursula realises the big piece of hash has disappeared from the edge of the table, looks at the tall black dog bucking and rolling its eyes, and back at the empty space on the table again.

Nein, says Ursula, *nein!* She ate that shit! Can you believe this?

She brings her hands up to her face in despair.

Caya's pregnant too! *Mann!* Am I going crazy?

She locks herself in her room, moving the furniture around. Thumps and crashes from Ursula's private war zone echo through the apartment, underscored by the moaning of the stoned Doberman.

Ja, says John, a Lucky Strike smoking between his fingers, it's okay. Really, don't worry, I know you can't understand, so don't even try. She comes from a fucked-up place but, you know, man, I love her. This seems crazy but, you know, we're going to be okay. *Ja?* Okay. *Alles fein!*

John smiles at me, daring me to believe him as one lazy eye goes out of focus, trained on invisible mysteries in the aether behind my head.

Caya has fallen asleep in the middle of the kitchen floor, her distended belly rising and falling as she breathes and twitches, an ecstatic grin across her face.

Ja, says John, you see the dog is alright. But the politics are something else! That's something you could be worried about. You know, West Berlin is a little island in the East. We are surrounded. I know nobody in the East, I have no relatives there. It is, you know, like a dream. East Germany? What is that? Some kind of joke?

At Friedrichstrasse railway station David and I queue up through slow-motion border controls for a five-mark transit stamp, walk a corridor and a few flights of stairs across to the Communist side. Down on the platform, the spartan Reichsbahn carriages of the Vindobona Vienna express are ghostly and desolate: brown vinyl upholstery, brown curtains, faded faux-teak panelling, the scent of beer, gherkin and tobacco. A smattering of commercial travellers and foreign students sit in the flickering half-light as a whistle blows and the train picks up speed into the black, starless haze of the DDR.

I'm never going back, says David. Melbourne sucks, it's not even real, it's a half-life at best. Why go back when there's all of this to explore?

We stare out the warped windows across the flat plains of Leipzig where a nuclear stack spews steam into the chemical air.

Yeah, I answer, why would you go back?

Well, I guess I have to see my mother sometimes.

Maybe she can come to you?

An oncoming train belts past, vibrating our carriage like a toy.

I'm not going to hold my breath, says David. How old are you?

Twenty-five.

Well, I'm twenty-three and I've got all the time in the world.

The domes of Dresden hove out of the gloom as the train enters a deserted station smudged by coal smoke and scarred by the English carpet bombing of 1945. This is the last rail stop before the Czechoslovak frontier and most passengers have alighted from the idling train when in the next carriage a scene unfolds as uniformed and plain-clothes cops forcibly remove a girl onto the platform. The few travellers around her pretend the arrest is not happening. I grip the window and watch transfixed as she cries and protests until the engine kicks in with a reverberating blast of horn.

Don't get involved, says David, stretching out across the seats for a power nap. It's not worth it. You know what I mean? Everybody's got their own shit to deal with. God knows I have enough of my own.

Crossing the frontier, border cops search the carriage with dogs and interrogate the few and silent passengers; their dark police uniforms and insignia signify the institutional weight of a vast, indifferent bureaucracy. No one resists this systemic implementation of power. Time slackens to a speed some existential seconds slower as the language shifts into the alien, heavy Slavic tongue. The cop studies my passport looking for the transit stamps, places it on an armrest, punches in an inky affirmative.

The Vindobona crawls to a dead stop on the raised outskirts of Prague. The serpentine undulations of the Vltava river below glisten in the moonlight. No one gets on or off the train. There are no announcements. While David dozes in a corner, I wander into the empty Mitropa restaurant carriage where a pall of cigarette smoke hovers over a fossilised array of cabbage rolls and sausages. The bolted windows mirror me against the weaponised unknown of eastern European night in a warped funhouse reflection, a ghost out of time myself.

Another shot of InterRail Stroh rum, another bootleg Princeton cigarette.

I could get addicted to this feeling.

Dawn breaks over Vienna's Westbahnhof station. Early-morning business commuters in woollen suits and overcoats wait on the platform surrounded by an overkill of corporate neon – Siemens, Bosch, Bayer, Daimler-Benz, Deutschebank, Western Union, GE. Carrying guitars, we merge into the morning peak-hour crowd and check in to the Hotel Fuerstenhof on the far side of the Guertel.

I sleep all day in a suite with red-carpeted walls, drink soup at a Chinese on the strip. At the U4 club, I set up and play an hour before midnight to a full room. Afterwards, people tell me they enjoyed the show but the real news is elsewhere – thousands of East German citizens are queuing up on the nearby border roads inside Czechoslovakia, demanding right of travel into Austria.

Revolution is in the air.

Shit, says David, what if we can't get back home? What if there's a war, man? A fucking war? There'll be no train to ride back to West Berlin on!

We're here for several more days anyway, I reply. Another show and then the live broadcast from state radio. We'll figure it out somehow.

Ach, you don't need a train, says Karen, our local promoter. You can stay with me. Let's go to a bar I know down the street, a very historical place. You will love it.

Karen and her friends bring us to a bar five minutes' walk away. Hyper-realist murals of powerfully built men fucking each other decorate the walls. Whips and cuffs are displayed on purple velvet cushions in glassed alcoves. George Michael sings on the stereo.

This is a very old bar, she says proudly, here since the thirties at least.

Sex club? David asks.

No, she laughs, it's just a private club for people with

sophisticated tastes. You see, sexuality is deep in our culture. Remember Sigmund Freud? We have a very long history here, not like your New World, *ja?* She laughs icily. After all, what history have you got?

We come from the future, David replies solemnly, to a place where history stopped fifty years ago.

Don't kid yourself, darling, Karen says, you are children! All of history is happening now, all these people shouting to be let out of those poor countries. Don't you realise? There will be blood, but we are used to this, *ja*? We are, how you say, experienced. She raises her glass. *Prost!* To the free world!

Siberian winds caress the streets of West Berlin with cold, skeletal fingers. The trees are stripped of leaves, the sky gunmetal grey. Caya has delivered her puppies. They roll around on the floor gleefully while Ursula stresses about finding homes for them. Kilos of potatoes to nourish their mother boil on the stove next to pots of Mary's pasta sauce, the only food we can afford to eat.

Just get lost, Mary tells David. I don't want you around here.

What about you? David asks me. You want me to get lost too?

I want to keep the peace and retain him as my manager, but I can't do both. Mary is forcing the situation. Clearly, she wants to be the only one advising me on what to do. She and David don't get along and there is only one viable solution – David has to go.

I'm sorry, I tell him. This isn't working out.

He looks at me, outraged, says nothing, walks out slamming the door behind him. I can't even look at Mary, the smug expression on her face.

Ursula and John argue into the small hours, their voices echoing through the apartment in a frenzy of mutual recrimination. The rent is late, the neighbours have been making noise complaints, relationships are frayed to breaking point and the brothers are clearly beginning to panic – if we don't get a record deal for my music, they insist, the studio will go under and we'll all be out on the street.

Got any more songs?

The investor who lent them the start-up money is becoming increasingly tetchy. Now when he drops by unannounced, everybody holds their breath while the doorbell rings, waiting for him to go away.

The radio whispers reports of mass demonstrations, one hundred thousand in the streets of East Berlin, seventy thousand in Leipzig. The situation is quickly escalating, nobody knows what will happen next and we don't have the resources to leave town even if we wanted to.

John and I are in the basement studio, recording folk songs irreverently revved up with acid and electronics, sampling single strings from my old guitars, making loops, losing track of time while we have circular conversations about what we think we're meant to be doing and how to get it done.

Chrislo Haas, bearded and wild-eyed, hunches over the MS-10 synthesiser, patching and repatching cables, grinding the remnants of his teeth together and talking to himself under his breath. Chrislo's machine is pumping out a 50-hertz wave that vibrates the pavement way down the street, and it's four in the morning. A neighbour is banging on the upstairs door, her dog barking out a polyrhythm. We turn out the basement lights and wait for her to give up her protest and leave.

Ja, says Chrislo, who gives the fuck?

In the basement there is no sense of time, only a continuum of abstract night punctuated by coffee and beer and sound. Chrislo is recording electronic noise across one of my songs, unconstrained by arrangement or duration.

Don't stop the tape, he says nervously, this is good, really good.

But the actual song finished ten minutes ago and he's continuing across an entirely different song that follows on the reel. Chrislo is not concerned with songs as such – he's about pure, raw sound and the freedom and the space in which to use it.

Yeah, I say, this is great! Don't stop.

At six, when I wake up, Chrislo is still working.

Ach! Fucking great, he says, listen to this! And he laughs soundlessly, mouth open, neck muscles working as he chomps on thin air, warning lights flashing in his eyes.

The Korg synth he's taped is like nothing I've ever heard before. I'm so captivated I don't immediately register that he's recorded over all the tracks on the tape, erasing everything I recorded before. Now there are eight tracks of white and pink noise, no voice or guitar or drums.

You don't need that shit, he says, that was yesterday and it doesn't matter any more. This is new pop, this is the new pop music. You will thank me.

I stare at him blearily while we listen to the playback, but Chrislo seems to have lost interest in the recording. With a childlike cry of delight he mounts a mechanical beetle, the toy of Ursula's son, mounts it doggy style, grinding his hips into the dark, rotating plastic, then looks at me and laughs until I laugh too.

In ze ass, get it? Now you get it!

Then the laughter stops and he walks over to the tape machine, rewinds to the beginning and pressing play-record, erases everything on the tape from start to finish.

Besser so, he says solemnly, almost whispering, *besser so.*

Mikal visits the basement studio with a black eye and a sixpack of beer under his arm – he and his girlfriend are not getting along. Mikal has the face of Jesus straight out of some Catholic print, gaunt and bearded with sad blue eyes. The girlfriend is crucifying me, he says with a bitter grin, I can't take it any more.

They have a wild three-year-old boy, and they both like a drink.

Mann, he complains, I don't know what's going to happen next. But whatever you do, don't make babies! When the child is born, I tell you, it's your turn to die! Then he laughs hysterically until he starts to cough, patting down his pockets, looking for a cigarette. Maybe that's why we have kids, he says, to commit suicide!

Don't say these things, says John. *Mensch*, it's not right …

What's that sound? I interrupt them. Suddenly, we're all aware of a background noise subtly seeping through the gaps in our conversation: pop-gun fireworks, distant sirens, the ground itself seems to be shaking.

John, alarmed, gets to his feet as Ursula bursts in from the top of the stairs – Johnny! *Mann!* Quick, come here! They're coming over the Wall, right now! Johnny! It's on the TV!

I unplug the instruments and power down the mixing console while John and Mikal open the ventilation grate above the mixing desk and the noise of the external world fills the shadowy basement – car horns, shouts and strange cries, rockets whistling through the streets, explosions like small-arms fire in the distance. The sound of street fighting turns out to be a symphony of celebration; sketchy, panicked television reports show jubilant crowds, strobed by flash photography, dancing atop the Wall in stonewashed denims, passing beer bottles around, waving German flags and chipping away at the concrete with picks and axes.

Radio bulletins confirm a steady flow of thousands of people crossing over from the East side. Border guards have simply discarded their badges and walked off the job. The grand charade is over – the Communist government, against all predictions, has collapsed under its own entropic weight.

We cruise from Potsdamer Platz to Chausseestrasse in Ursula's beaten-up black Mazda, scoping the action: police and riot vans command arterial intersections, bullhorns bark staccato crowd commands; red-black-and-yellow German flags flutter in the grey autumnal night. The atmosphere is tense, explosive, mobs roaming the streets like a capacity crowd exiting the football stadium after a big game, jubilant and volatile. Helicopters buzz overhead; even the fire brigade is deployed. We drive on until we can't get any closer, then double back to Harry and Evelyn's Ex'n'Pop bar in Schoeneberg where the crowd is spilling out onto the street.

An impromptu German country-music session sound-checks a Hank Williams song. They try out the electric piano, the lap steel guitar; the drummer tunes his snare. In the background, a cassette tape blares out Amphetamine Reptile bands, all distorted guitars and pain-driven vocals. In the adjacent black room, revellers cut lines of glittery sulphate on a mirrored table.

Giselle drinks at the bar, inconsolable. Our beautiful West Berlin, she says with tears in her eyes, is ruined. It will never be the same. The dream is over! Here come the masses ready to rape you and slit your throat for a home video player. Now Berlin will be as fucked as the rest of Germany!

Next day, the shelves of the neighbourhood Aldi supermarket are stripped. Chocolate, canned fish, bread, fresh milk, sugar, coffee and tea have vanished overnight. A queue of tough elderly housewives complain to the cashier about sold-out products and the critical lack of toilet paper. Such women endured the fall of the Reich, rebuilding their homes brick by brick after their husbands failed to return from the frontlines.

The check-out clerk just shrugs and gestures hopelessly – the momentum of history has taken over, even down to the most banal details, and there's nothing to be done about it. Come back tomorrow.

There's going to be more cops everywhere, warns Micha, they'll be checking everyone for documents. You got a visa?

I shake my head.

Stay invisible, he recommends.

Chris Hughes is calling from a telephone box in a small town near Timisoara, Romania. Chris and Bruno and their band Once Upon A Time arrived from Melbourne a few weeks ago and have been staying in the doctor's surgery too. A tornado of interference on the line, I can barely hear him.

I just tried every other phone box around but they're all

broken, he says. I don't understand why this one works! At least the shooting stopped last week, but there are no buses or trains. So we're stuck here with Gabi's family. Nobody speaks English. It's fucked! I'll try to be in Berlin by next week. You got a gig? Is there any money in it?

Hughes's coins run out. The line goes dead.

I walk back to my room. Mary and I are playing a board game on the floor – Risiko, the conquest of empires. I lay myself down on the floor beside her. Mary doesn't speak a word of German. Neither of us have any money, we have nowhere else to go.

Today is Christmas Day and our families on the other side of the world feel galaxies away. In the background, the radio whispers the news cycle between clouds of light static.

The dominoes could fall all the way back to Moscow, says the correspondent portentously, creating ripples in the region that will change the face of Europe.

The audio cuts to the streets of Bucharest, a hundred thousand people all shouting at once, sirens, gunfire. The Romanian dictator Ceausescu is on trial. It seems so immediate, like the execution of the Tsar and his daughters was yesterday, in the house next door. But details are hazy. The speed of events outstrips telecommunications. Confusion reigns.

The apartment is strangely quiet. All the dogs have stopped barking. We've become so used to the high-octane emotional atmosphere that dumb silence is eerie.

Where are the puppies, says Mary, did you sell them?

Ursula looks away and rolls her eyes.

I had to do something, she says, so I, you know, drowned them in the bathtub.

A moment of shock and then Mary starts crying.

Echt, mann, Ursula says, they were a real fucking problem, you know. What did you expect me to do? Look after them all? What do you think I am? A dog servant? I've already got enough problems with you two around.

It's New Year's Eve. Birgit, tall and dark with penetrating indigo eyes, her hair pulled back in a tight ponytail, has drunk five tall vodkas in a row but shows no signs of the alcohol fizzing in her bloodstream.

There's no point, she shouts over the music. People are apathetic. I know you think people are basically good but really, they don't care about anything. It's everyone for him- or herself. That's why the world is neck-deep in shit. Somehow we keep breathing, even with all that stink in our nostrils. What you think is change, that's just repetition. Because you don't know history. Ach, you think you do? Then if you know history, you also know there's no point. No future. People have the power, *ja okay*, but people are the problem. Depopulate, she says, this is the answer. The bomb was invented for a reason.

Sounds like another final solution, I suggest half-jokingly.

Birgit laughs briefly. They are still with us, she says, the Nazis, you know. They are in the government. They are in the town hall. They run the police. That's what, you know, Ulrike Meinhof was on about. She was no fool. But *ja*, in the end even the terrorists are useless. Because people are so stupid. And that's why we're all doomed, *verstehen*?

Then she relents a little and turns to Mary, I'm sorry if I'm talking too much, but you know, I haven't slept for days. I need cigarettes and something to eat, you coming?

We walk down the Oranienstrasse, past the Spanish restaurants and art galleries and hole-in-the-wall all-night bars and tattooed street punks with their skinny feral dogs begging on the sidewalks. *Hey alte! Gibst mir eine groschen bitte?* … Mate! Spare us some change?

Occasional rockets whistle overhead, fireworks rain down from the six-storey apartment blocks on either side. It's easy to imagine the war here, projectiles shooting by close enough to touch and the scent of gunpowder on the breeze.

Behind us I hear shouting and truck engines; a wave of military green is massing at the far end of the street. Even in this half-light the futuristic metal hardware and perspex face visors of the security police and their Dobermans glint like one dangerous machine. A few hundred people in the street are bar-hopping, getting ready to party in the new decade. The future. 1990.

A jolt of keen electric panic flashes through my body as batons beat on the massed shields advancing towards us. Everybody turns around, looking for a way out; that's when we see another wall of shields and helmets at the other end and realise the whole block has been sealed off – it's a set-up. We hide in a doorway but they're coming on fast. Somebody pushes me and shouts, Run!

The shopfront shutters are rolling down all along the street. We scramble under one of the last to close, mere seconds before it slams shut. Police batons hammer a crazy, arrhythmic drum pattern on the metal blinds. The leather-clad biker next to me just smiles and shakes his head and says, *Immer scheiss egal!* – Always the same shit!

The barstaff line up dozens of shot glasses along the counter, filling them with chilled Moskovskaya. The owner calls for a toast to the new year – *skoll!*

Anne and Mary and I drink coffee on East Berlin's Kollwitzplatz, New Year's Day. It's cold and deserted and utterly beautiful, the deep winter light soaking the streets in spectral shades of grey. The apartment houses around the square are stripped back to their stone core, devoid of ornamentation or colour. Whole floors and entire buildings boarded up, windows smashed, gates locked with rusted chains.

A hand-painted anarchy symbol hangs from a fourth-floor balcony; next to it another pictogram threatens Nazi skins with a bloody red fist. Squatters have already moved into these dwellings, leaching electricity off the grid with long extension cables hung floor to floor. They come from parts near and distant as if to the beat of an invisible drum, whether Spain, Greece, Canada, Argentina, Australia or just some lost little town in the German countryside.

In the distance, the silhouette of communist *plattenbau* apartment blocks, monolithic and pale, stand jagged against the skyline. People moved out there years ago from these inner-city apartments imagining a new and cleaner life courtesy of the socialist dream, modelled on Soviet-style modernity.

You know, says Anne earnestly, soon enough they will renovate this entire district and raise the rental prices. They'll kick everybody out and the *Wessies* will move in – lawyers, bureaucrats from Bonn, politicians. Everything will look new, pink and yellow, like Lego bricks.

Eduard Ruehmann at Normal cuts me a deal. A letter arrives from Bonn with a cheque attached – the mythical advance in black and white, a signed contract. After John and Berndt have quickly sold off the studio and paid back their investor, there is still some money left over. I'm elated; we have lift-off because a band has formed around the recording sessions – the True Spirit. And now, once again, the van is waiting.

You ready? John asks.

Reinhold, behind the wheel, smiles maniacally.

Where's Hughes?

We got to go and pick him up.

Jesus wept.

We're heading to the East German town of Neuruppin, less than an hour away, to perform on a left-wing 'Red Wedge' festival program. The old autobahn beneath the wheels delivers a bone-crunching jolt every 20 metres where the slave gangs of the Third Reich dropped their concrete slabs and the cement grout dissolved over time; the Mercedes van rattles like a tin can full of nails

Shit, yells says Reinhold over the noise, where is it? *Links? Rechts? Links?*

Circling through the dark and deserted streets we eventually locate an old dance hall with a sprung floor and a handwritten sign out front advertising our concert there tonight. The promoter is a depressive young student called Klaus whose negativity proves infectious. The ersatz security personnel are his despondent student friends, and they cluster around the main entrance nervously testing the chains slung across the front doors.

You are *auslaender* band – foreigners, he says, that is problem, *weiss du?*

Rainer, a guitarist from the Berlin band Die Haut, has joined our group along with his girlfriend, who quickly becomes our manager. With a scarf tied around his neck and a worldly, commanding attitude, Rainer discusses right-wing gangs, such as the local neo-Nazi skinheads, with the promoter. John and Reinhold listen attentively.

I will fucking smash them, reckons Reinhold. I get my baseball bat from the van, *ja*?

No, no, don't worry about it, Rainer laughs nervously, nothing's going to happen. At least, I hope not …

So why did they book us in the first place? John asks.

Because, Rainer replies, they want to promote Western culture to the next generation and I guess we're guinea pigs for their experiment.

Lab rats, says John.

Fuck it, says Hughes, let's get a beer in.

A small audience gradually shuffles into the hall and spreads out in front of the stage, a little uptight and difficult to read. A student with intense eyes and thick glasses stares fixedly at my head while behind him people in the crowd seem distracted by what might be a small commotion happening beyond the heavy curtains at the street entrance. I introduce the band to warm up the crowd but there's no response at all and barely any clapping between songs. John stares at the floor during the whole set, feeding back through his amp with an electrifying howl. We are seriously loud but nobody seems to want to leave and nobody does.

Afterwards, a blonde girl is watching us packing up the amplifiers and drums. She's dressed in black and very neatly made-up with cropped peroxided hair. A group of crewcut young men with sour, belligerent expressions follow her around like bodyguards. Something isn't right about the way they're watching us and when she notices me observing them, she gives her boys a code gesture and they all quickly disappear.

Did you see that? I ask Rainer.

See what? he replies, looking around the empty room. Are you nervous? Take it easy, man. Everything's cool.

We're ready to load our equipment out of the venue when we hear chanting in the street. Shaven-headed youths wearing army boots have gathered in a semicircle around the entrance, singing old Nazi songs like a choir of psychotic sailors. Seconds later, another posse of skinheads charge into the hall past the terrified security staff, shouting slogans, blowing referee's whistles, kicking and slapping at anything in their path, splintering tables and chairs, shattering empty beer glasses, quickly exiting out the back of the building, leaving their hard little voices hanging in the air.

Lugging the gear out of the rear exit into the sidestreet where Reinhold's van is parked, we can still hear distant chanting and whistles echoing around the block. Better get a move on, says Hughes, it sounds like they're coming back. Just then we see the gang a hundred metres down the street but it seems they've changed their game; one of them is on the ground in a foetal position and the rest are taking turns kicking him with their steel-capped boots. I guess that's their idea of fun, reckons Hughes. We lock ourselves inside the backstage for a long half-hour until the police finally arrive, but by the time they do, the skinhead choir has mysteriously melted away into the flagstone streets.

Klaus, ashen-faced, thanks us for coming and hands over an

envelope containing several hundred Deutschmarks and a shaky hand-drawn map of the way to our overnight accommodation. The map guides us through the old town and out into the starless countryside, driving a long arc across the fields until we arrive at a housing estate of towering *plattenbauen*.

John and Rainer locate tower block B.

The blue glow of television sets pulses in a few of the apartments but mostly the windows are dark. Gutted Trabant automobiles lie marooned in the car park between sporadic clusters of garbage and weeds. We haul the guitars and electronics from the van across the loose gravel and mud into a lobby coated in a film of sticky, chocolate-coloured dust. A huge portrait of ex-DDR premier Honecker hangs in the concierge's office; the office itself is locked.

Our rooms are high up on the tenth floor and the elevators are all out of order. We climb stairwells reeking of disinfectant and giddily wallpapered in 1960s-style geometric designs to collapse into unlocked rooms furnished with narrow beds and bulbless Bakelite lamps. In the morning, I part the stiff, acrylic curtains and gaze across to the horizon where a huge power station chimney belches thunderheads of steam. Down in the yard, children play in the gravel and mud, shouting and digging with little plastic spades beneath a sky saturated with slag-grey cloud. I can hear the other boys moving around in the room next door and we shout to each other through the walls, making plans to meet downstairs. I slip into last night's clothes, pick up my guitar and rucksack and exit the room, leaving the door ajar.

A convoy of battered Mercedes sedans and caravans clutters the fields around Berlin's Reichstag, spilling over into the verdant public park of the adjacent Tiergarten. These Balkan gypsies, Roma people, have slipped in through a legal loophole from the Eastern dark. The *polizei* appear to lack the power to move them on.

I'm working nights in the Tiergarten Tempodrom, serving drinks at outdoor events. The gypsy kids, with their hard eyes and chunky bodies, seem more like miniature adults than children. They gang up around my kiosk, ordering beer and soft drink and quickly relaying the cups to other kids behind them.

Fuenf coca! Fuenf marken! Five Cokes! Five marks!

Es war nur drei! It was only three!

Nein!

Ja, sicher!

They are masters of the ancient shell game – three thimbles on a table, under which lies the prize? I move them left, I move them right, watch my hands! How much you want to bet?

I don't even try to compete with their razor-sharp street smarts.

The Roma men move slowly in their heavy gold jewellery, gamble at cards on picnic tables, drink slivovitz from plastic Pepsi bottles and watch the scene with hooded eyes, their women nowhere to be seen. The kids are their eyes and ears, coordinated by a collective mind, like flocking birds.

Soon they'll be followed by human slavers, drug dealers, plutonium smugglers, body-parts suppliers, the Russian mafia, the whole circus headed for Potsdamer Platz, Berlin's own ground zero, firebombed into ruins at war's end then razed flat by the Communists with the Wall rammed in one side and out the other.

The dirt and gravel above the bunkers where Hitler popped his cyanide now host a flea market. East European escorts patrol this wasteland by night in glow-in-the-dark thigh-high boots. By day, you can buy imitation guns and knives, illegal Nazi memorabilia, Wall fragments, Russian cameras, machine parts, spectacles, maps, binoculars, fur hats, Chinese batteries, books in Cyrillic and books from the DDR, photo prints of model workers in the agrarian and factory collectives – patriotic, selfless and loyal to the socialist dream.

Anything goes in the quest for the hard currency of US dollars.

Some have nothing to sell. They simply sit with their babies and small children cross-legged in the dirt, scarred and furrowed faces wrapped in head scarves, messages scrawled in several languages propped against their knees:

Bitte, hilfen sie mich, ich habe keine geld, gar nichts zu essen, bitte sehr hilfe mein kind … I have nothing to eat, please help me, please help my child.

With thumb and forefinger joined together and jabbing at the mouth, you don't need a translation. Eyes radiating suffering, they come from Albania, from Ukraine, from the 'Stans of far-away Soviet Asia, from places you've never heard of before with languages from somewhere back in time.

There is no hope for these people, says Ursula. Germany will not help them. Nobody will help them. They are stateless. They are here looking for the New World, for the dream. Can you believe how totally mistaken they are? It's all wrong. This is the Old World, and there is no dream, just another nightmare beginning. *Ja,* but I don't want to frighten you or anything, she laughs.

Kombi vans of *polizei* watch from the kerb with blank

expressions. They seem in a trance, waiting for a sign from their master puppeteers to move everybody on. It's a Mexican stand-off and nobody's blinking.

Those cops, they're just kids, says John, kids brought in from some nowhere little town in West Germany to police the streets of Berlin. They haven't got a clue.

A blind woman wearing a thin faded dress and army boots is hissing at me, pointing at the small children rolling listlessly around her feet.

Bitte, she says, *bitte* … Please, please …

Impulsively I give her fifty *pfennig.*

Oh *mann,* says Ursula, are you gonna save everybody? Then she laughs that brittle laugh of hers and punches me on the shoulder. Keep it for yourself. You're going to need it!

In her turquoise-veined blue eyes sparkle humour and infinite hurt in equal measure. Her ten-year-old son is hanging off her arm. *Mama,* he says, come on, let's go.

John and Ursula walk back to their car. Mary wants to leave too, wants to leave Berlin, fly home to the other side of the world. It's not safe here, she says, then asks me – What are we going to do? How are we going to survive?

I look around at the flea market and the volumes of human junk on display – the busts of Lenin, the broken compasses, the giant schoolroom maps and icons of a Europe rapidly disappearing before our eyes. The Cold War has thawed, the Wall has fallen and the New World Order is licking its reptilian lips at the thought of the feast yet to come with much talk of free markets, deregulation and the end of history.

How could we leave now?

Ceska Non-Stop | Czech Republic, 1993

Uniformed border cops eyeball our foreign passports, the Berlin-plated silver Passat, the little girl strapped into the back seat, the guitar cases in the boot. While one rummages through our luggage, the other cop zooms in on Enzo's plastic-coated EU identity card, signals him to step out of the car.

Passport? Passport?

Enzo climbs out guiltily and shakes his head; he has no passport, only an Italian identity card. Without any explanation we're immediately parked to one side for special treatment.

The surrounding high hills leapfrog into the distance, forests stripped by acid rain, 360 degrees of total exposure. Detained truckers and drivers stare vacantly into space beside their vehicles, smoking cigarettes and waiting for the Czech cops to green-light them through the East–West interzone.

A light snow dusts the windshield, melting as it touches the ground. Blind Willie Johnson moans on the car cassette player, growling about the keys to the kingdom and how this world can't do you no harm.

Enzo reluctantly follows a cop into a grim little guardhouse while my three-year-old daughter grows fractious in the back seat of the car, throwing toys around, occasionally vocalising in her knife-keen little-girl howl.

Get rid of En-zo! she chants with a fetching smile, her singsong syntax rising to a mellow peak at the end. Get rid of him! Daddy, are you listening?

The cops in their grey overcoats and peaked caps escort Enzo back to the car.

I don't know, man, he says, they won't let me in. I don't know what the problem. What the problem? I never had this problem before.

A gloved hand shoves our passports and visas through the passenger window. Mary puts them in her bag, drums her fingers on the seat.

Let's go, says Violetta, he's a naughty boy.

The cop shoots me a look and waves towards the exit lane, says something in spiky, sibilant Czech.

Drive on, says Enzo, I'm going to hitchhike back to Dresden tonight. You got to do the show, and you got the baby.

Swinging his pointy boots over the floodlit Armco railings, he jumps down into the outbound lane. The thick-necked cop shouts at him and his dog lets off a gunshot bark. Enzo just keeps walking – he's already seen a trucker ready to drive. I watch him in the rear-view mirror as he climbs into the cabin, clutching his personal belongings in a Kaiser's supermarket bag.

I told you to get rid of him, my daughter says. Daddy, I told you! But you didn't listen! And she raises the bottle of juice up to her tiny mouth and drinks.

Everything changes past the frontier: subtle shifts in the hues of scrub grass and exposed rock, skeletal silhouettes of unfamiliar trees, a deepening of the air's bitter chemical tang. Ancient meteor impacts sculpted this landscape out of crystals and rare minerals forged in million-degree heat. Then humans came, rearranging the topography with slaves and serfs and, later on, dynamite and bulldozers.

The Bohemian valley appears gripped by a collective hangover after fifty years of communist rule. The passing villages are dark and still and decrepit, offering few signs of life or activity of any kind. Occasionally farmhouse lights flicker in the distance but there are no roadhouses or route numbers or streetlamps or air traffic – just a two-lane blacktop posted with intermittent red cat's-eye reflectors. The only signs I understand are Stop and Exit, everything else is hieroglyphs. Occasionally, red and blue chemical smokestacks break the horizon, discharging mystery cocktails into a mass of bruised cloud. Here, all the birds are black.

Miniskirted girls stand by the roadside in the zero-degree mountain air, waving friendly obscenities at the passing headlights. One girl gyrates inside a neon-lit perspex box; others catcall the drivers, endearments or insults, you can only guess. They're brought here from deeper east for the truckers and sex tourists crossing the border for a blowjob and some cut-price slivovitz. Their faces are painted in bright colours as if they put their make-up on in the dark; through the trees burn the camp fires of their male minders, playing cards and drinking slivovitz to stave off the cold.

Frantic, our tangled-haired, long-suffering promoter, apologises as we climb the stairs, picking our way over the shards of broken glass. Prague, very difficult, he says. Since revolution, bah! He throws his hands up in the air. Revolution very good-bad. Everything little bit shit.

The situation we're in is hard to grasp in the dark of night.

This, he says, is very little. Please, please.

The apartment is booby-trapped – some lights work, some

don't, windows are cracked and broken, doors don't close. Clusters of exposed electrical wires hang from the wall near a gas bottle attached to a kitchen stove, the only heat source in the room.

Mary and Carmen fetch quilts and warm clothes from the car to make beds for the children while I read them stories by a candle's flickering yellow glow about a cat who prowls the gabled roofs of old Prague by night. Covered in piles of clothes, battered Barbie dolls and soft animals arranged by their pillows, they are angels, innocents, slowly falling into sleep …

Then I'm gone in a rush for tonight's show, walking with the Rattenfaenger down a Zizkov street, the huge flagstones slippery beneath our leather boot soles. The Rattenfaenger is a wild-haired New Zealander bass player with gypsy genes and the blood of a sailor. Keep it really simple, he says, and, you know, hypnotic. Be hypnotic. Better, be mesmeric.

The Rattenfaenger arrived from Berlin tonight in a van with Reinhold and John. Hughes couldn't join them, last-minute problems had arisen and no one could reach him as he lives in an East-side squat without a telephone – there are no drums tonight.

We've got the metal street signs instead, says the Rattenfaenger. In a medieval stone cellar, anything you do is loud. We won't need microphones, just stamp on it like the old blues guys. You know, keep the beat. Industrial strength, he grins.

John is waiting for us beneath near the massive steel girders of a railway overpass. Since he quit drinking he started smoking again and you can see it in his eyes, all glittery and unfocused. Not that shit, he says laughing, I don't touch that shit any more. Then he spreads his arms, taking in the angular, smoke-stained city looming over us. You can feel this place, he says, Prague. Its soul is under ice. The ice is smoking because it's a vampire that can't ever die. The heart is still beating down there, underground, in the caves. It even survived us Germans after we fucked everything up, because it's a tough old bastard, *ja*! Tougher than Nazis.

Smoke pours out of the street entrance to the Komotovka. Winding stone stairs cut into the bedrock open onto a cellar vault where the eye-stinging air tastes of coal and vinegar. The crowd is smoking furiously. Frantic is translating things people say into his psychedelic English.

Ceska, Slovakia, split, Frantic says over a huge glass of beer, very good. Today, not today, he waves his arms, small-big country. Good-bad, a bit shit. Moskva squeeze us for the juice, until juice run down their leg. Now, nothing.

The background noise of babbling voices and phasey out-of-focus rock music is overwhelming and the room buzzes with electric energy. There has been tentative exultation in the air since the Cold War finished four years ago, and today independence from impoverished Slovakia has finally come. Yet the old, cold times are close in memory and people seem sceptical of the German and American multinational neons ascendant over the city's crumbling silhouette.

The Rattenfaenger and I set up the amplifiers while the sound tech, communicating with us through sign language, places microphones across the stage. We have a small cassette Walkman patched to the sound system to play background loops, several electric guitars, and the electric harp – when John starts to blow with maximum distortion and reverb, he's a sonic tornado.

We play raggedly reinvented blues by Howlin' Wolf and Lightnin' Hopkins, twisting them into our own shape, as well as songs I've written myself drawing something from where the old blues stopped, merging that feeling with technology and experimental sounds. The crowd can't really understand any of the words but it doesn't matter because they read into us the mythology of the West and their psychic liberation from the Soviet bloc. Here, very few people speak English but nearly all speak some Russian.

Russian badly to speak, Jacob says, English worser. Drink? He gestures and small glasses of shiny green liquid line up on the bar, glinting poisonously.

Becherovka, laughs Natasha, good for health! The room is movie-set thick with blue smoke. A group of twenty or so have formed around us, ordering drinks and offering lines of backyard Pervatin crystal and discussing a bar crawl until dawn. I slip away to check on the girls, see if everything's alright back at Frantic's squat.

The door's unlocked. I walk across the creaking floors, fumbling for a light switch while branches scratch on the roof. I see my baby daughter sleeping soundly with a bottle perched to her lips while an icy draft floods the room through broken windows. I fire up the oven and sit by a window and watch a crescent moon fall below the horizon, too wired to sleep.

The club called La Spagna stands in a field at the end of a winding country lane lined with skeletal trees, an hour from Prague. From the small raised stage you can see the approach from out on the high road, a horizon line of bare earth and collapsing country cottages.

The sound system is a couple of old cones hooked up to a

customised home stereo. Standard lamps light the bandstand with a dusty glow: a carpet on the floor for drums and a battered microphone scotch-taped to a stand, stools and couches scattered about under a high arched roof of wooden beams. There is no money here, everything is old and worn and broken.

Jarek's pixie eyes swim behind ovoid spectacles.

Here, he says with a grandiose sweep of his arm indicating the long room of the farmhouse, the bar, the surrealist paintings on the walls, you see? The revolution started here, in this place in communist time, people come here to listen to jazz! Because it was banned! Hah, Western music, you couldn't get it. So you smuggled it in. The radio was … how you say? Jammed. Fucking jammed radio.

Progressive fusion oozes from the stereo, all rhythmic panic and rapid chord changes, but the vocals are in Slav and the effect of different time signatures and atonal horn clusters is savage – it's the sound of the Plastic People of Prague and their countercultural revolution, an intellectual cacophony of sarcasm and scat, the music of dissent.

In communist time, says Jarek, even private talking very, very dangerous. Because police hear everything. Your best friend, your brother, your own children cannot trust. Everyone must inform police. Police know people not be trusted. Because people know too much! They must pretend to forget everything they know. Everyone knowing and forgetting. This was a blackmail system. Sometimes friends and family must inform or take punishment. Better to forget! And now, no one can be sure of what they remember and who did what. So, you know … Big headfuck for very long time, some of us are … recovering … and some never will!

Jarek tugs nervously at his beard.

Then there is the brain doctor, he continues, for bad thoughts …

After a few seconds reflection he returns to his professional persona and asks – Does your band want something to eat?

Cheeses pickled in a pale greenish fluid are served with dark brown grain bread and pilsner. Shot glasses are lined up on the bar beside unlabelled bottles of homemade slivovitz. John sniffs the alcohol then wedges the cork back in. Oh God, he says, I'm glad I don't drink any more.

Yes, oh God! laughs Lubor, but there is no God … But the cheese is good! Very strong. In acid solution. Not really, but really. You try it? Very famous Czech acid cheese. And pickle. *Tac, tac.*

Darkening fields outside the farmhouse windows roll in mist under a cloudy sky. Men and women arrive in cars, headlights shining through the windows. A dog drinks from a bowl of water then curls up near the fire, a baby cries. Lubor sits down beside me with a loud sigh.

Mmm-da, he says, they said you have a manuscript, yes?

Lubor's expression is stretched; he doesn't trust his English and looks around at his colleagues and friends, who in turn confer with each other, searching for a translation.

I hand him a pile of paper printouts. It's all here, I say.

And what is story?

Hard to explain. Something based on the life of Jerry Lee Lewis. About the changing of the eras, how each generation invents new mythologies yet in the end they're all the same, the same myths with different faces, different clothes, different music.

Lubor and Jarek confer in rapid-fire Czech, their animated faces detailed by broken capillaries and long beards, the faces of

Dürer's apocalyptic horsemen galloping over the Bohemian hills on grinning skeleton steeds. A door slams, somebody laughs. Suddenly I become aware of the smell of gas in the room.

You didn't eat the cheese, did you? John asks me with concern.

Feeling a little nauseous, I say nothing.

There's something strange about it, he continues, I can't put my finger on it but I have this feeling, this weird feeling …

Local boys are setting up on the stage, acoustic guitars, electric bass and drums, performing Czech folk songs in punk rock style. The slowly arriving audience is clad in denim and leather and sporting long, pony-tailed hair, whether male or female. These are strong faces out of medieval woodcuts – zealot eyes and protruding lips – background extras straight out of Hieronymus Bosch.

A towering woodsman with hair down to his waist is giving us the evil eye from across the room.

Oh no, says Natasha, he's with mental problem. Oh shit, he's coming over here!

The woodsman drunkenly pushes the furniture out of the way as he draws closer and says – You guys never gave a shit, never gave a shit about us. You guys, you guys, he repeats darkly, never gave a shit about anyone! But communist time, he says looking from left to right as if checking for secret police, was total shit. Then he laughs and jabs the air with a toiled, callused finger and smiles, you guys. Why? Why? Why the fuck?

Natasha searches for words – Don't listen to him, she says, he's crazy.

Maybe he's got a point? I reply.

The two of them tangle in Czech awhile before Natasha says to me – He thinks you're somebody else, an American.

No American, I say. Australian.

Oh, he says, Why the fuck? Uncle Sam, Vietnam!

Not exactly, kind of …

You know what you did? he says looking right at me – You, you guys use us for your little war games then run away to watch when the shooting starts! The West are liars, that's how they win, so here's to the West!

The woodsman downs another shot of firewater. *Na zdraví*, he shouts with a hollow laugh and disappears out the door.

He's walking home, says Natasha, across fields, next village, hour by foot. He lives alone in the woods, and he's an asshole now but he used to be a hero. Yes, he was hero, a playwright in communist time, and now he's a drunk. Life is … I don't know what! She laughs then raises her hand – But that sounds so stupid! I don't know what life is, when heroes are assholes and revolutionaries are drunks!

My mood is rapidly morphing and I start to look at her differently. Natasha has a hard-to-define attitude, as if she's hiding things – secrets, a bad childhood, a recording device. The kind of girl who'd pin a feather to the back of your coat or slip a lock of hair in your pocket or maybe spike your drink, just because she felt like it.

Lubor passes me his pipe. Opium from fields, he says, pointing through the misted windows into an impenetrable night.

Mary and Carmen and the little girls are driving back to Berlin in the silver Passat with the rosaries hanging from the rear-vision mirror and my old cassettes stuffed into the glove box. I load their bags into the boot, check the maps, give them Czech crowns to pay for petrol and expenses. Daddy isn't coming? Violetta sulks and preens in her pink dress and hairclips. Not coming? You have to come too, she pouts, or I'm not leaving.

I'm back in a few days. You don't want to stay here any longer, do you?

No, I want to go home.

Be good, says Mary.

I watch the girls drive off and it makes me feel sad and strange and elated all at the same time, like looking down a long telescope into the past where everything is far away and ever-faster receding. You try to focus for detail, but the machinery is heavy, unwieldy, frustrates your need to see clearly; images dissolve. Memories can't carry detail indefinitely; they degrade to purest, mythic elements – the futuristic Prague space tower, four girls in a silver car, the spectral light of morning.

I wave goodbye into the exhaust fumes.

Tomasz meets me at the Lucerna in the old town for a drink.

I'm going to make a fucking sandwich, says Tomasz, a sandwich so fucking good no one will touch those fucking shit cocodrilos any more. Every petrol station in Czech Republic, every school and office block you'll see my sandwiches in the pay-fridge.

What makes you so sure, Tomasz?

He gives me his withering, you-idiot, snap-second stare. Because of special fucking sauce, what do you think? My own fucking patent!

It's noisy in the bar. We are shouting to be heard. American students are already here in numbers.

Fanny, yells a kid in a Notre Dame T-shirt, Kalashnikovs all round!

At the bar, Fanny turns and yells back across the room, Yeah, if they know what I'm talking about! These Czechs need to learn American. Move your ass!

The barman shoots her a look as he mixes vodka and an energy drink the colour of diesel into a dozen shot glasses.

More rowdy American kids pile into the bar and the reserved local Czechs draw back, creating space between them in the large, dimly lit tavern.

C'mon, says Tomasz, let's go somewhere quiet.

The decrepit old town centre is a labyrinth of medieval cobbled lanes and empty buildings, more beautiful than ever in this state of advanced degradation. A sulphur-yellow glow preserves the old-world culture in nostalgic socialist formaldehyde – abandoned buildings with shattered windows and decayed facades, their walls stencilled with the faded logos of manufacturers long gone bankrupt.

At the top of the hill the Zizkov graveyard is vast and ornate, a masterpiece of fin-de-siècle and art deco design spread out beneath huge old trees. There is movement in the mausoleums where the mad and the homeless sleep. We cautiously enter the mausoleum of a once-proud family, newspapers and blankets on the floor and childish cartoons drawn on the walls captioned with Czech writing.

Tomasz cuts a line on the mantel of a huge marble sarcophagus and we brace ourselves for the chemical rush – something that tastes like bleach in the back of my throat clears the webs of alcohol from my mind. We retrace our steps through the labyrinthine cemetery followed by rustlings and phantom footsteps. Those who dwell here prefer not to be disturbed.

At five the next morning we're still drinking in the cafe of a grand hotel, watching grim-faced factory workers crush into streetcars, going through the robotic motions of a life punching the clock.

'Robot', says Tomasz, is a Czech word, and the first robot was the Golem, created by Jewish sorcerers working for the alchemist King Rudolph. Rudolph had magic vision for Prague, and drew plans for the old city and the castle grounds with sacred fucking geometry. John Dee came from faraway England, and wizards too from all over Europe, following Rudolph's plan. Nostradamus cast Rudolph's horoscope and seeing the empire's imminent decline, refused to say anything because he knew Bohemia was doomed.

Doomed? Why doomed? You're still here!

Yes, but the fucking movie already finished and nobody noticed yet, he replies. It was a fucking shit movie, too! Look at Czech history! Or better, don't! Everybody's left the cinema but they think the movie is still going, the movie of their lives. Look at them, they are dead, they are just dreaming they're alive. In Prague, they put hallucinogens in the tap water – how else to explain the look you see in every pair of eyes in town?

An elegant waiter in a long white apron places the bill on the table.

We never close, he says, come back soon.

I wake up curled on a rug thrown over patterned linoleum scented by strange chemicals. Framed black-and-white pictures hang on the walls – a distant uncle in military uniform, a teenage work gang in a summer field, a terrier with a ribbon around its neck. The apartment is something of a family museum since

Tomasz's parents retired to a village, his grandparents having passed away some years ago.

They're going to sell, he tells me with his clipped bark of a laugh, and when they do I'm fucked. It's a shit world. Not only, but there's something else you need to know – we have no coffee sugar! We're going out.

The chrome elevator drops ten floors at high speed, opens out onto a high-ceilinged foyer decorated with futuristic sixties Star Trek chrome fittings. Somebody's screaming blue murder to wake the living and the dead.

Several white-coated nursing orderlies wrestle a tiny old lady out of another elevator while traffic cops cordon off the carpeted throughway to the street where an ambulance is waiting, its red and blue lights reflecting off the lobby's metal walls.

Possessed by unlimited rage and struggling to keep her housecoat covering her modesty, the old lady's voice chainsaws through my hangover while we stand and watch, transfixed by the sound of raw human pain. She doesn't want to leave, her resistance bolstered by adrenaline and dementia. One of the nurses uncaps a syringe and rummages in her bag of drugs; the old lady doesn't have any choice in the matter, not this morning.

Normal socialism, says Tomasz, this is it! Live your whole life in a place like this until totally fucking crazy. My parents know her, they say she used to be a spy. Husband died years ago. That's normal too – the men die young from all the pollution in the factories. This building is full of factory widows, their memories and their little dogs. This one, always screaming at nothing in the night, had to go sometime.

Tenants have turned up from all over the tower block to

witness her departure – some amused, others distressed and wanting to intervene yet perhaps restrained by an ingrained fear of authority. Most are impassive, just standing by as she lashes out helplessly with her hands. My weary, strangely sensitised mind perceives her pulsing red aura, the flames in her grey hair and a stream of giddying memories in her wake. And now she's in the ambulance for a sedative shot, restrained by four burly nurses in white coats with hangdog eyes.

The clouds hang low and heavy, the early spring air charged with intermittent lightning. A huge low-pressure system is coming from the east, from Russia, and it's time to drive south to Moravia; tonight I perform solo in Brno, three hours away.

I call up Berlin to talk to my daughter. My heart skips a beat and sinks as the call goes straight through to the answering machine I bought at the flea market in Potsdamer Platz. I pause for a moment, searching for words. Hope everything's okay there, I say. It's getting really cold here. Call you from the road later today when we arrive. Lots of love.

Tom Morawetz, my road manager from Berlin, knocks on the phone box door, pointing at the gunmetal sky as snow starts to fall. He's wearing a full-length leather coat, ripped jeans and a T-shirt that highlights his muscles and elaborate tattoos. Watching me steadily through his thick, black-framed glasses he says – The weather is not nice, *ja*? I don't have a good feeling about this but we will make it anyway, *wenn wir Glueck haben*!

At midday, the densely forested hills already seem steeped in twilight. We stop at a roadside gypsy tavern; to eat there is either a goulash of indeterminate age or there is sausage, and to drink there's Turkish coffee, beer or slivovitz. Radioactive cakes glow behind a glass panel near plastic tubs of red kraut. There's nobody here but us and as I start to wonder why, the first snowflakes fall.

We kid ourselves about how the threatening weather is likely to blow over as soon as we clear these mountains but in truth it seems a full-blown blizzard is gathering strength, and it's too late to turn back now. Morawetz ignites the engine and I insert a cassette of *John Wesley Harding* to ease the tension as the snowfall intensifies.

Suddenly, the road snap-freezes into a black sheet of iced asphalt, the wheels lose traction and the car swerves violently. Survival instincts kick in as we concentrate on not getting ourselves killed.

The afternoon becomes a nightmare on ice under blizzard conditions – the power's out and the highway streetlamps are down, masses of badly maintained ten-tonne rigs clog the lanes and there's no sign of emergency services anywhere. We are both aware of issues with accident insurance outside the EU and a police force with a bad attitude left over from the defunct regime.

Within an hour the snow-white darkness is impenetrable. We've slowed down to a 15-kilometre-an-hour crawl. The windshield frames a vision of deep chaos unreal as any video game; automobiles skate across the road on mad trajectories and collide in groups, some are abandoned with doors hanging open or plunged deep into snow drifts, their rear emergency lights blinking red.

Human figures flee the road wrecks, waving their arms for help. Two drivers locked in a fistfight slip over on the ice and get up again, still throwing punches. A group of twenty-odd Vietnamese shiver by the roadside in T-shirts and plastic raincoats, thumbs extended, flagging for a lift – but even if we'd had space enough for them we can't brake to a stop on that frozen slick.

In this continuum of sleet and headlights, direction signs have all been erased by a veneer of reflective ice. The only legible signage is intermittent and hastily erected, a blinking lamp illuminating the word *pozor* – Danger.

We've shut off the heating to conserve petrol and donned thick winter jackets and gloves – inside my full-length leather army coat I'm sweating up a storm of my own. While Morawetz drives with teeth-grinding concentration I wipe down the windscreen with damp sleeves, telling stories to boost our spirits. The snowfall has hushed the external world, silencing the capsule's interior. Stones of ice grind beneath the tyres. At this speed, we'd make better time on foot; by the time we've covered another hundred miles, it's already show time in Brno.

Defeated by the elements, we roll to a stop in a petrol station restaurant car park. The cessation of movement is a strange sensation and we stagger from the car lightheaded and weaving on the ice.

Two cops watch us from a parked sedan, its slowly pulsing blue light on the roof triggering instant paranoia. We don't need to have done anything wrong to attract their unwanted attention; the Czech police force has remained pretty much the same since before the revolution – a law unto itself.

Quickly, we slip inside the pub's warm funk of beer and cigarettes. It's a shock after the storm, this dark and smoky room, warm and still and packed with road refugees. Two television sets mounted on either wall screen a softcore porn film – steam rising from the jacuzzi, a fat big shot in the tub with a lit cigar in his mouth and a couple of doped-up showgirls for company.

Rubbing our eyes and reeking of human sweat, we squeeze into seats between surly truck-drivers at a table thick with lager foam and ash. Two fair-headed teenagers move swiftly between the tables, ferrying litre glasses of dark Czech beer; their faces similarly pretty and tender, they seem far too innocent for this place. Forgetting our own predicament for a moment, I stare around me at the screens and the truckies, worrying about what could happen to them out here on a night like this.

At daybreak we slide to a stop against a kerb in the city of Brno. We've been on the road for fourteen hours. I finally find a payphone that works and call the promoter – he's remarkably unsympathetic and deeply pissed off that we missed the show, telling us to meet him in a cafe near his Mersey club. Inside, workers and students are warming up for the day ahead with shots of slivovitz or Turkish coffee. Roadshocked, we sit and order black tea. Morawetz and I haven't spoken much for the last several hours. We stare at each with glassily concussed expressions.

Next to me, a young man sporting a mephistophelian goatee catches my eye; he smiles kindly and says something incomprehensible and offers me a pipe loaded with smouldering Bohemian grass.

The bone church is discreet, slightly concealed in a depression in the corner of a field of brown earth and crows. Inside, the bones of Black Death victims from six hundred years ago have been interlaced by skilled artisans into bizarre shapes and forms.

Votive chandeliers of smooth femurs hang on 50-metre

steel chains. Intricate suspended phalanxes of skeletal parts form macropatterns resembling marcasite-encrusted Bohemian jewellery. Tapered pyramids of skulls, chalices of clavicles and vertebrae vibrate to similar frequencies as the relics of the Maya, everything gently coated with the dusty wax of the crypt.

Nearby on the edge of town stand a few concrete housing blocks and a cafe which is closed. Not even a dog barks. The trees are knobbly and contorted and devoid of leaves. The sky is a cool grey mass of undulating cloud. There is no wind. Any sense of temporal urgency has been replaced by the sense of time moving in vast cycles.

The muscles in my lower back have been flaring up since the all-night drive. I'm lying on a trolley in a long fluoro-lit corridor of absolute spartan simplicity, other trolleys spaced randomly along the scarred, grey linoleum floor. The walls are painted in an almost transparent pale Eastern Bloc green prized for its emotional neutrality. The muted smell of tangy disinfectant hangs in the air. I hold my breath, trying to block it out, waiting for the masseuse to come. Around me, voices talk in rapid-fire Czech, sizzling emphases with virtually no vowels to be heard, a hard, sibilant, machine-like language renowned for its high level of grammatical complexity.

They wheel me into a minimalist consultation room where the various steel instruments and rubber tubes seem strange and unfamiliar, as if I've wandered into a veterinary surgery. These are oversized apparatuses, stylistically different from Western hospital kit. On a bench are scattered a few mirrors, some bedpans, a set of scales, a hypodermic syringe from ancient times big enough to inject a horse. Sounds penetrate from the outside – rubber wheels squeaking on linoleum, a machine belt humming in the basement driving the heat and ventilation, a dog barking on a chain.

The masseuse is standing over me, smiling: a huge middle-aged woman with footballer's forearms and skin pale as processed flour. Talking in Czech, she slathers her hands in a soapy carbolic substance and works my spine. The massage is strictly functional. Any pleasurable moves have been excised from the training manual. My body is a collection of machine parts depersonalised in her grasp like a roll of linen, a pot of dumpling mix, a string of sausages.

Now Alice walks me back down the hall to visit her grandmother.

This was the deal – she would organise the massage and in return I would greet her ninety-year-old nana, not long for this world.

Windows at one end of a dimly lit salon frame a grey winter afternoon – heavy-rooted trees decapitated by fog, abandoned scaffolding, outlines of crumbling buildings worn soft by time. The nana has been here for several months already and hopes to be well enough to go home soon, but Alice has already prepared me for this encounter with the knowledge that she is unlikely to ever leave. No one in the family can really give her full-time care; everybody is working or looking for work. Times are extremely tough and getting harder, with little prospect of change in the near future.

Nana smiles at me and in her sparkling grey eyes I flash on the decades of her history, spanning the entire twentieth century – a young adulthood in the brief decade of 1920s democracy before the West sold Czechoslovakia out to the Nazis – then the war, the pogroms, the camps – followed by the few months of Czech independence before the murder of Czech premier Dubcek and the arrival of Soviet tanks in the streets of Prague, heralding nearly fifty years of economic oppression and attempted cultural brainwashing; the uselessness of it all, the mass sacrifice of lives and personal destinies to the abstract conceptions of power politics, self-interest, nepotism, corruption and conformism.

Nana smiles again and looks at me kindly and says something in a cracked little-girl voice. We grasp hands. She seems happy enough with her companions in the salon, girls dressed in the fashion of many years ago. They share the tribal affinity of a common culture, one rapidly fading in the blinding glare of a capitalist modernity they will never even want to get to know – alien, disenchanted, decadent.

Attendants with trolleys serve soft medallions of meat, gruel, dumplings and onions. The kitchen is frugal and austere, running efficiently on a shoestring budget like a poor house, a working person's clinic. Is this socialism? Or just the bare minimum the state is expected to supply? Private hospitals for the rich are elsewhere. This was never a classless society. The percentage ratio of people earning multimillions every year is similar to the West – the 1 per cent of 1 per cent; those who know their way around the loop of the rulers, the cabal, the inner circle.

It's time to return to Berlin. My family is waiting there. I offer my friend Jiri a thousand kroner to drive me up to the border; his handsome face turns dark at the request but he assents anyway. I assume he needs the money. Throwing my bags and guitar into the boot of his Skoda, we drive out into a stormy night towards Zinnwald on the German border, a few hours to the north.

Lightning bursts across the mountains in freeze-frame silhouettes, rain slashes across the windscreen, the wipers grind rubberless on glass. A sudden, stronger flash illuminates Jiri's face and he appears to me in that moment a total stranger.

Everything okay for you, he sneers. You don't come from here, you don't know what it's like. Rock star! Fuck! He slams his hands on the steering wheel. Fuck it!

Then he looks at me and smiles a mad, snaky grin.

When I see the way my girlfriend looks at you, he says, I feel like this – and takes his hands off the wheel; the ride slews across the rugged mountain road as the two-tier lights of a lorry round the bend. I try to grab the wheel but Jiri pushes me away and rights the steering just as the truck blunders past.

You like? He spits, foaming at the mouth. You like? How you like it? Like this? And releases the wheel again. The car veers towards the soft edge, threatening to plunge down into the muddy gorge. Headlights of oncoming vehicles transform the windscreen into a pane of liquid light.

Do you want to die? screams Jiri.

No, I yell, I don't want to fucking die!

You do, do you?

No, I don't!

By now we're both screaming.

Okay, he says and relaxes a little. Nobody want to die.

No, I reply, we don't want to die tonight.

The border control station slides into view and he pulls over to let me out. Tom Morawetz waves with gloved hands from the German side, the fluorescent yellow security lights glittering across his glasses.

C'mon, he calls out, we're late, and it's snowing again!

Jiri smiles at me wolfishly. I hand him some *koruny* and grab my road kit from the boot.

The thick-necked border cop behind the metal grille flips through my passport and points to a waiting room full of cigarette smoke. I slip fifty Deutschemarks under the grille and he stamps my visa with inky contempt, hands back the document and waves me through, back to the free West.

Valley of the Moon | Europe, 1994

The shouting rips through my dreams like a chainsaw – it's three in the morning in Genova, Italy – and our tour manager, Enzo, is standing in the doorway of my room, his liquid Latin eyes bulging with shock and outrage.

Jesu Christo, the bus, he shouts, it's been raped! *Rapino!* All the guitars are gone! Those beautiful guitars! *Tutto sparito!*

I'm lying on the bed, my stage shirt still glued to my back, grasping at what he's saying but the words slip through the cracks in my mind, interleaving with residual dream fragments of smoky stages, shattered windscreens, endless corridors of doors signed in unknown languages.

In the *pensione* breakfast room, the rest of the group are scattered around the table, heads in hands, dishevelled and delirious from the afterparty. The Rattenfaenger holds up one large callused hand in front of his face and begs for calm.

Slow down, Enzo, what are you talking about?

I'm talking about the bus! There's a big problem, what do you want me to say? That there's no problem? Oh yes, man, everything's okay, I don't think so!

Despite his high-pitched Milanese drawl, Enzo is speaking way too fast. He can be hard to understand at the best of times, expressing himself in ambiguities so as no one can ever pin down his position on any topic, but right now he's on fire, relishing the drama of sudden disaster, his tour manager resolve shattering into pieces as he looks for one of us to blame.

I notice Max, our dapper English roadie, fumbling in his teddy-boy jacket pockets, searching for a distraction. He produces two wrapped Swedish lollies and a metro card with a telephone number scrawled on one side. Offering Enzo a lolly he says, Well, I hope you're not thinking of blaming me! I'm always being blamed for everything! I can't look after a bloody bus! I was at a party, Ash will tell you, he was there too, but I didn't take the guitars, I wouldn't do that!

It occurs to me as I watch Max shaking like a marionette with the DTs that he may have taken a stimulant.

They forced the doors with a focking crowbar, says Enzo, and him – he points at Max – he just hides while they rape the guitars!

It's not my fault, exclaims Max, I'm not a bloody bodyguard!

Hughes looks at me and I look at our sound engineer, Ash, and Ash looks at John who looks back at me and for a second I'm unsure if I'm still asleep or onstage; we regard each other blankly, waiting for one of us to break the spell and explain that this whole drama is just a ghastly misunderstanding.

I told you Genova is too dangerous to leave the bus on the street, yells Enzo. It's a port city, man, they steal shit and ship it out of here all the time! I tell you but you don't listen! Now what you going to do?

Tom the driver is awake now, bleary-eyed and shaken. My bus, he says, what happened to my bus?

Under the streetlights' sodium glare, with the Mediterranean heaving black and unruly beyond the breakwater, Tom's huge, reconditioned German army bus is hanging wide open. The military-green doors are bent and scratched, the interior turned upside down as if a tornado had spun right through it. My two vintage American Fenders and the Rattenfaenger's Ibanez bass are gone.

Max unwraps another Swedish lolly, the wrapper lingering forlornly on the ground by his feet; his legs shake uncontrollably. The lolly sticks to the front of his teeth as he starts to complain about his nagging toothache but Enzo shuts him down with a sharp look and Max curls in on himself guiltily and squeezes his eyes shut, hoping to disappear in plain view.

Crushed and hung-over, we drive into the February snows. This is only the second day of a six-week trans-European tour, and the first time we've entirely organised such an ambitious tour from scratch: we had a falling out with our record label and agency last year regarding tour support and promotion, so we've invested our own time and finances into becoming a completely independent road act. We don't have money for new instruments but Tom has the first mobile phone I've ever seen, a Motorola big and heavy as a brick with counterintuitive green buttons, its battery constantly expiring.

Tom shouts into the luminous brick over the engine noise as he drives, wheedling and demanding guitars from the promoters. Substitute guitars appear at the next sound check in Alessandria but it takes time to understand what any guitar can do; not only this, but during the show my effects stop working, blowing a hole through the band's sound.

Gremlins, says the Rattenfaenger, electrical gremlins. We need a voltameter and a soldering iron. He upends a tool box across a bench seat and methodically pulls the effects units apart to examine the wiring and circuits; it's too dark for surgery – several small Japanese components vanish into the aggregate chaos of the bus never to be seen again.

I don't want to sound like a hippie, John says, I fucking hate hippies – but I'm getting a bad feeling, you know what I mean? Where is this all going to end?

As he say this, it seems to me that the little light there is around us becomes trapped in his pale blue eyes, lending them the blind clairvoyant light of a medium.

Maybe it's the bus? Chris replies nervously. Who knows what's gone on in here, what kind of depravities and privations? Think about it, young men taken from their homes by the *Wehrmacht* and dehumanised …

What about an exorcist? says Max cheerfully, after all, you can still hire them here in Italy!

A strange mood is taking hold of me. I find myself both attracted and repelled by people and situations that never interested me before. Life on the road tends to be a cycle of crises separated by long periods of boredom and frequent frustration, slaving to a schedule that demands more than you can handle. A deep sense of uselessness haunts me after performing the music – the mission – through a haze of stage lights and excitement. When an opportunity presents itself for you to lose your mind for a brief while, sometimes you take it …

Late that night, I find myself in a luxury apartment drowning the how and the where and the why of being here with vodka and pills; there's a fountain and scented candles, marble bathrooms and pretty people dancing at what seems to be some kind of fancy-dress party. I'm not sure who anybody is – their faces are strange but friendly and my own face feels glued on. By now I've forgotten who I really am, enough to be easily lead astray, like another version of myself that I don't think I really like.

At dawn, the streets of Milano are draped in ghostly clouds, Bangkok-style. I find my way back to the bus, recollections of the night before involuntarily flashing through my thoughts, fragmented and inexplicable as a dream.

We cross the border at Chiasso during a lightning storm, the engine groaning on the Alpine gradient like a choir of galley slaves beneath the lash. Hughes watches *Toxic Avenger* on a video screen; John and the Rattenfaenger learn Howlin' Wolf guitar riffs from a cassette on the raised mezzanine up the back, the traffic warping around them through the curved rear windows. Max's nose is buried in a book entitled *Observations of the English Tufted Duck*. Ash and Enzo are riding shotgun. No one attempts to speak over the rattle and roar of the battered bus.

In a rock club in a Swiss mountain-top town, broken vintage trophy guitars hang on the walls and we restring and resolder and play them at high volume and the crowd bays for encores like the wild dogs I hear howling in my sleep. I'm picking a circular pattern of notes on the Japanese guitar that the head girl in the club gave us to keep.

What are you going to call it? asks the Rattenfaenger.

Wolf, I reply without really thinking.

Ah, he says, why Wolf?

Because I keep hearing dogs, or wolves maybe, really far away, way out on the edge of hearing. It's like surf, like an ocean beach crashing in the distance, except these are dog voices, howling.

I hear 'em too, he says with that faraway look he gets when the seen and unseen worlds become entangled in the now. I've been hearing them off and on ever since we left Berlin.

I flash on the memory of leaving Berlin – the snow falling

on the huge bus at Checkpoint Charlie, saying goodbye to my family, the sense of urgency to get out on the road. We lock eyes. The sun rises. It's already time to go.

Arriving at the Czech border, Hughes, still wearing his day-glo-bright polyester shirt, two-tone winklepickers and electric-blue suit from the night before, realises he has left his luggage and documents back in the Alps. The frontier cops regard him warily as he explains his documents are missing through no fault of his own. Somehow he charms his way through the control using a tattered passport photocopy left over from a Czech visa application, uncannily fished from his jacket pocket. We've seen him pull these stunts before so many times before, it seems like he attracts these kinds of situations. I ask him about it.

Don't get me started, he says, it's a long story. When I settle down to hear his tale of woe, he just waves me off, saying it would take far too long to explain.

I can hear the wolves louder now, their breath hissing in my ears like drops of fat spattering on a hot grill. Strange events are happening at speed and behind it all I sense a dark star spinning, marking out our time, our fate.

At a club in northern Germany I meet a girl who tells me she can read the future. She looks like an ordinary Goth girl on first glance, wild hair and heavy eyeliner, but there's something mysterious and magnetic about her, an otherworldly aura that draws me in.

How do you do that, I ask her, read the future?

Come around tomorrow and I'll show you, she says, writing down her phone number and address.

The next morning Tom and I drive out onto a rainswept,

brainmatter-grey plain dotted with the ghostly shapes of twisted trees.

I don't know about this, Tom explains warily, in this area of Germany there are the cults, you know, Wiccan, Satanic, strange things happen ... he hasn't even finished his sentence when a windscreen wiper bent by a vandal the night before snaps off. We wind down the side windows and lean out, squinting into the void.

We find Wibke in a tiny town out on the flatlands past Osnabrueck, dealing tarot cards onto a batik sheet printed with symmetrical Kali motifs.

You are the protagonist of your story, she says glancing at me with her intense seagull-blue eyes, but you have lost your way. You are not hearing the call of your higher nature. If you don't listen, in time you will be forced to listen. Anyone who ignores the call of their higher nature is living on borrowed time. She points to a card where a full moon drips golden blood between two hills. You are in the valley of the moon, she says, you can't turn around and go back, you can only go forward and although the night is long, the choice is no longer yours.

Outside, darkness has fallen and an incessant rain beats down as we crawl slowly, blindly back along the road we came, the Westphalian flatlands bleakly mystical like an old Ingmar Bergman film that we can't write ourselves out of, so deeply entangled in its narrative have we become.

I don't want to make you nervous, says Tom, but the engine is getting really hot.

I flashback on visiting Tom a few weeks ago in Berlin; he was lying underneath the bus in the street, his hands black with grease. The *polizei* closed off the street last night, he'd said, because my bus leaked oil from one end of Mansteinstrasse to the other. I have a huge fine! *Ja, peinlich,* this is not good, but give me time and I will fix it with my two strong hands!

Tonight he's decidedly nervous at the wheel, squinting into the featureless void through thick spectacles. Out on the plain, I hear a canine keening over the engine noise and mention it to Tom. That's just the drive shaft, he replies with a forced, hollow laugh. Don't you think about it, you've got a job to do. Like she said, you can't turn back, *stimmt*? What else are you going to do? You were born for this, *oder*?

In the haunted backstage of an old dance hall in Muenster, the band's haggard faces cluster around our tour itinerary by torchlight as the next jagged penny drops – a clerical confusion of dates seems to indicate that we are booked simultaneously at two shows tomorrow evening, one in Brussels and the other in Amsterdam, over a hundred miles apart. Cold fingers run up my spine as I realise the error is mine. I can't understand it, I check the dates and crosscheck then double-check again … The wolves are still howling, and the only consolation is that the Rattenfaenger and John can hear them too – at least I'm not losing my mind.

Tom walks into the room, his hands black with engine grease. *Ja,* the bus, he says, I really don't know if I can fix it. Something is not right with the water pump, maybe it's a hole, I don't know, but if it keeps leaking, the engine could explode.

Onstage, John is on fire too; he's the random element in the band, blowing his harmonica as a constant psychedelic undertow, blowing until the howl becomes a screaming through a battered amplifier maxed into distortion, a scream to shout down the sanity-threatening world.

I'm going insane, he insists, because of the bureaucracy, because of my wife! It's making me crazy! Everything *is* crazy!

I ask him what he means and he says he doesn't want to talk about it, then laughs and brushes the sandy hair off his face to reveal searing blue eyes staring out in two different directions and says, You know, I just want to be a good man. How hard can that be?

The smell of burning plastic seeps across the stage as my guitar gradually fuzzes out; a power transformer has just melted down. The audience, rapt in the music, don't seem to notice the smell or the fate-struck expressions on the faces of the band – or if they do, think its part of the act.

A large black Chevrolet with Belgian number plates is waiting at the stage door of Amsterdam's Melkweg with the engine running. We throw the guitars and effects into the boot and the Chevy takes off in a spray of gravel. The quaffed, denim-clad driver looks like Elvis in night-vision sunglasses. Friends in Brussels sent him to get us to the gig on time and he breaks the speed limit all the way, delivering us to the Botanique at exactly the time we are due onstage. We get out of the car, plug in and play to a packed house with doomed intensity.

Arriving late into Hamburg the next day after stopping every 50 kilometres so the bus can cool down, we discover our hotel booking has been cancelled. Late in the night over a bottle of whisky in the Fabrik backstage, we review our options.

Can't we just book another hotel? I ask Enzo.

No way, man. There's a football game or a convention or something big going on, we already tried.

Where's the promoter?

He never showed up.

We could drive to Berlin?

I don't trust it, replies Tom. The bus has to go to a *werkstatt.*

Well, we can sleep on it then, says Max.

It's too cold to sleep on the bus, Tom answers, the heating system is *kaputt*. Outside is minus 2 degrees. But if you really want to … He opens his arms wide and smiles.

The band look around at the dimly lit, graffiti-daubed backstage reeking of beer and bleach and realise our options are the deep-frozen German night or this concrete floor. But two Greek sisters, overhearing the conversation, invite us to spend the night at their home out on the edge of town. There's enough room for everybody, they say, our parents are away on holiday.

The sisters sit in the front seat to give directions, but Tom, at the wheel, keeps looking down at the climbing temperature gauge, ready to shut the engine off before it blows. They're directing him through a shortcut along the Hamburg docks when Tom suddenly looks up from the dashboard, screams, and drives headlong into two concrete dragon's teeth barring the way.

My head connects with a hard surface. I come to on the asphalt beside a frozen canal looking up at an ambulance crew. Around us are police and powerful arc lights and a giant crane dragging the disembowelled army bus off the concrete posts. Next thing I'm on a hospital trolley. The attending emergency room doctor looks strangely familiar. Right there in casualty, we recognise each other – Mimi, the bass player from the Carnival of Fools, with whom we played that opening night in Genova before the guitars were stolen.

Mimi, what are you doing here?

This is my other job, he replies.

Is this really happening?

Scientifically speaking, yes. But then again, everything is illusion, is it not?

Doctor, can you give me a brain scan? Sometimes I have hallucinations, barking dogs, wolves … Maybe it's just tinnitus?

Dogs? A scan? Look, I'm just a medical orderly and you're very lucky, you only have a concussion. But when you get the chance, get a proper scan done. Problems can arise later that they can't know about yet, like blood clots on the brain.

Thanks, Mimi, and by the way, you play a mean bass.

And may your G-string stay in tune, he says.

You for real?

Are you?

Back in Berlin, John has just discovered his ex-girlfriend lost custody of their child. They separated over a year ago now but while we've been away she's had a run-in with the police that brought a sadistic social worker into their lives with ghastly consequences.

Frau Weiss, John says bitterly, is more than a bitch, she's a symbol of the entire German state, the Nazi guilt, everything that's foul about this country. Where do these people come from? Do they have parents or children? They act like we're some kind of science experiment!

The last time I saw Ursula, she'd started using the hard stuff and her face and arms were all scarred from cutting herself and she frightened the hell out of me. I avoid addicts and didn't even realise she'd become one herself. Her descent into hell happened so fast no one saw it coming. We were standing in a playground with the kids rushing around us like mad things, laughing and chattering and crying all at the same time. Ursula defiantly told me she was in deepest trouble. Then she kissed me on the cheek and told me not to worry, that it would all be all right in the end.

And now, suddenly, she's dead. Even John doesn't seem to know exactly what happened, how she died, if it was a suicide or an overdose. Frau Weiss is disclosing nothing and obstructing John's efforts to find out what happened to her and where his baby is now. But he has friends and he finds out and fashions an emergency plan.

The long grey winter is showing the first signs of spring. John and I are standing on the Pallasstrasse by the indestructible Nazi bunker opposite his now completely empty apartment.

Goodbye, my friend, he says, and we hug for the last time. I ask him if there's some way I can help and he stares right through me.

It's all over, he says, just keep making the music, do that much for me. And when I can, I'll send through a harmonica track, a guitar track, something to stop me from going crazy. You know, I can't ever come back. If I come back they'll arrest me! Can you imagine that? Getting arrested for taking care of your own child? This world is insane! Totally fucking insane!

In the early-morning hours John breaks the little baby girl out of a state facility and heads straight to the airport, vanishing into the atmosphere on a one-way ticket to Canada. It's not easy to grasp how final John's decision is – he has to invent new means to survive in a country he's never visited in his life. My own family have already left Berlin and returned to Melbourne; life-changing decisions are happening around us.

Nothing will ever be the same again.

I'm at the Ex'n'Pop. Someone calls my name and I turn around. My old friend Oliver is drinking at the bar. He looks at me ironically through his small round glasses and says, Ah, the Australian singer. How was your tour?

Everything that could go wrong … well, they say everything happens for a reason … I'm just sitting here asking myself what those reasons might be.

That's bullshit, Oliver replies, everything doesn't have to happen for a reason. You just can't accept that everything's random. The fact that you and I are here at all is completely random. There is no master plan, all of this – he gestures at the dirty yellow walls, the little stage, the other guests drinking and talking – just happened by chance. There's no meaning to any of it, no matter how much you want there to be a reason, a meaning, or a sense of purpose. All that's required of us is to survive and reproduce but that interpretation isn't romantic enough for you. So your mind invents stories and connections to link things that have no real connection at all; that's what we're hardwired to do – make sense out of the uselessness of existence. Otherwise, we'd all just kill ourselves …

Enzo has set up some solo dates for me in Yugoslavia.

The war, I ask him from a payphone in Lyons central station, isn't there a war going on?

Well, yes, he says, but don't worry about it, man. I mean, we're nowhere near the action.

You sure?

Absolutely. C'mon, man, don't be a pussy, we wouldn't go there if it was a problem, right?

In the hazy morning light after the Italian–Slovene border, the Orb's techno prog oozes from the car cassette player as mountains and fields flash by. A figure looms on the three-lane expressway wearing a check flannel shirt and navvy pants held up with braces. Drawing closer we realise his bare arms wield a huge woodsman's axe. As if in slow motion, he raises one hand and points directly at Miriam behind the wheel. She swerves at the last second to avoid a collision.

Porco dio, exclaims Enzo in the back seat, crossing himself like a monk.

What are you worried about? says Miriam, I've got it all under control.

Miriam is a friend of Enzo's, a short, compact girl with a Mona Lisa face and permanent black rings under her eyes; a battered Pentax film reflex camera trembles on the seat beside her, ready to shoot. Miriam wouldn't take no for an answer when she asked us if she could come along as photographer and driver. I'm glad she's here. She's tough, and she's smart too.

Ljubljana is stark and empty. A pall of coal smoke hangs in the air, acrid and dense. The unpainted facades of the old townhouses radiate abstruse secrets. The Metelkova club is a squat in the old disused military barracks. The promoter, Dragan, wears dark glasses by night. Dragan's look is both gangster and establishment, accommodating both ex-communist bureaucracy and free enterprise; his taste in music and artists is surprisingly eclectic and underground. He won't speak directly to me, only to Enzo. He says, When the Stones come to Ljubljana, when anybody who's anybody come to Ljubljana, I'm the only promoter they'll talk to. And even they don't get to talk to me. I never chat with the artists.

I leave them to their secret discussions and wander down to the performance venue. Kids with dogs hang around in a dimly lit cellar warmed by an open fire in an oil drum. Smoke saturates the air. I fire up a Camel to filter out the petrol fumes and set up my equipment. A few hours later the room is crowded with rowdy anarchists and students wearing John Lennon glasses and long ponytails. I play a lot of the old blues songs, knowing that no one understands a word but it doesn't matter because the feeling is what counts and it runs deeper than language.

The Croatian border is locked down under a warlike, colourless autumn sky. Hours pass before we finally reach the control, where a girl in a black police fleece with an AK-47 strapped over her shoulder seems thrilled to see an Australian passport. Have a wonderful time in Croatia, she says, handing it back to me with a smile.

The highway beyond is almost totally empty. Nothing moves, not even the police cars parked by the side of the road. A fuzzy tape of *Pre-Millennium Tension* plays on the car stereo. Zagreb is cold and grey. There are no street signs, and nobody speaks English when we stop to ask for directions.

The club is full of skinny peroxide-blond kids wearing black clothes. They watch me perform with impassive faces, barely react to the music and remain distantly silent in the pauses between songs. Maybe they've come to the wrong concert or it wasn't promoted right or maybe they were expecting a rock band, not a solo performer with a guitar and a sampler – or they're just too cool, I don't know. The promoter, an anxious guy with matt-black eyes, doesn't speak English. I don't know what language he and Enzo are using to communicate; they huddle secretively in a corner counting out currency.

No problem with the money, Enzo says, making priestlike movements with his hands. We got it all in Deutschemark.

I turn around and the club is empty, a hundred kids vanished without a sound.

What is with everyone in this place? I ask him. What's the vibe?

It's the war, man. Everybody's scared. I think they enjoy the show but you know, in the end, I don't really care, it's up to them. I mean, what else they want?

The streets are deserted after curfew. We drive in circles around the old centre until a giant hotel appears, twenty massive floors braced by exposed girders of steel and futuristic concrete. In the centre, a massive clock face displays the wrong time. The high-ceilinged *Metropolis*-style lobby is crowded with heavily built men in old-world suits and overcoats, some sitting and talking quietly or dropping coins into the payphones, others pacing or reading newspapers. The clerks have pomaded hair and sly masklike expressions that could be mistaken for friendliness were it not for the mass of tension hanging in the air.

Your passports, please?

On the fifteenth floor, things are weirder still. Uniformed soldiers hang out in packs in the corridors, blocking the way as we shamble through with our equipment looking for the right room numbers. Maybe this is their reward for the fighting – a three-star hotel behind the lines, bright lights, big city.

A bottle of Croatian grappa stands on the table beside the ashtray. Enzo pours some shots; the liquid is rough and strangely sobering. In the next room we can hear a confusion of voices. One man begins shouting wildly, his voice breaking into a scream as he hits a psychotic crescendo. Thumps reverberate through the thin walls, somebody turns up the radio – it sounds like a fight is going on, like a nightmare.

Che diavolo sta succedendo? Miriam whispers under her breath – What the hell is happening?

She paces up and down in the small room, clenching and unclenching her fists, her dark eyes clouding with an emotion I can't identify.

We can't just leave them like that, she says heatedly, it's not right!

Leave it alone, says Enzo, don't make trouble.

No, really, you expect me to just not do anything? What if they kill each other?

They're not going to kill each other!

How do you know what they're going to do?

It's not my problem!

Cowards! she exclaims and sweeps out to knock on their door. I hear them open up and talk to her roughly in Croatian. She enters, and their room quietens for a while. Minutes drag by until she slips back in to our room and says, They are so fucked up! They're just boys. Their friends have disappeared or been killed. They just need somebody to talk to them. Then she picks up her pullover and walks back to the door. I'm going to sort them out, she says. They need help.

Why don't you stop her? I ask Enzo.

I can't stop her, says Enzo, she's crazy, man. What can you do?

This is why I didn't want to bring her along. You know what she's like.

I step outside into the corridor to scope the situation. A girl in a plain, dark green dress is standing in the hall, a couple of soldiers talking down to her in a nasty tone of voice. She catches my eye and I realise I've seen her before, at the show.

Pomozi mi, she says very quietly – Help.

The soldiers look at me in an unfriendly way and then back at her, their hard dark eyes asking all kinds of questions that I don't want to know about. Suddenly I sense that we're all targets, that all of us are somehow under threat but I don't know what my role should be; I feel her sadness, something damaged that needs protection and I ask her if she wants to come into our room. Wearily, she nods her assent.

The girl sits down on the floor, tightly clasping her black-stockinged legs. She's very thin and I wonder if I should get her something to eat before realising there's nothing in the room except for the grappa. She tells us her name but the sound of it is unfamiliar and it slips by me like a faraway whisper. The soldiers' angry voices echo around in the corridor outside and I turn on the radio to soften the mood; an imperial symphony of choirs and cymbals hisses from the speakers. The girl stares silently at the faded pattern on the carpet.

Enzo bristles with raw nervous tension. I'm going down the hall, he says, to see if she's alright. This isn't safe and we both know it.

I tell him to take the key. As he closes the door I see the soldiers out in the corridor staring into our room.

The girl says, I shouldn't be here. I think I have to go.

Like he said, it's not safe out there.

But it never is.

I sit down on the floor beside her.

How far away do you live?

Oh, the next village from the city. I do this often, by walk. But I don't want to go tonight, because of police.

Police?

There are patrols everywhere. This is what they wanted, the army chiefs, to have the whole area under control for miles. I don't want to meet soldiers walking home tonight. I'm frightened of them, so many girls have been raped and no one seems to care about it. Can I stay here just a little while?

Sure.

Just don't get any ideas.

She touches her dress, very serious.

You don't want this, she says, you don't want me.

I look into the cloudy gloom of her eyes and tell her the truth – I hadn't even thought about it.

Well, don't start. There's so much you can't understand, you don't want to get involved. I'm sorry, I should go.

No, it's okay. I get it that you don't want to walk home. The patrols. It's late. I understand.

No, you don't.

What?

Understand. I live with my mother in a very small village. My brothers are conscripted. My mother, I have to look after her. She was hurt from a bomb and she's … well, her legs are gone … She's on wheels.

The soldiers next door are shouting and bumping the walls. At some invisible cue they all start laughing roughly and their room gradually quietens down again. I turn up the radio – a movement for strings is playing, interrupted by bursts of static.

Do you feel safe? I ask her.

The girl doesn't answer – she's already fallen asleep against the wall, her hands balled into little fists. I pull the blanket off the bed and gently place it over her, a pillow by her head. The hotel is suddenly very quiet. I look around at the nicotine-brown curtains and the dirty beige carpet and the faded oil of a rural scene hanging near a telephone that doesn't work. I hear her shallow breathing in the half-dark, and far off in the distance, the baying of feral dogs.

A few hours later when I wake up, she's gone.

Unknown #99 | Europe, 1999

Humans, says the medium with a sigh, drift apart and separate. Marriages and relationships break up. It's inevitable; in fact, it's in your DNA. But we're all connected, so no one and nothing is ever truly lost; we lose sight of each other only in this time reference, this illusion – the illusion of the human game. And you don't need me to tell you the human game is not all there is, because you already know it, you feel it.

We're sitting on plain plastic chairs in a generic office space with the blinds drawn. I can faintly hear the dull, low rumble of city traffic emanating from another world. The medium is volatile and hyperintelligent and so deep into the channelling that a breaking sweat glistens on his hairless pate as he looks right through me at a vanishing point in the back of my head with chilly, alien detachment.

Don't shy away from change, he says, you need to accept it, use it. Big changes are coming, big changes in what you consider to be real. Maybe not this year but in the beginning of the next century, portals are opening around the planet, and all kinds of holographic illusions will start to appear. Some of these will be frightening and violent, but that is all they are – illusions. He inhales with a violent rush of air and raises a finger – Don't be fooled; there is only one reality, and you are it. You are all that is, sourcing all that is. So be it!

Melbourne's peak-hour traffic crawls past colonial military

shrines and statues of dead generals coated in bird shit that even this monsoonal downpour can't erase. Office workers unfurl their umbrellas and dodge between the cars, orange streetlamps streak across the windshield. I hold the wheel loosely in a kind of trance, listening to 3PBS on the car radio, the symphonic devastation of Arvo Part's *Cantus* beaming down from its transmitters in the Dandenong Ranges: funereal tubular bells and shimmering glissandos from deep in the Baltic soul, all minor keys, crescendos, choirs, polyphony. Music as brutal as this recognises the infinity and the sacredness of grief; you can let it overwhelm you or you can turn it off, one or the other, no in-betweens.

The boot of the green Toyota is full of computers and papers from my studio on St Kilda Road, a falling-down house splattered in every colour, shaded by a massive willow tree in the backyard. Every creaking floorboard and cracked window is now condemned and everybody else who worked there has already gone – mostly painters, pursuing an even stranger ambition than music. That house was my refuge before the speculators came with a price tag for everything that exists including the human soul; at the end of the 1990s, the barcode is the bottom line.

After months if not years of paralysing psychic unease – the touring and travelling, the high-tension phone calls, the lack of phone calls, the Western Union moneygrams, the girls, the hurt, the long silences, the guilt I feel and the guilt I don't feel, the uneasy gut sensation that I'd done something terribly wrong – finally, my wife and I called an end to us. I'd already failed to embrace the marriage counsellor's sympathetic, well-trained voice of reason; the idea of being shot with red-hot bullets of guilt and regret in a shooting gallery a mile long held little appeal for me. I could see the deep disappointment in Mary's eyes, framed in the dismal silence of all my wrongs lined up ready for anyone to take aim at and blow away like clay pigeons. I could feel the history of us slipping away in an ocean of tears and I was raw and arrogant, hurt and lost, but mostly curious about other worlds waiting to be explored. This formula of mine doesn't perform well in the reconciliation proceedings; they frown upon this kind of thing. I could hear the bullets being loaded one by one with every tangled emotion I tried to express.

Why can't you do something about it? Mary asks me. Why can't you do something? It's not my fault. I didn't do anything wrong.

The bullets of truth and lies penetrate every part of me, all those years of love gone with one final smoking bullet in my brain. But I knew what I had to do, and so did she. As the medium said: So be it.

A fortnight ago, I locked my belongings away in a cage and since then I've been living in that empty house with the mice and the ghosts and the last of the painters for company. Tomorrow, it's the airport again; I'm flying back to Europe. I'll be there for some months, I don't know how long, whatever it takes to restart my life; post-divorce depression filters the world into multiple shades of black, each darker than the last.

My five-year-old son, already agile and graceful as a panther cub, drums his little feet, gathering speed until he appears to be walking on air. You can't be like this, Daddy, he insists, you can't just go away!

My heart recoils like it just took one bullet more. I hold him in my arms and promise I won't be away long. I ask Ruben what presents he'd like me to bring back and Violetta, overhearing the conversation, straightens her pink tutu and adds her requests to his. They squabble over the details while the list expands exponentially. I try to memorise everything they say but last night's conversation with Michelangelo in the small hours over a bottle of wine keeps echoing in my thoughts:

You can't stop now, he'd said, and you can't go home and you can't start all over again either. You've already tried that. Any which way you look at it, you have no choice, not if you want to keep doing what you do. There's no walking away from this, so just keep on going. What else are you going to do?

Saying goodbye to my children this morning rips me to shreds. I don't know how to manage this kind of grief, a searing pain that bypasses all thought and goes straight for your soul with a numbing hurt beyond words. At the same time, I realise I've come a long way to arrive at this place in time, and my dream of another world is so close I can almost grasp it. I tell the children the truth, that I love them and that I'll be back soon and then it's the freeway, the city skyline gradually fading into the private hell of my own thoughts.

The system rapidly consumes me: check-in, security controls, transit lounges, airline food packs, films formatted for the small screen inside your mind. In the seats in front of mine, several women nurse their noisy newborns while I throw back rohypnol and repress the years of tears burning behind my eyes. The horizon curves tightly around the earth, a half-moon shadows the wingtip, the Himalayas spread out below like rippled fudge. In the diazepam no-time of infinite midnight another baby cries, the fuselage of the Boeing shudders like jelly, insomniacs stalk the aisle. The children's faces haunt my dreams along with unsettling visions of both the distant past and the unknown future, all mixing together into a ball of confusion spinning through my brain at thirty thousand feet until the sudden thump of rubber on concrete jolts me from my unsettled reverie. More passport controls and terminal corridors follow in a seamless continuum of jet lag where time is only relative until the whole sequence fades into a foreign darkness on the far side of the globe …

CNN is blasting the twentieth century's final war out of the television screen across the room in widescreen technicolour. Jetlagged, I watch with one eye open as the killing escalates in the ex-Yugoslavia. NATO rockets and bombs pulverise Belgrade; the Black Hand execute Moslems in Kosovo. Media commentators high on their own spin expertly surf the flow of corporate advertising between video clips of hovering B-2 stealth bombers and Apache helicopters manoeuvring in supernatural ways, cruise missile nose-cone cameras exploding crosshaired targets, drone footage of refugee columns stranded in mountains fleeing death squads.

I'm lying on Reinhold's couch in the Kreuzberg quarter of Berlin, a high-density zone of Turkish families, squats and low-rent housing. Curled up like an embryo on the floor of his bedroom, Reinhold is yelling the word 'fuck' over and over again in escalating crescendos as he processes the pain of some monster hangover.

Sidestepping the panhandler and junkies at the Kottbusser Tor *spaetkauf*, I buy him some Berliner Pilsner and bring it home; he cheers up instantly, telling me a story about a fight with a Kurdish hashish dealer.

A fucking knife! laughs Reinhold with tears in his eyes. He pulled a knife on me! Can you believe it? What does he think this is, *West Side Story*? And me, I used to beat up skinheads for sport, ha ha! With a goddamned baseball bat, ha ha! Stupid fucking knife. Who was he trying to kid?

The room is dark, lit only by explosions of colour from the CNN war porn on the television.

Ja, and I can't believe that shit either, he says. NATO! Another stupid rock show, even louder than the Grand Prix!

It's Friday evening and Kottbusser Allee throngs with young Turks in hotted-up cars pumping hip-hop from massive, custom-installed woofers. I can feel the bass like bomb-blast shock waves even up here on the fifth floor, overscored by the howling sirens of a squadron of riot police vans on their way to another downtown fracas.

How can you stand the noise? I ask Lucas.

What noise? he shouts.

The drone of a helicopter hovering above the building mixes into the police sirens fading into the distance and the obscene noise from the television.

What fucking noise? Reinhold yells.

I have to go, I tell him and he just stares at me, trying to lip-read my words. I use sign language and he finally punches the mute button on his remote control.

What? You're leaving tonight? Where to?

The Ruhr. I'm meeting Chris Hughes there in the studio.

Ach, he says, why didn't you tell me before?

My half-restrung guitar lies across the couch, books are stacked on a coffee table, dirty clothes scattered on the floor. The open suitcase spews papers, journals, contracts, lists of phone numbers and addresses, cables, wires and transformers, train tickets, broken boots, everything flung in blind. I throw my clothes on top, kneel on the lid and force it to close, clicking the locks shut.

Snow falls on the old steel town of Bochum in Germany's industrial valley, the Ruhrgebiet. The twisted shapes of ancient industrial machinery loom like war ruins against a slate-grey sky. I pull up the collar of my leather jacket and stamp the snow off my boots, blowing warm air into cupped palms.

Hughes looks at me and asks, What happened to Norm?

My mind searches for a quick explanation, but there isn't one.

Nobody seems to exactly know, I reply hesitantly, he was going okay, or at least that's how it seemed. The last time we were together at a barbecue in this big garden in Northcote, we discussed getting him over here, he was excited, we made an agreement – it was on. He called me a few days later saying he'd booked his flight, we talked, I don't know, more than several times, we had it figured out. That was a month ago; then last night I get a call from the Rattenfaenger ...

Horst, the shaven-headed studio owner, opens the heavy steel door and heat blasts out: the control room is hot as a sauna. Machines blink and hum, the patch bay is half ripped out and trailing cables, the hardware racks are packed with knobs and dials and meters and LEDs in varying degrees of health and decrepitude.

I've never engineered a mixdown in an old-school studio like this; in fact, I've never engineered a mixdown at all, but that's why we're here – to mix an album for our band, the True Spirit. Our handlers at the KGB Agency connected us to this studio because as it's already partially deconstructed for moving to a new location, it's extremely cheap to hire; but today we discovered our old friend, our road manager and sound engineer, Norm, never caught flight QF10 out of Melbourne to join us here.

Norm died a few days ago at his parents' house in a dusty Victorian country town, swept into another avalanche, another young death, another one of our band disappearing into the unknown. We are gutted by the news. Speechless. Sadness fills the studio until it gets hard to breathe. Norm? Norm, what the fuck happened to you? I keep expecting him to walk through the door until recognising he's left this plane of existence, I crawl into a sound-proof booth and howl. I can't stop and I can't forgive God for taking Norm, can't forgive this careless God who smashes up our lives, who fucks up time and time again then dematerialises into a harem of lyre-strumming angels shouting his name, leaving us to clean up the heartbreaking mess left behind … I have to control this. I have to make this record. My instincts for life kick me back into action and into the studio, stuffing my sadness deep down inside and pushing me on through into the future.

Horst rushes through explaining how to operate the mass of semi-functioning equipment, how to set the alarm systems and lock up after work. I've been nodding knowledgeably all along, struggling to understand his German English and ask the right questions, but he seems distracted and eager to get away as if preoccupied with other matters. He hands me the keys and I think I hear him say something about returning later in the week. As he disappears into the snowdrifts, Hughes shoots me a look to say, *Do you know what the fuck he was just talking about?*

We have a week to pull this together in isolation, working

twelve hours a day. I don't know exactly what I'm doing, but I have some idea – over the years I've watched engineers mixing and asked questions. I turn on the power, load the tapes and gingerly move some faders around. A loud hissing comes out of the studio monitors, then the isolated tracks kick in at high volume, sounding strange and distorted. Hughes covers his ears and grimaces. I quickly turn the volume down but at the same time, I notice the VU needles are still dancing wildly.

Can't you hear it? asks Hughes.

Hear what?

Man, that high-pitched sound acupuncturing my brain!

The speaker cones are quivering paranormally. I rush into the tape room and turn down the masters on the power amps then give Axel a quick call.

Calibrate the system, he says in his clipped German English, switch off the speakers, power down the desk and the amps, return everything to unity, *ja*?

Hughes has opened the street door to let the zero-degree air cool the control room; outside, the snow has frozen to ice. He fiddles with the heating system controls, swearing quietly to himself, until slowly the temperature drops.

The rebooted studio hums faintly; lights blink and flash, needles jerk and quiver. We coax a sound from the desk, mystified and intrigued by how the different sounds are falling into place. Like a Frankenstein's monster, the album manifests riddled with scars and sutures and starts to walk, clumsily at first and then with gathering speed, into full-blown life. It's a sprawling mess of a record, *Last Frontier*, recorded in four different countries over the space of a year; the way it's mixed is similar to the recording method – shooting blind in the dark. It comes together through no fault of ours – something or someone else is guiding the process. Maybe it's Norm, tweaking the pots and faders as he whispers in my ear, *That's not how you do it, dolt, you do it like this – now pay attention! Are you listening? Can you hear me?*

At Fulda Bahnhof the rail lines glint with frost. The unnatural brilliance of a satellite hangs low in a voided sky. I'm the only person on the platform and wind the only sound. The surrounding hills are dark and empty. It's after midnight and my hands are turning to ice when I hear that keening electrical hum in the overhead wires and feel the wheels rumbling through the soles of my boots. The Intercity Express ICE 1952, several hours late, pulls in to the platform.

Inside the carriage, the scent of cigarette smoke hangs in the air. Another lone traveller sits opposite me in the darkened compartment, an old man small as a dwarf, like a ventriloquist's dummy, his tiny legs drawn up on the seat beside him. He is slumped and immobile as if asleep but the flashing lights of an oncoming train reveal that he has one eye open and one eye shut. The open eye is bloodshot and clear-coloured and staring straight at me. I move one place to the side and his eye follows; I shiver and look away, gazing out through the window into the featureless intercity night.

The 1952 rattles and thumps as it slows in to Zurich Bahnhof, rousing me from a broken sleep. The tiny one-eyed man is gone and a dirty white light suffuses the compartment windows.

Outside is chill and silent. I walk out into the city, ask directions to the stock exchange and find myself in a museum-like wing of the Zurich SIX; a singer with wild, cult-leader eyes and long blond hair is sound-checking at the microphone on the stage at the far end of the room, the high vaulted roof painted with faux-Renaissance clouds and cherubs.

There's not enough reverb, he says strumming his folk guitar and staring blindly into the stage lights, give me a church. Give me a goddamn church!

Clouds of hydroponic marijuana and burning patchouli oil meld together under the arched ceiling. The hall becomes a temple, his vocals floating in the digital soup.

You people are finally getting it together, he says, it's got to sound like a goddamn church, okay? Om, he sings, long drawn-out oms droning through the haze of reverb and dope smoke.

Backstage, Antonio, the young and wealthy promoter, is surrounded by a group of technicians and musicians talking in three or four languages simultaneously.

Cops! pontificates Antonio, the cops don't exist. It's all in your mind. They're just hot air fronting the shadowplay of the state, a big, dirty fraud. You know those ancient gods, like Zeus? And what was he called, yeah, Apollo? Well, they're just the remnants of a previous age that fucked itself out of existence. We are time, man, old as the stars. Who gives a fuck about cops? Antonio notices me standing there and grips me by the shoulders, looks into my eyes and states with chemical conviction – We are immortals!

A New York drummer called Khan begins triggering samples with his tablas. Machine-gun volleys of percussion ricochet off the stage in a hectic breakbeat, fast and polyrhythmically intricate. Khan's band fall in behind the groove, jazz players, phenomenally quick. I've never seen breakbeat performed live before, this confluence of trained musicians and their new-generation digital machines.

Then it's my turn; I plug into a Fender Twin guitar amp by the drum riser and make samples using metal slides on the open-tuned strings, stacking C chords on top of each other in clusters, letting the resonating harmonics fade on an almost infinite delay.

A guy watches me curiously from behind the onstage DJ decks. He's attaching all kinds of stuff to his white label vinyls: scotch tape, paperclips, links of broken chain, tiny ball bearings. He starts dropping sounds on my loops, tiny molecules of quantum interaction massively amplified, scratches and echoes, atoms under a sonic microscope.

He tells me his name is Dimitri.

I'm interested in very, very small sounds, he says, the kind of sounds that normally you can't hear. These kinds of sounds are, I don't know, like an invisible world that's always around us but we're not really aware of it. The stylus is a key to unlocking this other dimension because it's really a sort of microphone that touches what you can't hear. My amplifiers are always turned right up to capture the sound, so loud they can damage your hearing if you're not very, very careful.

Next day we're recording together in his small studio near the river, on the third floor of an old terrace with creaking wooden floors and a view over the wild garden out the back. By nightfall we've recorded several hours of improvised music for guitar and turntables in long, ambient drone pieces conjured from a phantom world. For titles I use the names of places recurring in the Yugoslavian war reports – Novi Sad, Pristina, Mostar.

I listen back to the recordings on a train headed south for the border and it's like nothing I've ever heard before even though it contains traces of many things I love: abstract orchestral pieces, inexplicable electronica, space recordings from telescopes and satellites, the sacred melodies of Arvo Part. Electrical fires burn in the back of my brain; I sense new vistas opening up, all I have to do is pay attention and wait. Right then the name for this music arrives fully formed – *Transfargo* – grafted from Scandinavian cross-continental trucks glimpsed on the autobahn.

Finally, for the first time in my life I feel totally and utterly free; I'm cashed up and nothing and nobody is tracking my movements, I have no phone, no way of being contacted, and on the other side of these crepuscular mountains lie the paradoxical mysteries of Italy.

Enzo's battered white Lancia pulls up on the Piazza delle Medaglie D'oro at Bologna station. We drive through the fruit and vegetable markets to the Link, a squat converted into an underground venue. US band Labradford are sound-checking a thick mass of ambient frequencies in the *sala blu,* students scuffle and joke in the rough-and-ready venue cafe, technicians scurry about checking wires with voltameters. There's a sense here of being hermetically sealed off from the hectic surrounding city, a kind of free-will zone normalcy cannot enter.

Business is not bad, says Enzo, except every time the modern dance wankers put on an event we bleed money. But, you know, it's a collective … what can you do when there are thirty people trying to agree on something? Better to have a blowjob … These people just destroy your mind. At the same time, if you really want to make money, if that's what you really want, work with the

DJs. That's where the money is and that's why the good music, the band scene, is really in trouble. Who wants to pay thirty million of lire to bring out a band, and then the backline, the hotels, the food ... Kind of easier to have a couple of guys play some records – you can see the problem. It's not going to go away.

That night, some English DJs play the big *sala bianca* and the room is packed, at least a thousand people, and they dance and get off on themselves, paying no attention to the DJs on the stage. The music is electronic, generic four-on-the-floor house beats, vapid and indigestible. With all the chemical stimulation of the ecstasy and special K in the room, behind the party vibe lurks the tyranny of the machine.

The television news is saturated with images of the NATO bombing of Serbia. High-tech military manoeuvres show the people what good use their taxes are being put to – queues of armed jets taking off from the Aviano airfield, light-speed smudges in the night sky little more than a hundred miles away.

Man, it's all happening so close, says Davide, another member of the Link crew. You can almost smell the explosives drifting across the Adriatic Sea, feel the earth shake when the bombs hit. They're people just like you and me, except they're getting blown to bits while we watch it on TV. The world is fucked and this is what fucked looks like, like that – he indicates the screen where a small crowd of protestors at Aviano are being coerced by military police into a van. It's all about the money, man. Always was, always will be.

The Apennine Mountains flash past the windows of a Naples-bound train between stretches of long tunnels cored through the rock, the gallery walls inches from my face. A valve amplifier trembles on the seat next to me, the guitar and hard cases stacked in the overhead racks. My friend Tim, an American luthier living in a priest's cottage on a high peak in the outer Florentine hills, picks me up from the station. It's springtime south of the Alps – birds twitter, huge zeppelin-like *calabrone* bees buzz from flower to flower and soft clouds float in an acid-blue sky.

Tim grew up in the sixties, saw Captain Beefheart sing the blues, dropped acid in Haight-Ashbury, demonstrated against the Vietnam War; he moved to Italy to escape the noise of New York City and perfect his art in solitude. By day he tends the grounds and the grapevines and chops wood; by night he writes and builds handmade violins.

Tim glances at my gear through his wire-rimmed spectacles and scratches his beard and says, Ah, you're recording ... Well, in the chapel the acoustics are great. You've got to hear this space, the echo. Now, where are those keys?

The heavy wooden doors groan open in a shower of sawdust. Wood shavings and leaves blow in around our feet while mice scamper out of sight. A life-sized wooden sculpture of Our Lady of the Sorrows pierced by eight curved swords surmounts the opposite wall. There are vases of eternal paper flowers, a lectern, faded images of saints. I drop my suitcase on the ground and the chapel acoustics reverberate like a thunderclap.

Before the Roman Church, this site used to be a temple to Hera, queen of the gods, says Tim. It's a very powerful place.

He disappears and returns with a bottle of Chianti and two glasses while I set up my equipment in the chapel's perfect silence: the electric guitar runs through a valve preamplifier and distortion device into a sampler and an analogue delay before hitting the

Lombardi amplifier. A stereo microphone hangs from a high crossbeam and feeds into a digital tape deck, recording the entire ambience.

Channelling the psychic residuals in this sacred place, improvised pieces emerge in long swathes of reverberant noise. Haunting harmonics, overtones and microtones resonate in the chapel's high stone eaves like eerily symphonic echoes of a ghostly choir. In the vacuum isolation of headphones I feel discarnate presences cluster around me, their origins in distant constellations, their intentions ambiguous.

When it gets too intense I walk outside and lie down in the grass and smoke. The night is exceptionally clear at this height, and staring into the Milky Way it seems the earth and the heavens invert, as if I'm on a precipice looking down into a vertiginous canyon of stars.

Tim's eyes light up when he hears the recordings.

That's trippy stuff, man, he says, I knew the chapel had something to say, I hear it talking through you. But still, I don't get what it's saying. Maybe it's all in Latin!

The overnight sleeper train bound for Messina is booked solid. Two weathered Sicilian octogenarians watch with stoic patience while I stow the guitar and hard cases away in our narrow shared compartment, then offer me a soft drink and a creamy *cannolo* in a plastic wrapper. Kids on a camping excursion yell to each other down the corridors. The toilet is smeared with human shit by some deranged hand – *va fancu!,* the excremental scrawl spells out, up your ass!

I read a Gideon's Bible in the bunk bed while the old folk

sleep below. The sound of the wheels on the steel rails, the roar of machinery and air in a composite wall of noise filled with nuance, harmony and detail fill my skull; it sounds like *Transfargo*. Sleep comes in stops and starts while I dream about a metallic object flitting and spinning over a stand of trees against a pale grey sky. The object's form is mutable, morphing between disc and orb, its size, orientation and distance hard to guess; the thing could be huge or minuscule, a new-generation stealth fighter on manoeuvres or a bogong moth batting itself against a wire flyscreen door. An authoritative, telepathic female voice states the three letters 'UFO' with deliberate clarity.

I wake up suddenly in the roaring vibration of the train compartment with clear access to one of my oldest dormant memories; I'm six or seven years old and experiencing eternity for the first time, cross-legged on the floor of the school gym.

Miss James is at the lectern talking about Jesus and the Lord in a voice rusted by time and repetition. The other boys fade away as my gaze fixes on a ceramic pipe fitted to the wall behind the medical-nylon beige of her stockings. The pipe is just below eye level and slightly overshadowed by the gym bench above it. A seam of cement where the pipe suddenly bends and disappears into the brick galvanises my attention. As my mind follows the seam into the wall, I hear a gentle popping sound and visualise more and more pipes beyond, millions of pipes interweaving in an infinite network like an M. C. Escher diagram. It's a mass synaptic explosion and for a moment I'm teleported out of my body into a state of hyper-consciousness where nothing and everything are the same.

The train comes to a grinding halt in the railyards at Villa San

Giovanni. The carriages are very slowly detached then shunted back and forth onto a ferry across the Strait of Messina. On deck, the air is warm and the choppy water faintly slicked with oil. Seagulls drift overhead. I chew on a stale *arancino* from the ferry's own greasy-uspoon cafe while a giant Madonna statue with open arms welcomes me back to Sicily.

A light shower of tiny magnetic particles rains down on Catania. People on the streets wear surgical masks to avoid breathing in the black grit. Cars skid and collide on silica-slicked roads inclined at improbable gradients. The volcano Mount Etna, beneath which they say lie the Vulcanic forges of creation, is spewing ash.

Sleeping on the floor at the D'Agata sisters' apartment with my ear to the ground I wake up to the neighbourhood kids' bloodcurdling screams echoing around the courtyard and somebody knocking on the door.

C'mon, says Antonello, I want to introduce you to the best tits in this whole stupid town. We walk down to the fish market and shuck some lemon-doused oysters while he knocks back his first chilled white for the day.

Sicily, Antonello explains, is heaven and hell in one. For you, foreigner, it's a kind of heaven. For people like me who were born here, it's a special kind of beautiful hell.

Tommaso and Emma and Marta pick me up in an ash-streaked white Panda, edging through the narrow traffic-jammed streets until we reach the *stradale* for Siracusa and leave the city's volcanic crush behind. Slowly the landscape flattens out, surrounding us with olive fields and ancient dry-stone walls.

The Villa Teresa is a beautiful, dilapidated country house,

limestone white and sunspot hot, its gardens all grey ash and skeletal shadows. Distant fires spread black smoke across the sky. The fire department, reckons Tommaso, is busily torching the fields so they can then put out the blazes themselves, then justify the extra funding squeezed from the forestry department. The whole thing is a rort. Stick around here long enough and you'll get the idea.

The house is very old, no parallel lines, the plaster hand-smoothed with no hard corners. The floors are tiled, the walls bare and unadorned. The influence of nearby North Africa is subtle but present. Marta and Emma wander around whispering to each other in soft voices as they choose their rooms and hang mosquito nets.

Roberto nonchalantly spins records in the *grand salotto*; effortless, ambient summer beats echo through the empty, high-ceilinged rooms.

The fridge is loaded with bottles of white wine. There is no hot water and there are no mirrors; I very quickly forget what I look like and cease to care. My beard grows and my skin burns and the days blur into a haze of heat and light, nights into a continuum of music and conversation. People come and go, occasionally bringing more wine, drinking water and fresh fish. Sometimes we drive into the town and eat at the restaurant on the hill, everybody talking at once, the courses vanishing as fast as they arrive.

We walk through the swamp reeds to the Oasis of Vendicari on the Ionian Sea. The most beautiful girl I've ever seen, a girl I've never met and never will, walks into the shallows at twilight. The sunset fuses her hair with light, her body silhouetted against the glowing disc. She launches herself from the ledge of an underwater Greek ruin into a perfect wave and disappears below the surface.

I follow her down into the ruins but lose her in the depths. My skin is dark and soaked in salt water; the salt crusted on my lips makes me thirsty. Emma passes me a lemon granita. The frozen ice and citrus juice explode on my tongue. We sit there, stunned and hypnotised by the sun setting below the horizon in waves of burnt orange and magma red. No one wants to leave.

Wisps of cloud illuminated by Mediterranean moonlight merge and dissolve in an ever-changing, free-form pattern. Just as I'm drifting off to sleep, I notice way up high in the earth's upper atmosphere a small fleet of inter-dimensional orbs hovering in the heavens. I try to rouse the others to witness this incredible sight but by the time they open their eyes the tiny luminous discs have faded behind a cloudbank.

Did you see that?

Marta rubs her eyes, shakes her head, turns over and falls back to sleep.

A billion silent stars hang there in the sky, looking down on us with intelligence beyond mortal comprehension.

Matelico Moods | Sicily, 2000

The highway shimmers in a heat haze through the windows of the Catania–Palermo morning bus. In the Sicilian interior's desolation of singed cactus, scorched fields and stony ravines, nothing moves. The livestock is invisible, sheltered by hidden valleys and barns in a landscape so timeless and still, it's hard to grasp that there are more than five million people living on this island.

Staring out at the rolling hills with the sun on my face, I feel cut loose of the past, like I'm floating in free space; no one can reach me here to question my actions or interrupt the strange flow of events that brought me to this place. Last week in Porto Empedocle, I experienced something like a past-life flashback, a deep and overpowering sensation of having been here before that I can't explain, something in the light, the sound, the smell, the shape of things. Sicily appears to me as a paradoxical parallel world where I can lose myself in the exploration of other ways of being, free of the shadows of the past and the shackles of expectation. And then, I met a girl who brought everything into focus. It feels like I'm meant to be here, that there's a mission to be done, only I don't know what it is just yet.

I'm lost in these ruminations when the driver makes a sudden, unscheduled departure from the A14 highway, following a series of tight turns up a two-lane blacktop leading to the forbidding precipice town of Enna. Just outside the gates, he pulls over, climbs down off the coach. A short, balding man in Wayfarer sunglasses, shorts and a polo shirt stands 20 metres away, waiting for him. In the external side mirror I notice them kiss lightly on each cheek and a small package change hands.

The other passengers scattered around the bus seem indifferent to this unscheduled pause. A pop song plays loudly over the radio, all saccharine strings and wounded macho pride, while a nun concentrates on her *panino* sandwich, a young girl whispers into a mobile phone, two teenage boys in front of me read the same copy of the pink-papered *Gazzetta dello Sport* and an off-duty soldier boy snores in his seat.

As the radio song draws to a hyperbolic crescendo, the driver, unshaven and unreadable behind his wraparound polaroids, gets back behind the wheel and ignites the engine. The bus descends through the ragged hill country onto a deserted four-lane autostrada potted with holes and shepherded by faded, illegible signs before slowing down at a roadblock, the engine howling against the gradient as the driver shifts into low gear.

Armed *carabinieri* board the bus and search all passengers. They find a kid with some grass in his backpack and their satisfaction is palpable, like they just won the lotto. A grinning cop standing close to 2 metres tall in his peaked military cap pinches the kid's stash between thumb and forefinger. The plastic bag is packed with weak homegrown weed, the junta of Mafiosi and crooked cops having cleared the island years before of strong African grass in order to flood the market with smack and coke.

And then they turn in my direction. The driver is watching me in the huge rectangular rear-view mirror – even through his thick, black shades I can feel his eyes boring into my head.

I documenti? the cop asks me – Documents?

I'm nailed to the seat with surprise – last night I played solo in a Catania art squat until three in the morning and I've barely slept at all. I'm not carrying any personal documents, never having expected to be interrogated on a Palermo-bound Greyhound. But I'm also aware that the fight against illegal immigration is intensifying; on nearby islands like Lampedusa, the detainment camps are massively overcrowded with *clandestini* smuggled across the sea from Libya. There are tens of thousands of undocumented strangers on the island at any time. In Sicily, a person can just disappear – although, as they say, a body in the water will sooner or later get washed up by the tide.

When I admit that I've got no ID, the *carabiniere* just smiles.

Tu resti con noi, he says, sitting down beside me – You stay with us.

We grind into town through gridlocked streets lined with concrete mega-*palazzi*; these are the suburbs of Palermo, areas bombed flat in the Allied invasion of 1943 then rebuilt by cement-mogul Mafiosi under contract from *Democrazia Cristiana* politicians in the 1960s. The traffic devolves into chaos as the streets narrow near the bus terminus. The asphalt is teeming with families sending off or greeting relatives. The general confusion is bewildering – but my friend, Andrea, stands tall and it's easy to locate him towering over the crowd. In a lawyer-like tirade of local dialect and sign language he assures the cops that I'm of no further interest to them and casually, they let me go. It seems the deal is done within the unspoken boundaries of a mutual understanding – I may have no papers, but I've got local backup. In the general melee of the terminus we grab my suitcase and guitar and disappear, the midday sun beaming overhead, the city resonating with chaos and heat.

I ask Andrea, What the hell happened back there? No answer. Then I ask him why the *carabinieri* boarded the bus; he replies that they had an insider tip to intercept something valuable stolen in Catania and quickly spirited out of the city – I was just in the wrong place at the wrong time. I tell him about the bus stopping in Enna and the mystery package changing hands and he just looks at me steadily for a few seconds then starts laughing.

We walk down the crowded Via Roma, past the franchise luxury goods of Louis Vuitton and Dolce & Gabbana and the Italianate culture of conventional beauty. Out the front of a Rinascimento superstore, a wizened little man pushes a handcart loaded with bootleg cassettes; tacked to his vertical display board are cassette covers of the old-school singing stars of the Italian south. The voice of one of these artists, Roberto Murolo, sings from a beaten-up tape deck lashed to his handcart. The passers-by barely notice the music vendor or his wares; they're focused on the handbags and shoes in the fancy boutique windows.

Local-government elections are in full swing: coloured portrait photos of candidates are scattered across the footpaths, poster-sized versions glued to power poles, shopfront awnings and walls. It's a rogue's gallery of hundreds of bizarre-looking candidates representing not only centrist political programs but also the extreme left and right wings, including that singularity where the two 'wings' meet each other on the far side of the political spectrum, becoming as one with organised crime.

A sinister carnival atmosphere pervades. At the Piazza San Domenico, a funeral procession descends the steps of a baroque church; the black-clad mourners pick their way through the flowers and election flyers, lead by robed priests waving metal crucifixes that catch the sunlight in blinding reflections, almost as if they're wielding laser lights powered by God above.

We walk on through the narrow, winding streets, a breakneck wind blowing at our heels. Sheets and shirts dance a tarantella on clotheslines strung high overhead between the buildings; shutters and doors slam like gunfire. Passing the open door of a restaurant kitchen, I see a cook gnawing on the head of a boiled octopus before reckoning it to be too tough and throwing it back into the oily, bubbling water.

This is the Vucciria district by the old port, and it's a wild zone of the city somewhere between dream and nightmare. Shielded by local mafia from the direct reach of the police and city hall, the baroque buildings bulge with saline humidity, precarious and decadent, disintegrating by slow neglect.

Occasionally, a balcony detaches and falls into the street below, sometimes a whole apartment. Last year, an entire family of ten were buried in the debris of their own home yet all of them survived, even a three-year-old pulled from the rubble hours later by the fire brigade. Garbage ferments at the foot of these decaying facades.

This is all Sicilian heritage, says Andrea, gesturing towards the sandstone terraces. Property speculators, he explains, are waiting for all of this to slowly collapse before they get to work – they can't easily just waltz in with the wrecking ball – and anyway, why go to all that trouble when the place is already falling down? One way or another, it's all going to get turned into shopping malls!

Families cook over gas-bottle barbecues, sidestepped by sleepwalking barflies. Little kids snatch the shoulder bag from a dumbstruck German tourist and speed out of sight, laughing.

Street kittens scatter, sheltering under a rusty dumpster. A clean-up crew hose the fish market's blood and scales off the stones; the shops have already pulled their shutters down. I figure it must be a saint's day or a Vatican holiday, only to discover the district is shut down in the aftershock of a Mafia assassination a few days previously.

This explains why, back at the apartment where I'm staying, Croce, a painter with a predilection for gruesome Catholic themes – visceral abstractions of blood and fire on huge canvases – has embarked on a drinking binge. *La Sicilia* lies open on his kitchen table, a report on the killing featuring photos of the blood-soaked corpse on a city street. The slain *guappo* was a key figure in the local network and I can smell both grief and fear in the room. There are obviously a lot of things happening here I don't understand.

Nearby, fat, bearded monks in long black robes sell tickets at the entrance to the catacombs of Palermo. Underground, in the natural cool of the ancient grotto, mummified bodies are on display – monks, merchants and aristocrats preserved in eternal rictus by the embalmer's art. Most of them are very well dressed, the children like little vampire dolls in satin and bows. The grimacing faces of the mummies are echoed in the expressions of people in the streets around me, a gentle death dance between formality and the inferno. Emotive overstatement is in everything – relationships, art, food, love, a heightened reality of passion, transgression and redemption.

We stop for a drink in a hole-in-the-wall bar swarming with extras from some Carravaggio masterpiece before arriving at our final destination – the Palazzo Rammacca, an old Bourbon townhouse with a marble spiral staircase and an art squat on the top floor, its front door stickered by decals that read 'Mafia-free zone'. I've been invited here to create a sound installation, part of an art project designed to pump new blood into this decrepit zone of the city.

Using a fifty-dollar shortwave radio, I tune in to broadcasts from Tunisia and Algeria. Palermo was a great Islamic city in its time, and traces of that era still remain. I tease out this connection with Arabic songs and monologues phased and filtered by fading radio waves into transparent noise, like background radiation, mysterious voices from another world close by across the sea. I'm mixing the radio with loops sampled from a record player, dirty old vinyl snatches of Mantovani, baroque orchestral diversions, frothy string confections – how these elements interact is a dice roll in the direction of chaos theory. There are no permits or supervision. Here in the Vucciria, different rules apply.

As the light fades, Uwe returns from painting glow-in-the-dark footprints on the interior walls of the collapsed building opposite. It's too dark and too dangerous to continue, he laughs. I can't see what I'm doing. But these footprints are creating a sensation in the neighbourhood. People love them. You know, people here are unpretentious; they just accept art for what it is, which is nothing. In Switzerland, people want to know how to interpret it, they ask why. But the question is meaningless – there is no reason, there doesn't have to be.

It's a hot night, and the wind is thick with airborne dust from North Africa, the ragged old mixing desk sticky with humidity. Boris and Ciccio strap speaker boxes onto the iron railings of the balcony, testing the weight against the wind's violent tug. Jürgen, the mastermind behind the installation, attempts to hook my music up to the internet for live streaming from his battered PC. To me, the web is new and unknown territory. We regard the dial-up modem warily, guessing at its blinking little lights.

A Muslim call to prayer surfaces through the warped radio hiss. A loop of Stanley Black's exotic piano runs parallel. They are strangely in key. I scramble down the winding staircase and out the marble-floored atrium into the streets below to listen. Down here it's more diffuse; the installation blends in with scooter exhausts and domestic disputes and the clamour of car horns. Soundwaves wash through the narrow alleys and cul-de-sacs; unrecognisable fragments of the muezzin's call from the minarets mix with cascading Latin glissandos, the music seemingly radiating from a black starry sky caught in glimpses between the towering buildings overhead.

I pass families clustered around televisions in the street watching *varietá* broadcasts from Berlusconi's Mediaset in Milano. Between blasts of sexual innuendo and saturation advertising, showgirls dumb down to the beat of radio hits written to industrial formulae. I get the impression no one seems to notice my sound installation over the noise of Mediaset, but it turns out I'm wrong about that – back at the palazzo, Jürgen and Boris are waiting for me on the spiral stairway.

Looks like you've got some explaining to do, Jürgen says nervously. The guys from the butchery and grill on the other side of the piazza want to have a word with you. Inside, a group of young local guys wearing jeans and T-shirts logoed in sporting colours – mostly pink for the Palermo FC – are muttering and jostling around, their hair neatly razored like military cadets. One of them catches my eye across the room.

Hey, you! *Straniero!* Are you the boss of this noise?

Yes, why? Is there a problem?

Your little joke is finished, he scowls. Now it is time for some real music to begin.

Jürgen continues nervously typing bright green computer code onto his screen; everybody is pretending to do something else, fiddling with cables, shuffling papers or just staring at the blinking red lights on the cryptic little modem.

This isn't a joke, I reply.

Shaking their heads sadly, the guys toe the ground with scuffed trainers. Then one of them pulls a handful of cassette tapes from his jacket pocket and holds them towards me, daring me to take them. On the dog-eared, 1970s-vintage cardboard cassette covers I recognise a truculent, heavy-set face familiar from pictures in local kiosks and bars in the rougher districts of Sicilian towns.

This is Mario Merola, says the kid with the tapes, and he repeats the name several times, heavily enunciated, like I'm a bit slow in the head. I have no idea who Mario Merola is, or what these guys want.

This is good music, not like the rubbish you're playing right now, sneers another of the lads. Put it on!

All of them stare at me intently; this appears to be an offer I can't refuse.

Very quickly, Boris produces a TEAC cassette deck and patches it into the system. I flick open the cover and drop a Merola cassette onto the spindle drive. Hitting the play button, out comes the music of the Sicilian streets, fronted by a sensuous voice dripping with melodrama and singing in a dialect I don't recognise.

Now the butchery guys are beaming. This is real music,

popular music, music that people want to hear, they say. One of them puts his hand on my shoulder and asks – You are a musician? Pay attention and you might learn something from this. If you learn these lessons well, maybe you too can one day sound this good – but I doubt it …

The cheesy orchestrations of Mario Merola blast out of our speakers at high volume. Ciccio brings in a sixpack of Moretti beer and passes some bottles around. The room fills with talking, drowning out the installation. Under headphones, I fade up the loops of white noise and Islamic diatonic melodies and it seems to me that in this context, Merola's voice evokes a Sicilian dream world touched by both ancient Africa and the insidious science-fiction premise of this new millennium. This makes some weird kind of sense because Sicily lies in the centre of the Mediterranean Sea, a crossroads between east and west since human time began.

The guys from the grill and butchery finish their beers and prepare to go, leaving their Merola tapes with us to be sure his music keeps serenading the neighbourhood. Everyone shakes hands and smiles. It always takes a lot of time to exit a room in Sicily; you risk offending people if you don't formally acknowledge them. A lot of cheek-kissing and small talk is standard protocol.

A quarter of an hour later, after they're gone, we finish a bottle of homemade wine and turn up the other sounds backgrounding Merola's voice. Chance, random elements interact with machines and radio waves. Merola's star ascends over the Vucciria once more, but with psychedelic electronica for company. Just then, as I'm realising a strange and significant new discovery that could lead to unexplored territory, a baby gang of streetkids – *zingari*, gypsies, *romani* – rush the apartment, bobbing and weaving and chattering in high little voices. Chaos breaks out as they take over the installation. These kids, whose age is hard to tell, are out of anyone's control. One of them, waving a grubby cassette tape in the air, demands to hear his music – which turns out to be some species of Balkan techno. The night dissolves into a delirium of Eastern Bloc beats and ragged, coal-eyed children dancing to the metal machine music of the computer age.

Back in Catania, I work obsessively on what I now call *The Merola Matrix*. To me, it's like a trapdoor into the underworld of the Sicilian psyche, or maybe a gateway into my own subconscious, I'm not sure which. I fall regularly through this trapdoor into an alternate universe that breaks every musical and legal rule. I sample Merola's voice, stretching and splicing it to become the mythological narrator of this new reality, a Dante-esque guide into the island's mysteries. I begin to dream in Italian since no one really speaks to me in English any more; memories of life beyond Sicily grow fainter the longer I stay. I know I don't have much time, that I'll have to leave soon. It's good, this disconnection, and it helps knowing a little Italian language, but that's still not enough to decode the lyrics of Merola's songs because they're sung in another tongue – Neapolitan dialect.

Merola is actually from the city of Naples, 500 miles north across the Tyrrhenian Sea. He grew up working on the docks and rose to stardom in the *sceneggiata*, a form of romantic melodrama rooted in folk songs and opera and music-hall variety. Betrayal, disappointment and heartbreak figure repeatedly in its depiction of humanity's struggle to extend happiness beyond a passing, freak instant. It is both formulaic entertainment and public ritual; the audience sing along with every word, knowing full well how the story ends: sometimes a woman must die, less often, a man – the lover avenging his honour is usually male. Either way, the man has his own ordeal, reconciling his relationship to the all-powerful criminal underworld that is the real society of men – *la malavita.*

I start watching Merola's movies from the 1970s and early 80s. They're readily available as bootlegs at the big *La Fiera* market in the centre of Catania. These blurry video cassettes with their faded photocopy covers include titles like *Napoli serenata calibro 9* (self-explanatory), *Mammasantissima* (The Sacred Mother), *Carcerato* (Imprisoned), *Zappatore* (The Peasant), *L'ultimo guappo* (The Last Gangster), *Napoli, Palermo, New York – Il triangolo della Camorra.* Merola figures in these narratives as an honourable citizen in the pressure-cooker slums of Naples, squeezed between the Camorra and the secret agendas of corrupt politicians and bent cops.

Something tragic in these movies renders them strangely poignant, even if the histories of the meaner streets of southern Italy and the black chronicles witnessed on their streets are much worse. And at the end of each movie, like Bollywood, there's a banquet scene where Merola conducts a singalong and everybody eats endless courses of rich food.

I approach Sergio and Felicita at the Zo to further develop the idea of the *Matrix.* The Zo is a new cultural centre under construction in an old sulphur warehouse on the Catania docks, and they seem intrigued by the idea of including the *Matrix* in the celebration of the centre's opening. A team comes together around the project – musicians, writers, video makers, sound engineers. The following months become a full immersion in *Sicilianitá*: cutting and recompositing the voice of Merola onto sampled musical backgrounds, manipulating archival recordings, editing old super-8 home movies, recycling photos from long-ago family photo albums, listening to the blues-inflected work chants of the sulphur miners, and cutting fragments from period films – such as *La Mattanza*, a documentary of the annual tuna fish slaughter – searching out essential signals from the dissipating cultural core.

It becomes clear that ancient and pagan flavours run through Sicilian folklore, from the *sagre* – the fetishist festivals of foods – to the exorcisms reported in local newspapers. Late every winter, Catania hosts the *Festa di sant'Agata*, the patron saint of the city, her icon hauled on floats along city streets caked with the wax from huge votive candles, followed by chanting priests and flagellants. Saint Agatha was brutally tortured by Moorish invaders in a vain attempt to break her faith. The image of her breasts hacked from her chest reflects not only the ever-present profile of Mount Etna looming above the city, but also the popular cream-filled pastry known as the *panzarotta*; the intrigue between rich food, sex, death and Catholicism is at the root of all things Sicilian.

Opening night at the Zo Centro Culture Contemporanee: some local politicos and their wives are here, arts administrators, local collectors and patrons, wheelers and dealers of all stripes, celebrities, media identities. We're launching *The Merola Matrix* as a live multimedia performance. With only a few hours to go, Luca, my chief collaborator, is still exporting the basic backing tracks of the show from an overheated computer. Plumbers and electricians work around us in the studio space, fiddling with pipes and wires, readying the Zo Centro for its premiere; dust is everywhere and the tension is rising.

Minchia, exclaims Luca. The machine keeps freezing!

It's got to work, I reply. Keep trying!

It's the electric current, he replies. We need something to stabilise the current.

How?

I don't know – get Superman! Or call a priest!

Sergio, the Zo creative director, draws me outside to meet an arts administrator from city hall. The concept has grown, Sergio explains to the *assessore*, since the seed was planted in Palermo several years ago. We've expanded this *Matrix* beyond Mario Merola into a modernist revision of Sicilian culture. The results are astonishing!

The *assessore culturale* looks at us like we're both crazy and unfurls an umbrella to shield off the light rain of volcanic ash falling in a shower from the sky; as the ash hits the ground it hisses like rain, like something alive from the forgotten geological past.

Bene, he says, *molto interessante …*

A volunteer passes by with some canapés and the *assessore*, distracted by the food and by passing celebrities, fades into the crowd. Frazzled, I search out my girlfriend, Marta, and find her talking outside with a friend. It's a cool, clear night. Behind us, the waters of the bay lap against the breakwater. I can hear Luca and Emilano sound-checking the *Matrix* in the hall, Merola's voice echoing through the open space. Once again, I'm pervaded by a sense of déjà vu. I seem to remember dreaming this moment long ago – these people, this light, the awareness of a mutual destiny.

I'm freaking out, I tell Marta. So many problems. This was all a mistake.

Calm down, she says. It's a beautiful show. I think people will love it.

What if they lynch me?

Why would they? It's good, and more importantly, it's even funny. You can't predict how people will receive it, so why worry?

Maybe I went too far with this thing, I reply. I've been known to before …

The concert room at the Zo is full. I'm overwhelmed by the emotional experience of the music and the images, and also by the technical aspect of the production: different guests sing or play instruments, depending on the piece, while Luca and Emiliano and I work the sound with instruments, samplers and a mixing desk onstage. Around us, Orazio projects colour-saturated, slow-motion loops on multiple suspended screens. It's a complex production, and at the same time a private trip through the eerie dream world Sicily has become in my mind. The music is hallucinogenic, but it's the images that haunt me most – a predatory lawyer behind his desk, fishermen sailing at dawn, Merola pulling a gun, Catholic street processions, a super-8 movie of a girl dancing at a party, red fingernails on a telephone, a Camorra bandit in eternal somersault. *The Merola Matrix* is both a time warp and a seance. The question 'why' is meaningless – there is no reason, there never was one.

A few weeks later in Naples, the show is tense and emotional; we are messing with the sacrosanct. The audience is strangely quiet within the high-ceilinged stone chambers of the Palazzo delle Arti. Suspicious of what we are attempting to do, they seem both stirred and perplexed by the avalanche of images and sounds from the city's collective memory. It's the older generation who really take the irony and subtext to heart because they know our sources so well, citizens of a city under siege by the Mob since they can remember.

The live shows and the release of a *Merola Matrix* album attract attention. Gianni Valentino, a journalist with the Neapolitan edition of national newspaper *La Repubblica,* calls for an interview and promises to let me know if Mario Merola chooses to invite us to his seventieth birthday party – a luxurious public event to be held on a summer's evening at the *porto di Napoli*, attended by luminaries such as Sophia Loren and Massimo Ranieri.

Gianni is just back from an interview with Merola where he played him our recently released album of cut-ups of his music, and insists the invitation is a strong possibility after talking with Mario's son, Francesco. Gianni explains that it was through Francesco Merola that he managed to reach Merola padre.

In the elaborately mannered style of Neapolitan society, our record company arranges the delivery of a large basket of Sardinian cheeses and tart white wines and floral delectations, as a *regalo* for Signor Merola on our behalf, preparing the ground for the delicate discussion to follow.

The invitation and the phone call never came.

I'm sitting in the garden of Marta's family home high on the slopes of Mount Etna reading Gianni's interview with Mario Merola in the national newspaper *La Repubblica*:[1]

---

1. G. Valentino, '"Guapparia" Electronica And "The Merola Matrix"', La Repubblica, Naples edition, 10 June 2004, translated by the author and E. Cinquerrui.

Mario Merola sits at the head of the table, and without interruption manifests expressions of curiosity, irritation, happiness. 'Damn, how did he get this idea into his head? A record of electric experiments stemming from my interpretations of "Zappatore" and "Guapparia"? Let me listen to it.' Merola is astonished when he gets his hands on the CD of *The Merola Matrix*.

The face of the legendary Neapolitan singer is incredulous. 'But he's expanded me, stretched me! He's twisted my songs. I'll tell you the truth, Mario Merola is like a pig, from me you don't throw anything away. When you contacted me I thought this was about somebody imitating me and remaking my hits in a personal way. Instead now I realise this work is something completely unexpected. I don't know, I'm impressed. What do you think, is it really appropriate?'

Reversing the roles, I find myself now being interviewed and in transcribing this interview I'm forced to consider – for personal reasons or for recklessness? – what this operation really serves; it's got roots in the deepest and most sacred anthropology and in the real research of the social effects of these songs …

As we listen here in the Merola household, the house itself is populated (with the extended Merola family) and their expressions are incredibly varied, enthusiastic faces mixed with worried faces, and a couple of children who seem to feel their granddad has been rendered somehow unknown, mythological …

I put down the newspaper as the drone of a distant helicopter grows louder. Soon it's hovering overhead, pinpointing our house.

What the hell, says Marta, *che c'è?*

We're suddenly aware of heavy vehicles thrumming at the

gates, blocking traffic on the steep and narrow road that leads to the house. Giacomo, the family's misanthropic Russian bear hound, springs into action, barking furiously and running along the high walls surrounding the family property. Marta darts off barefoot calling her mother, Jenny, as the gates swing open and a posse of motorbikes and paramilitary vehicles enter the compound and park without any great sense of urgency. A few men are armed and masked, the rest in plain clothes, fourteen or fifteen of them in the family driveway.

Instantly, I'm concerned. The situation is clearly unusual and cops always make me feel paranoid and nervous for no reason. I can't help thinking that their presence may be connected to my treatments of Merola's music. I know he's politically connected, so who knows how far he'd go to shut down the *Matrix*?

The barking stops – dog-squad specialists have cornered and muzzled Giacomo. Two plain-clothes cop pick over my passport suspiciously while they interview us in our apartment. You're an artist, they ask me incredulously, a musician? What are you doing here in Sicily?

Research, I explain. After all, Italy is a world centre for art and music.

They like the sound of that response but won't be drawn on the reason for their raid. Marta gets on the intercom to her sister, and it's soon clear that everyone here is being interrogated but no one knows why.

The cops lose interest in us when a gleaming Alfa Romeo pulls into the driveway and a tall, debonair, middle-aged man in an immaculately tailored suit gets out. Gesturing with gloved fingers, he leads his team into the house of Marta's father, Franco. The rest of us follow them inside.

The top cop tilts his head and pulls a large, white, monogrammed handkerchief from his suit pocket. He wipes his face with it and stares intently at the sweat glistening on the linen, then introduces himself in a strong Roman accent as a detective from the Comando Carabinieri per la Tutela del Patrimonio Culturale – in short, the Italian art police – and requests entry to the underground storage space where Franco keeps his art collection. This storage space was only ever spoken about in hushed whispers as works by Sicilian painters came and went, disappearing into the archive that Franco had been building for his family over the last forty years. It was to be his legacy.

You are welcome, he says, to see what I have. There is nothing to hide down there. Everything belongs to my family and me, and if it doesn't, it's not ours … Franco laughs nervously – a little joke, *sì*?

The detective smiles grimly and spreads out the architectural plans to the house. This is your art storage space here, he says. But what is behind these walls? That is what interests us.

They are just the old farmhouse walls, cut from the volcanic rock, says Franco.

Well, we are waiting, says the detective, for a drill to arrive, the kind they use to drill tunnels for the autostrada ... The trailer bringing it here is having some difficulty fitting on your narrow mountain street, but we expect it before too long.

A drill? Franco says, his eyes widening. What do you need a drill for?

The detective ignores the question and turns instead to his

team, returned from scanning the storage space. The floor plans don't match up, they say – this is the wrong place!

What? the top cop exclaims incredulously, dabbing at his face with the handkerchief. The drawings are incorrect? This is all absurd! I cannot trust anyone. I cannot trust anyone to do what I ask. *Signore*, I am sorry but we are in the wrong place! This is not the house we want. His voice trails off – there is nothing here that we want …

The sun outside sinks fiery crimson in the afternoon sky. The clouds darken and the wind sharpens and whips around the ankles of the team as they realise their mistake.

Hold it! Hold everything, the top cop booms, flicking his mobile open. Hold the special transport, he shouts into it, I repeat, hold the transport. Intervention no longer required. We stop. That's right, stop. *Si! Fermare tutto! Hai capito? Tutto!*

The disappointed team swiftly, silently evaporate; they didn't want to stop, this was the house they had been assigned and they wanted to cause some trouble. But the top art cop lingers on, drinking whisky with Franco in the magical Sicilian twilight.

I can see you're a good man, the detective says quietly. Franco? I may call you Franco, yes? It's a shock, I understand – but this is good Scotch, this is very good Scotch – so I will tell you a story, Franco, a story which may or may not be true …

The detective coughs and clears his throat – Well, a *pentito,* a Mafia informer, he provided us with certain information for a price … There is a piece of art, Franco, a priceless piece of art that I have been searching for since many, many years. Maybe you know something more than I do, I ask for your help on this, I ask for this today. Do you remember the Palermo of 1969? The

San Lorenzo robbery? A man of your generation and knowledge would remember this … yes?

I watch with surprise as Franco double-takes, his eyes wide with disbelief. *Santo Christo*, he cries, not Caravaggio, the Nativity?

Signore, we have an informant who traces *La Natività* back to your house. It might even be here, Franco. The masterpiece was torn from its frame, you remember this? You remember it was torn from the frame and maybe, just maybe hidden in the foundations of this building?

It feels like I've been drawn into the continuum of Italy's incredible history where both Caravaggio and the Mafia are zero degrees of separation away; history is being rewritten now, and we are all part of it. I look around at Franco's *salotto*, the paintings and discreet sculptures lining the heavy stone walls, and feel the weight of the past bearing down in a very real way. Marta and the family look on with ashen faces, wondering if Caravaggio's Nativity really is hidden among the collection of artworks in the vault underneath the house.

You know, somebody knew the layout of your home very well, says the top cop quietly. Someone you can't trust.

Shady acquaintances of the previous owners, replies Franco. Or tradesmen, you can't trust them either.

Maybe, says the detective, maybe. But people do very strange things indeed when tempted by artworks beyond value. And *signor*, as you well know, here in Italy we have so very much that is priceless …

I watch him closely as he wearily gets to his feet, his white handkerchief a curled-up ball of sweat, and steps out onto the terrace. In the distance, the lights of Catania twinkle in a giant electric tiara around the volcano. He lights a cigarette and exhales a cloud of smoke. The shrill sound of his mobile phone interrupts this moment of meditation. Three assistants appear out of nowhere, guiding him swiftly back to the chauffeur-driven Alfa. They gently push him onto the leather back seat, the doors closing smoothly in perfect Alfa silence as the unseen driver guns the engine into the darkness of night.

Return to the Source | Mali, 2008

We're in the backroom of the Djembe bar in Bamako, Mali, over on the northern edge of town where the streetlights start to thin out and the shadows gather. A hip young audience hangs out here, tuned in to the hard-edged urban sounds of extended jam sessions using rock instrumentation. Complex Malian syncopations and relentless drum and bass dance beats are laced with African electric guitar, soulful, electrified. The vocalists come and go, singing the praises of bigshots and beauties in the room, angling for a *cadeau* or reward in return.

These songs of praise are delivered with murderous attitude through a PA system cranked so deep into a distortion zone that it's on the voodoo borderline, a sonic tonic for the soul, all bite and grit and heart. Tomorrow we're flying out of Mali, but for now the night is running hot. The club promoter figures we're passing through from the Festival au Désert, and asks me in the French lingua franca if we're a band …

Well, as a matter of fact …

The African musicians, whose brilliance has annihilated the last several hours, hand us their instruments with curious smiles – Chris Brokaw on the drum kit with its raw hardware and cymbals; Chris Eckman on the subsonic bass; me, a beaten-up Chinese electric guitar. The MC, with a quizzical smile, holds the single battered microphone so I can sing into it – there are no microphone stands in this place.

We segue into a slow African blues and Brokaw switches to double-time, keeping the vibe strong and punchy. Then the MC takes the mic, singing in Bambara, the beginning of each syllable delivered like an icepick to the heart. Tall, thin men in sharp suits and women with beehives are chilling out on couches in the smoky air. Our band is Dirtmusic, and this is where we belong.

When Dirtmusic first got together on tour in central Europe, Eckman had recently returned from visiting the Festival au Désert, and he raised the inspired idea of going to Mali. Later, we made it happen, meeting up in the transit lounge at Charles de Gaulle airport with our guitars, rucksacks and yellow fever certificates.

A mixed bag of African businessmen and European tourists and adventurers board the packed Air France flight to Bamako. I sit with a posse of middle-aged Spaniards headed off on an African safari, their stained denims, brandy breath and drooping moustaches vibing post-colonial decadence. A Raj-era Englishman has swapped seats with me so he can sit with his wife. She glances at my copy of Cormac McCarthy's *The Road* and turns to her partner.

Well, look, she says, he's reading *On The Road* – you read that once too, didn't you, dear? Years ago?

The vast gulf between Jack Kerouac's beat generation and the apocalyptic doom of McCarthy illustrates the distance Western culture has travelled in the last half-century; beat generation expectations of the groove-fuelled search for kicks and endless highs has morphed into a race against time with planetary self-destruction and a general reckoning with the collective heart of darkness – and maybe that's why I'm ten thousand metres over the

Mauritanian Sahara heading south en route to the city of mystery par excellence, Timbuktu.

Airport security appears loose at first glance until I notice some travellers being steered into customs offices in the arrivals lounge by plain-clothes observers. Masses of luggage are thrown higgledy-piggledy onto a rubber belt and X-rayed by a security guard whose intermittent gaze is unlikely to unscramble the images seething across his screen. Two elderly porters pull my luggage and guitar away in the general melee of the arrivals hall, and I stay close lest the bags disappear into the moving scenery.

This is the only incoming flight tonight at Bamako airport, and beyond the perimeter a gentle chaos is milling around under huge palm trees. Two teenagers – Hey boss, give me a job! – stake their claim on us as we exit into the roiling humidity of the parking lot, four-wheel drives and taxis milling around in a chaos of bodies, vehicles and bags. Our escort of confusion now bargains for compensation and with the only note I have to hand, 10 euro, the deal is settled in their favour.

We climb into a Land Cruiser and drive through the Bamako sprawl. Few Western-style big-city lights here. The tallest building is a Sofitel installed in a Stalinist cement high-rise, harking back to Africa's ties with the Eastern Bloc before the fall of the Berlin Wall.

The *pension* is on a flat, red dirt road. Huge trees tower overhead, waxy-leaved, succulent palms and stringy eucalypts. You sense the equator is near. The clustered minarets of a nearby mosque watch over a vacant lot the size of a stadium; shanties proliferate across the packed-dirt terrain between hairdressing kiosks; wrecked automobiles are stacked in sculptures of rusted iron. A galaxy of smells: spiced meat cooking on roadside grills, mixed-fuel exhausts, open drains and the pervasive smell of burning African grass that is everywhere in the city and seems part perfume, part anti-mosquito and part narcotic.

On the nearby strip of bars and clubs, sharply dressed girls and guys throw back cocktails before bundling into taxis for clubs and parties unknown. I haven't yet got any idea of what this vast alien city is about, although it becomes clearer as the night goes on that if Bamako ever sleeps, it's only for a brief catnap between four and five in the morning.

Families sit outside cement-box homes watching television, a Peugeot crawls by raising clouds of dust, a stray dog takes a dump in a puddle while the mosquitos zero in on my body heat. The dark is deep here after sundown; it's too easy to get lost. At the *pension* I crawl under the mosquito net and listen to the distant thud of street djembes, the saccharine soul of Lionel Richie coming from the karaoke club across the way, and the orgiastic guitar solos of Santana from the bar below, all slamming together in my skull like a flashback to a psychedelic party scene from the 1970s.

Music is omnipresent, pouring out of clubs, bars and kiosks, from boom boxes and private cars and taxis – it's the background against which both mundane and extraordinary events occur, and it's the reason we're here.

Dawn breaks over the oscillations of the Niger River, flashing off the surface in dazzling shards of raw light. Cruising overhead in a Mali Air DC-10, the terrain recalls the saltpan country of Australia's dead heart. This massive river cuts a winding circuit of oxbows and alluvial islands around the southern edge of the

Sahara desert. Besides defining various zones of political and tribal influence, it literally brings the water of life to the many peoples scattered throughout the Saharan interior. It also signifies the last frontier before the high-alert terrorist zone into which Western governments strongly recommend their citizens refrain from travelling.

The Festival au Désert is located out here in the dunes and scrub beyond Timbuktu where skirmishes were fought between nomadic Tuareg desert tribes and the federal government throughout the 1990s. Legend has it that young Tuareg guerillas returning from refugee camps in Libya and Algeria after the ceasefire traded their AK-47s for electric guitars, feeding into a desert rock music best symbolised by the Tuareg band Tinariwen,

After the ceasefire, the Festival au Désert was created as a meeting point for Tuareg people dispersed by war and the confiscation of nomad lands and moved into refugee camps along the Malian border with Mauritania and Algeria. The festival symbolises peace, unity and regeneration after crisis – a meeting of the tribes.

The desert beyond the oasis of this festival is still volatile, however, and the future uncertain. East, across the border with Niger, French and multinational corporations are mining uranium. The nexus of military and industrial activity here encounters land ownership claims by the local indigenous people; sparks fly in the media blackout zone.

Even further east lies the Sudan and the ongoing civil war in Darfur. The ground is ripe for extremists; in neighbouring Mauritania, the Lisbon–Dakar stock car rally has just this week been cancelled because four French tourists were kidnapped and executed by bandits. Not to mention the shooting a few days later of three soldiers investigating the execution. Two French journalists are currently remanded for trial in Niger for undermining state security, after reporting on abuses of the environment and the population in mining zones. There's a lot we know nothing about regarding 'special interests' on this part of the planet.

On the ground at Timbuktu, we negotiate the chaos of the arrivals hall – local guides search to identify their tour parties; taxi drivers, their unmarked four-wheel drives parked outside with engines still running, hustle for the clients without prearranged contacts. I'd heard wild rumours of Europeans being bailed up by their drivers in the wild dune country beyond Timbuktu. Instead, we're fortunate enough to meet charismatic festival director Many Ansar, whose courtesy and influence soon have us in the back of a four-wheel drive, with a member of the Malian musical collective Tartit riding shotgun in coloured robes and designer sunglasses.

In the arid, medieval desert city of Timbuktu, bizarre columns and facades are silhouetted against the whitening sky. Women and children sell dried banana skins and fish scales on the shoulder of a packed-dirt road. A skinned pig is draining from a meat hook near an evangelist church mission, a reminder of a not-so-distant past in which missionaries, slavers and mining companies 'explored' Africa, and working in concert sent the loot back home to bankroll European wars. At what price fortune beyond your wildest dreams? Long ago, Timbuktu was reputed to be another El Dorado, a city of gold. At the single traffic light we encounter traversing the city today, an ancient woman of indeterminate age extends one withered hand for alms, her face cast in shadow by a veil.

The Land Cruiser plunges on past graffitied mudbrick walls and prehistoric mining derricks, onto a kind of gravel highway, red dirt spraying out from under the wheels. The vegetation thins out to virtually nothing as our driver turns off at a hand-drawn sign reading 'Essakane' plunged deep into the sand. Tyre tracks lead away into the rough terrain and several other Land Cruisers are nearby – it appears we're about to form a convoy for some cross-country scrambling. Brokaw is talking to a mature-age American couple and the woman says – Oh, you guys are a band? Maybe you've heard of my son's band – they're called the Dandy Warhols?

This isn't the kind of conversation I was expecting out to have here, but then the Festival au Désert brings together people from all around the world with a taste for music and a will to adventure – as I'm about to realise over the next hour's knuckle-whitening, body-slamming, stomach-churning freestyle drive through the dust-drenched morning light towards Essakane.

The temperature's high by the time we enter the real Saharan dune country. Broadsiding on this loose white sand, we nearly sideswipe several trees as our driver whips the steering to stop the Toyota from rolling. The trail has deteriorated to nothing, we're idling in deep nowhere, the driver lost in thought. But our guide from Tartit knows the terrain and she steers us through the fields of sand right up to the stone gates that mark the entrance to the site.

The Festival au Désert spreads out across the dunes in a labyrinth of white tents, distant stage scaffolding silhouetted against a cobalt Saharan sky. Continuing on foot we meet the friendly French-speaking organisational crew, and after signing in and collecting our security passes we relocate our vehicle and driver, bogged in loose sand a half-kilometre away. The temperature has risen to around 30 degrees by now, and carrying our personal load of 40 kilos each over the waves of soft, fine sand, the dry heat begins to cook our brains.

We find ourselves billeted opposite the tent of a young Tuareg band called Tamikrest. An American *Vogue* photo shoot is using the extended Tamikrest tribe as a picturesque backdrop (and musical soundtrack) for a lithe model clad in poverty chic. The ten or twelve guys and girls of the Tamikrest group seem indifferent to what's going on – they have their own kind of nomad desert cool.

I'm talking with the Tamikrest percussionist Aghaly about the idea of him guesting with us tomorrow night on the festival stage when Brokaw grabs the dobro and wanders over to play cross-legged in the sand – kicking off a jam session that will continue for the next three days through the common language of sound, rhythm and rock and roll. All around there's a sense of movement and expansion as several thousand people converge on the camp site and the sun drops behind a sine-wave horizon – something's going to happen here, now.

Vieux Farka Touré is one of tonight's big-name acts; Baba, the band's djembe player, guides me through the mysteries of the festival after dark.

People from all the world, he says, they come here because there is nothing like this festival anywhere else. Music was born here in Mali, a long, long time ago, and that's why they come – because this is the source of the music people listen to today.

We drift past the inner core of kiosks and administrative

and artists' tents and across the sands where people talk around campfires in African and Arabic tongues, French and English of all kinds, as well as Spanish, Italian, German and more.

Tuaregs ride in out of the desert on their tall, rangy camels in groups of two or three, draped in robes and turbans, only their eyes showing, long curved swords hanging by their sides. Camels own the desert; saddled in coloured blankets with intricate trimmings, tattoos of ownership carved into the skin of their huge, powerful thighs, they move silently on the sand. When they loom up out of the darkness, the desert night is clear enough that you can see the long black lashes fringing their pale, shiny camel eyes.

All across the wilderness of Essakane there are camps and fires – women swathed in black robes, roaming groups of kids, goats, chickens, tethered camels, a profusion of cooking smells. Above the scattered trees, the stars begin to appear and I'm struck by how the constellations are displayed in a different orientation in this equatorial African sky. Orion is high over the dunes, and on its heels comes Sirius, the Dog Star – the brightest in the sky, described thousands of years ago by the Malian Dogon people as a twin-sun solar system, a fact only recently confirmed by Western science's high-powered astronomical observatories.

Accurate Dogon knowledge of the galaxy actually extends much further than this. In tribal performance they drum on spherical calabashes with metallic fingers, gyrate in orbital dances to the rhythm of abstract mathematics. Humanity originated in east Africa, not so far from here. We're near the Source, and these are the stars they saw back in the beginning of human time – year zero ...

Baba and I are sitting near a fire having a smoke when a

Tuareg guy in his robes and sword sits down and strikes up a conversation. He says he's from a faraway town, sweeping his hand vaguely across the dunes.

How do you navigate in the desert? I ask.

Les étoiles, he replies gesturing at the stars. Then he says in English – The Seven Sisters, pointing at the Pleiades.

I try to explain how in Australia the constellations are inverted and he shakes his head and laughs and offers me a joint.

Several thousand people have gathered at the mainstage, pulling on coats, scarves and headwear as the temperature rapidly drops. A thin wedge of waxing crescent moon hangs low over the dunes, the full lunar orb silhouetted by an astral halo. The sound in front of the speaker stacks is a little confused, but as I wander this sand-bowl ampitheatre it morphs and mutates and eventually I find a sonic sweet spot high on the rear sand dune about 500 metres from the stage. Vendors stroll through the crowd selling ubiquitous Dunhill Reds, bottles of warm beer and soft drinks, or carrying trays of thick, sweet Tuareg tea. By the time the Africans take the stage the mood is electric.

Tamikrest, transformed under lights in their traditional robes and turbans, lay down a set of amplified desert chants and drones that resonates off the cooling sands – to look and listen, you wouldn't know they average around twenty years old.

The regal Noura Mint Seymali fronts a traditional Mauritanian band in her robes and tiara; these long hypnotic tracks are shifting tapestries for her extraordinary voice to prowl along, as if Bessie Smith fronted a North African funk orchestra.

Vieux Farka Touré *et les amis d'Ali* are road-honed sharp and play with such precision it makes you reconsider what it means to be musically 'tight'. The fact that Vieux is the son of Ali Farka Touré and heir to the tradition of Mali desert blues assures him a spectacular reception from the crowd here at a festival closely identified with his legendary father.

After the early start and long journey from Bamako, the desert's crushing heat and the night's clean chill, we regroup in the Dirtmusic tent and drift away listening to the pounding of distant djembes and the oceanic hiss of camp-fire voices speaking in tongues.

With our sound check set for noon, Aghaly wants to get an early start, ready with his djembe before I've even had coffee. Beyond the procession of cruising four-wheel drives and mounted camels criss-crossing the sand is a nomad kiosk with plastic chairs under an awning where crew gather to eat and drink. Opposite me, a stringer from the *New York Times* is texting his story on a palm computer; behind me, Europeans talk currency exchange rates, schedules, battery rechargers. Kids drift by selling jewellery and cast-iron Dogon gods, making casual offers of Ghana grass and henna tattoos and postcards.

Back in the Tamikrest tent we're seven or eight musicians spread across mattresses or plain white sand. Aghaly is an incredible percussionist and we try seven or eight Dirtmusic songs before heading over to the main stage where a French production manager is sweating into his cell phone, saying the generator's run out of diesel. Keeping cool in a cave-like stone room, we run through more songs, fine-tuning beats. It soon transpires that the sound check is cancelled – too many technical problems and too many musicians.

As I'm wandering back through the camp, a turbaned musician with an ngoni (a kind of African guitar) on his knee beckons me to come inside his tent. Now, this is the same tent out of which earlier this morning emanated some of the wickedest oil-smoke African blues I've yet heard – an electric scimitar of sound distorted to the max, fierce stuff – the tent of Super Khoumeissa, masters of Takamba.

With a gleam in his eye my host indicates a mattress next to him in the centre of the tent. Around us four or five older men doze in the noonday funk. Kicking off my boots, I sit cross-legged and open-tune my guitar. I follow his ngoni patterns with my ears and eyes and soon we're riffing clean circular loops, traditional desert tunes. The master has a very intense stare; it's hard to hold. He smiles, I talk my broken French, he replies in an impenetrable accent, somehow we communicate, mostly we just play.

Then silence falls and a distinguished-looking man sits up and asks me some questions about who I am and I do my best to answer plainly. I ask him if he's playing tonight and he says – No, I'm the president of the commission for the surrender of firearms in Mali and in the Sahara wherever the Tuareg lands extend. The profusion of weapons is very difficult to control. It's equally difficult to win the agreement of different peoples, that's why we're here – to conduct a seminar seeking reconciliation.

How big is this problem? I ask him, how many guns are there out here?

He stretches out his arms out wide 180 degrees and shrugs as if to say the problem is almost infinite.

Back at Tamikrest's tent, an older Songhai guy drifts over and picks up Eckman's acoustic guitar and plays forty-five seconds of real Delta blues, Lightnin' Hopkins style. It's like a cue to start jamming and pretty quickly our group grows to maybe twelve or so musicians.

I hit record on the Aiwa cassette portable and start taping.

During the course of this scalding afternoon we play freestyle Saharan rhythm and blues in various configurations, usually a couple of acoustic guitars, some unplugged electrics, two djembes, handclapping and of course everybody's vocalising, including the two Tamikrest women whose ululatory cries make the hair rise on the nape of your neck.

We're trading songs, stories, riffs, rhythms and tuning. There's real discovery going on here and a shifting crowd surrounds the tent entrance, the excitement palpable. By late afternoon our instruments and feet are dusted in sand and desert burrs, hands and throats raw, cassette tapes all used up and batteries flat.

After dark, with a gentle wind blowing in, we set up on the mainstage with fifteen minutes to line check. The audience is already more than a thousand strong, most of them covered in robes and turbans sitting on the bone white dunes, silhouettes of camels on the ridges. The onstage sound is tricky with these rickety old transistor amps, and the microphone is giving shocks to my lips. There's nothing to be done about that given the miracle of electricity being delivered here at all under the circumstances, and the French stage mixer is doing his best to bring it all together. He spreads his hands and shrugs.

This is a rough-and-ready, skin-of-your-teeth technical situation – and would you expect anything less? The festival MC hands us the spotlight – we take a breath, find a groove and go for it, remembering the long road travelled just to get here; in performance you enter into the moment, and if you can, you surrender to it completely. Dirtmusic is about playing music and what that means to people on an energised, symbolic level beyond just the tunes and the words.

It's Saturday midday and we're walking around Essakane. Incredibly loud reggae music is coming out of a clear blue sky as if from giant speakers in the heavens – in reality, it's the sound check of Tiken Jah Fakoly, and these fat Ivory Coast bass riffs are bouncing around the dunes like giant rubber balls. I realise then how you can hear the festival music from kilometres away, even from Essakane village – brick houses and scattered trees, goatherds, a faux-Mexican arched stable inhabited by a tribe of donkeys, scattered dry camel turds, some white-collared blackbirds gliding over the fields, people dotted across the plateau collecting wood.

A family – the nine-year-old home from school kicking a plastic bottle around in the dust, the mother and sisters coming back for lunch, the father walking home with a rifle resting on his shoulder. I ask the boy, Yaya, what his dad is hunting for and he says, *les lapins*, rabbits … He is allowed to visit the festival but he has to be home by 1 a.m. curfew – so how does he tell the time? Yaya just glances briefly at the sky and smiles; this desert is his home, and the sun and stars strike the hours.

In the same way, it's impossible to be alone here. Sooner or later, somebody will appear. An Italian couple who motored all the way to the festival through Morocco and the deep Saharan ergs of Mauritania mentioned that getting lost in the sandscapes was a daily recurrence, as was the remarkable appearance of desert dwellers to set them back on course. Testing this, I walk out beyond the festival camp, beyond the camels and the tents and the groups of men observing Mecca until there is nobody in sight to meditate under a shade tree. After ten minutes or so, two figures appear on the horizon coming from different directions on tangents that converge on me, both shouting out to me as they pass, '*Ça va?*'

I'm washing from a canteen hanging off a tent support; the air is filled with faraway djembes, the bray of a moody camel, distant handclapping. A group of African musicians move across the camp site, accompanied by an incredibly distorted electric ngoni loop coming from an invisible source, as though a beatbox is concealed beneath their robes.

A traditional Tuareg ceremony set up in the dunes beyond the mainstage is drawing spectators around a huge rectangular red carpet. On one side are seated ngoni players, fifteen or more. In front of them, the women in their shiny maroon-black shawls clap and chant. The music is … well, trance geometry. Tuaregs ride decorated camels through the crowd and onto the carpet. The riders press their heels into the camels' necks forcing them to kneel, then jump down from their ornate saddles and begin to dance, telling stories by movement. Every now and then the generator cuts out but the rhythm continues.

Tonight we're joining Tamikrest on stage for their second performance at the festival. We're primed after more tent sessions but there aren't enough amps for the five guitarists onstage – besides the violin, djembe, electric bass, there are two sword-toting MCs and the Tuareg backing singers. The monitor sound is so deeply weird we all just look at each other and smile – what else can you do? All thirteen of us lock onto the beat, unable to discern where these unearthly harmonies are coming from. Again, the feedback from the audience is charged positive. But the polyphonic tsunami we heard onstage? Later, Brokaw explains as we sit down to eat – Well, Ornette Coleman gave us twelve tones, to set us free …

Behind him, moving across the carpeted sand of the VIP tent, is a kid in rough safari gear with an AK-47 strapped to his back. Some other guys appear out of the shadows and they usher him away from the lights, talking quietly; it's easy to forget the camp is armed while music continues all through the night.

Bassekou Kouyate is both scathing and majestic, playing some of the most unbelievable electric guitar I ever heard, except that Bassekou is playing an electric ngoni, with two tenor or bass ngoni players as backup, a singer with an incredible bittersweet voice like Billie Holiday meets Betty Boop, milling percussionists, beautiful turmoil.

Near the end of Saturday night the crowd is just beginning to show signs of thinning. Dogons in tall, eerie masks climb onto the stage roof, watching the action from the sky.

The silver-tongued festival MC takes the microphone and says – So, the world, when they think of us, thinks of Timbuktu as a mythical city from centuries ago, from back in time, an old legend. But we are here to say that Timbuktu is right here right now, and that people here deserve the same level of education and opportunity as anywhere. Timbuktu was created in the eleventh century, it's now the twenty-first …

He goes on to thank everybody who made the festival possible in the face of logistical problems with water, food, transport and electricity; all who cooked or organised; the indigenous Tuareg hosts of the festival; the artists; and of course, the audience for actually making it out there – a tribute to peace and cooperation. Then he thanks the security for their discretion at the camps and for the armed perimeter they maintain around the festival site to a circumference of roughly 60 kilometres, a reminder of how vulnerable our location is in the bigger scheme of things.

After all, this is still Africa, the continent that delivered blues, jazz, gospel and rock and roll, the cultural package of soul and style with which we identify today in our so-called 'developed' world. The midwife was slavery and the diamond mines. Africa is still recovering from the aftershocks of colonialism and globalism, but its beating heart is strong. There's a primal power here, vibrant and animated, and you feel it through the street murals and the body language and the music and the very air you breathe – but it can swing either way, and just beyond the peaceable surface of things you feel the shadow side, the poverty, the rivalries, the history. We've only briefly been privileged guests of this remote oasis, and after the circus has gone there'll be just dust and sand and echoes left behind. It's an early rise on Sunday morning, breaking camp. A burgundy dawn breaks over the dunes and we soon score a ride for Timbuktu, following the clouds of thick red dust raised by the rest of the departing convoy.

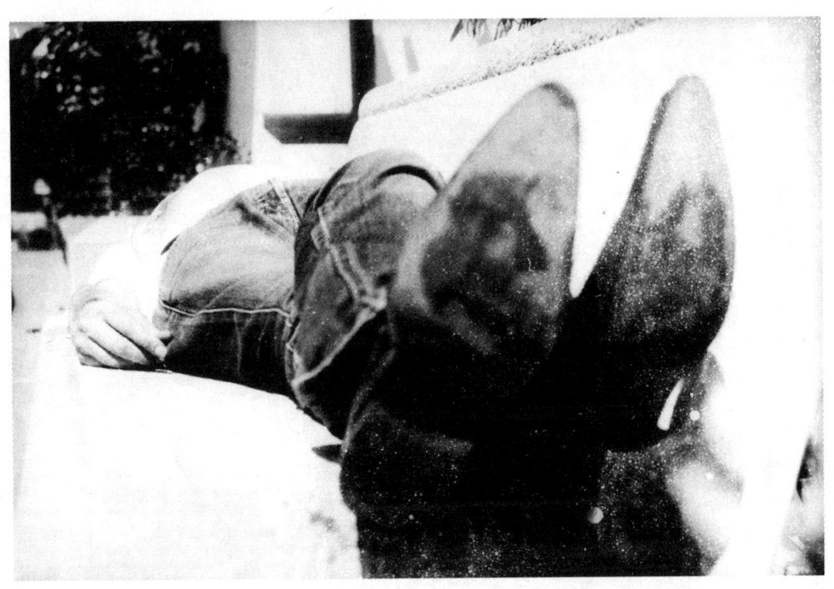

Fatalism | Europe, 2009

A bewildered mass of business travellers, tourists and airline staff stumbles through the air gate in the comedown daze of another sleepless twenty-four-hour intercontinental flight. A border cop scans my tattered passport with dead grey eyes, stamps the page automatically, then waves his hand at the Chinese travel party wearing surgical face masks behind me to come forward.

I clip a German SIM card into the phone. Almost immediately, the screen illuminates and I take the call.

We're all going to die, Mary says, are you listening? We're all going to die! Do you get it?

Phone to my ear, I drag my luggage out of arrivals onto the concourse of Berlin's Tegel Airport, the sky overhead cloudy and impenetrable. EU flags flutter in the lavender autumn light. A creeping sense of unreality infects everything.

What are you talking about?

Immunisations, she says, these new vaccinations, I read about it on the internet, how they're going to try and trick us with these new diseases they keep talking about in the media, SARS and all the rest. Don't say I didn't warn you, and by the way – where's the rent?

I'll get down to Western Union soon as possible, I reply, just need to get out and make some money first.

I could be dead by then, she says.

We could all be dead by then, I reply, so what difference does it make?

Don't play games, she says, just send the money.

I am on a two-month tour of Europe and she is in Australia with the kids. It's the classic bind. There's a core truth about being a traveller and a musician – that you can't do everything. Stuff slips through the cracks – you just run fast as you can, trying to catch it all before it hits the ground and shatters.

Inside the taxi the radio recycles eighties hits refitted with autotuned vocals and four-on-the-floor house beats – the retro and the now colliding in the centrifuge of German modernism. Once-familiar city streets slip by; the futuristic steel and glass corporate high-rises of Potsdamer Platz recently erected on the old dead heart of Berlin superimpose across my memories from years ago.

Time is winding down to the decade's end in a twilight world of black and white and phantom grey. I'm ghosting the city again, struggling to get up to speed with the plan – thirty concerts with three different shows and crews in an eight-week tour crisscrossing Europe from Romania to the UK. A lot of road and a lot of risk.

The taxi drops me and my luggage at the Kottbusser Tor Turkish street market in the shadow of Reinhold's old apartment, where laughs and cable TV would surely be found were he still alive – a stomach haemorrhage he suffered alone in his lounge room last year took him out to sleep with angels. The busy street feels emptier now.

The prospect of it all sends a shiver of terror through me – what happens if Mary is right and I catch some microscopic virus that renders me too sick to travel or perform? Winter in Brandenburg has come early this year, brandishing a swine flu mutation so slick the drug companies are already hyperventilating at the prospect of a pandemic and mass vaccinations. Jet lag is playing tricks – I need to keep on message, follow the job, read the signs.

An anonymous intern at the record label informs me our booking agent has disappeared. On a bender, he says, they're becoming more and more frequent, you know. *Ja*, people are talking, the man drinks too much. Last band of ours he booked, the tour collapsed a week before it started, and the whole time he was hiding in his girlfriend's apartment in a vodka-induced coma. Maybe that's where he is now?

Tour logistics are guesswork at the best of times, a walk in the dark where every kind of situation is possible – from a gig cancelled by some hardball neighbour complaining about noise levels to a multiple-fatality autobahn pile-up. But this year the situation seems even more fragile. Under pressure from direct downloading, the music business is imploding. Everybody is complaining about the money – artists, clubs, promoters, sound techs, studios, labels, journalists. If rock is dead and has been for years, the corpse is now radiating an infectious stink so strong even the dimmest operator can't help but notice.

This tour is meant to be an anniversary celebration of the True Spirit's inception twenty years before, but the release of our latest album has been delayed by eighteen months. Rumour has it that office politics dropped the German record label into a black hole and our album along with it. So here we are with no support and no backup, just the music and the infinite curvature of the road. As they say, living the dream.

Hughes still plays drums like a belligerent alley cat knocking over garbage cans, a style trademarked as his own across the good dozen studio albums we've made together. Deadeye plays bass with cool nonchalance, a Sydney boy who moved to Berlin a decade ago and never looked back. Hellhound, intercontinental drifter and inspired roots rhythm and blues guitarist, signed on for this tour as our fourth element and as solo opening act for every concert, laying down swamp blues on a steel dobro. Dugz has been our sound tech and tour manager for ten years.

The firm, ready for action, contracts in a briefcase.

The Frankfurt autobahn is packed with heavy-duty road trains storming down from Belarus and beyond, hungry for the lucrative markets of the West. We dodge in and out of the traffic to make up for our late start from Berlin waiting for Hughes, who's already on the beer and calling for a piss stop.

Dugz eases into the parking lot of a giant gas station illuminated by giant red neons. Pale bockwurst stand erect in an illuminated glass tube on the servo counter, Ultravox's 'Vienna' moans on the radio, magazine racks are electrified by weird northern porn. An elderly shop assistant glares from behind a warming bay where huge bolts of pork glint in yellow artificial light.

The show is good but the turnout is ordinary; a fan tells me this is the worst place to play in the whole city. Some guys from the record label are there in the audience – Not an auspicious start to the tour, they say, but then what did you expect? There's no promotion anywhere.

I thought that was your job, I reply.

No, they say, we had to… *wie sagt mann?* Downsize the company, *ja.* So now all band promotions are at the band's expense.

The conversation dies away as they focus on their beer.

Dugz interrupts – I can't find the promoter, he says, you want to track him down, get the cash?

Deep in the bowels of the venue, the office door is half-open. The promoter is slumped across his desk staring at a bottle of schnapps, a small, grey, metal pistol next to his face. The telephone is ringing but he ignores it until it stops, then lethargically pushes it from its cradle; a disconnect tone pulses in the silence while he stares at me wearily with bloodshot eyes and beckons me forward.

Are you trying to kill me? He whispers hoarsely. All of you, trying to kill me ...

No, I reply, pulling up a chair. We just want to do the business.

Yes, he says, everybody wants money, but nobody cares where it comes from, poor bastards like me have to give and give. Your agent is a drunk, your label is nearly bankrupt and yet you, he lifts his head from the table with increasing animation and aims a trembling index digit in my direction, and yet here you are, always wanting more, even when there's nothing left!

He pours some schnapps into a shot glass and throws it back.

So now, he says, now let's talk about your business.

I wait while he counts out the fee in very small denominations and shoves it across the desk towards me.

Thanks, I say, and recount the money. Do you want a receipt?

What difference does it make? he replies and lowers his head back down on the desktop, eyeballing the pistol.

The cities merge and blur in a smear of bad weather and heavy traffic. The hour and a half we're on stage is the best part of any given day – the rest is hotels, highways and waiting, always waiting in a dazed continuum of backstages, roadhouses, parking lots and more hotels. Money is tight, management is loose and we're always chasing the clock. The van keeps stalling, amplifiers blow, drumskins break, guitar strings shred and through it all the band play with a coherency and dedication of purpose that render every hour on the stage unforgettable.

I beat off depression's seductive advances with self-medication and alcohol. Vodka is the drug of choice, bleaching my brain cells and the light of day with its acid breath. I know this is part of the deal I signed up to, way back when I didn't know any better – back then I might have imagined all this as somehow romantic.

The last German date is in Berlin at a packed-out Frannz Club on the east side of town. The backstage rapidly fills with old friends of the band, many of whom played walk-on parts in the story of the True Spirit down the years, and the mood is high.

Don't ever stop, says Hughes, uncapping another bottle of Budejovice beer, just keep on going, doing what we're doing. Nights like this remind me of why we started in the first place. I know what you're thinking, but you're wrong. This is all worth it, get it? This is what we always wanted, to still be here doing this twenty years later, get it?

I've always admired his defiance in the face of adversity; we strike bottles together, showering the floor with bitter foam.

Next day, I watch the clock, hearing nothing and feeling everything, knotted up and toxic. I'm running too fast, my nerves raw and frayed from the rough riding and the magnetic black holes of the blues. Some kinds of depression can provoke the irresistible urge for oblivion, even though blue moods such as these always maintain they know what's good for us and only have our best interests at heart. Sometimes, the devil enjoys living like this within us.

My girlfriend's phone in Melbourne is ringing out. It's the morning where she is, but all clocks are relative – they run one way for me and another for her, as Australia is light years away. Disorientated, she picks it up.

Oh sorry, I've had a big night … I've been out drinking and well, what do you want me to say? You could be doing anything over there, I saw you on Facebook with God knows who! I think I'm going out all the time because I, because … Because I miss you, I don't know, I think I'm just …

She stumbles into a protracted, eerie silence then comes back swinging – Oh, but you don't care anyway! So what if I was out with some friends, you remember Brigitte and Paul and Romano? They took me out and we got so hammered …

She laughs that phony, menacing laugh and the satellite picks up it all up clear as if she's in the room next to me. Then the line goes quiet and she suddenly whispers – I can't do this any longer, I can't. I want more.

But darling, I'm doing everything I can. I know how hard this is for you …

No you don't. You're selfish.

The sound of her crying sits me up straight with its electrical sting. The connection crackles and drops out and then kicks back in with another rush of piercing static.

I'm nothing to you, she says. I don't feel like I mean anything to you and …

The line cuts out, credit gone. I hear the soft voice of the rain falling gently in the *hinterhof* courtyard beyond the kitchen windows. I'm in a strange bedroom that was once mine. I used to live in this apartment. My ex-girlfriend lives here now with her new boyfriend; time has passed, wounds have healed and I've learnt that friendship can be more real than feeling lost in another affair.

My ex has left me a note on the kitchen table among the breakfast dishes:

> *Hi. I'll be back by four but you will be gone by then. You have to do something with all that stuff you left behind in storage. I have no room for anything and I need the space. It's time for you to put it somewhere else and so please do something about it today. It'd be really nice if you could do that today. OK?*
>
> *LOVE*

The haunted little storage room behind the kitchen is stuffed with keepsakes and memories – books, photos, journals, 1970s tailored gentleman's suits I inherited from my Dad after he passed away two years ago. My mind turns to him frequently, and even though we didn't agree about politics and almost everything else, I often wonder what would he do in these situations I find myself in. I wouldn't put myself there, lovey! I hear him say, I just wouldn't do it! He could be harsh, but God knows I miss him now …

It was Budapest, a few days before Christmas. I woke up alone in a friend's apartment in the small hours and I could hear somebody breathing, constant and laboured, right there in the room. I had to ask myself – was it me? Were these my own last breaths? I lay there listening, open-eyed, slowly accepting that I wasn't dreaming and recognising that this was my Dad's familiar wheeze, half expecting him to wheel in and sit with me awhile, telling me where I'd gone wrong and not to worry. I could feel his presence all around me. It was strangely comforting.

Two years ago, we'd said goodbye at the aged care hostel on Punt Road, leaves blowing around his wheelchair as with mounting despair he once again gave up attempting to say what he had in mind to say. After the strokes, he'd communicated in non-verbal ways, all stammers and eye contact; sometimes it was like talking to a ouija board and I was never really sure what he was thinking. Cut off from the world through which he'd once moved so freely with dignity and grace, disappointment was a recurring theme, as was the misery of illness and old age. He stammered out that I must keep working – Don't stop, he said, you can't stop! Dad's watery eyes held mine as I told him I loved him and then somehow, as one does, I just walked away knowing I'd never see him again. If infinity exists, as mathematics insists it must, then everything and everyone is always somewhere; and so there was I, somewhere in Budapest, searching through the apartment for an explanation – Are you here, Dad? What's happening? Are you calling me?

Instead, it was my brother who called early in the morning to tell me he was gone. I couldn't get a flight back to Australia for love or money. It being Christmas, everything was booked out. Like death, distance is absolute.

I grab random things from the little storage room to take with me in the tour van – a picture, a shirt, a book on physics. The rest I scoop into giant garbage bags and deposit in the evangelical charity bins near the Kastanienallee. Gradually, I'm erasing any traces of myself from the city. These vanishing fragments of previous lives – I tell myself I don't need them any more, it's all just dead weight. The Prenzlauer Berg streets stare me down like I don't exist.

Walking back to the apartment, I'm overtaken by the van. Get a move on, says Hellhound, exhaling smoke from the driver's window, we're late for the jail.

Poland, All Saints' Day; the cemeteries are ablaze with floral arrangements. Women in vivid headscarves sell wildflowers and apples by the roadside. A narrow, winding country blacktop leads to the maximum security prison Zaklad Karny. The gothic nineteenth-century silhouette of the jail looms red against a battleship-grey sky. A light drizzle falls, the air acerbicly cold.

Outside the gates we meet Grzrg, the jail's volunteer activities manager whose idea it was to invite us to perform. Our Polish tour manager and friend Uncle Gusstaff had passed the proposal on to me and I immediately answered yes, thinking Johnny Cash at San Quentin, but the reality is somewhat different.

Grzrg and Gusstaff talk us through the machine's metallic viscera of ID checks, codes and intercoms. Grim-humoured guards take our passports and mobile phones, compiling an exhaustive list of every single item down to the last patch cable and guitar pick. Silent trustees load our gear through the supply dock and up two flights of concrete stairs to a large basketball court overlooked by tall leadlight windows. Dugz rolls out a mobile laptop recording rig as the band build up the backline of amplifiers and drums on a slippery parquet floor.

From the service stairwell we hear prisoners scraping chairs into position: right side, the top dogs who run internal affairs in the prison, with their shaven heads and buffed bodies, and on the left, rows of milder-looking prisoners. In all, maybe two hundred men watch us from their seats. Nobody moves. The gym is quiet as a church. Outside, shadow boxers wrapped in thermal hoodies punch the air in cages cut from the big wire wheel of the exercise yard. At the far end of the hall guards with automatic weapons watch the proceedings. We are in some kind of purgatory.

When the last chord of the first song dies away, the clapping initially falters then thunders to a sudden stop and in the ensuing total silence the only sound is the smacking lips of a huge guy in the front row blowing sarcastic little kisses. The four of us – aware of the clock running and the hard disc recording and the fact that Uncle Gusstaff has a multi-CD copier loaded in the truck and the album covers already printed – feel the pressure, check our tunings and the set list to know which song is next. Forty minutes into the show the plug is pulled and the audience exit with military precision. Time is tight. We load out into the frozen dark.

Fire blazes in the hearth of an old-world countryside tavern deep in the surrounding forest. Chairs are arranged before a small stage decorated with hunting regalia, stags heads, stuffed bears; shot glasses of Luksusowa appear from nowhere as the audience fills the room before we've even uncased the guitars. Hughes and Deadeye kick back with giant glasses of Tychy beer while Hellhound and me tune up as we go, segueing into a set of old rhythm and blues songs – 'Everybody Ought to Teach a Stranger Right' and 'Preaching Blues', scraps of Bo Diddley, or songs concocted on the spur of the moment based on a fragment of some Howlin' Wolf bootleg on a long-forgotten cassette tape from God knows where.

In the clear hard light of morning I wake up to a lake dazzled by sunshine. On the far shore behind stands of trees, a large golf course is laid out with military banners and flags. Soldiers buzz around in dune buggies. Huge storks flap overhead. There's no hot water and the refrigerator contains only meat, cheese and beer. All at once, I remember where I am – deep Poland. And tonight we're playing Warsaw, a six-hour drive with no highways to smooth the ride.

Last night's jail concert blasts out of the van speakers from a laptop cabled up to the stereo. Over the engine noise we're mixing it on the fly, calling in changes – less bass here, more guitar there, some drum echo, louder vocals, less vocals – watching the forests and industrial zones rolling by, with Uncle Gusstaff at the wheel playing chicken and the fox between the Russian semitrailers rocketing this highway of death connecting Berlin and Moscow. By the time we hit the outskirts of Poland's concrete capital, the mixes are ready and Gusstaff unpacks his CD copying system in the venue backstage, toasting new discs for tonight's audience.

The phone auto-illuminates. It's Mary again, calling to tell me she thinks she may have a serious illness. I can't explain it, she says, I just have this feeling I could die soon. And you, you're on the other side of the world and basically couldn't care less.

Of course I care, I reply. You can be sure I'd drop everything and be there in a day if what you say is true.

How do you know it isn't?

The van is starting to disintegrate. The red truck that hit us at a roundabout outside Olomouc a few days ago caved in the back doors, destroyed the rear lights and twisted the drive shaft. A thousand euro of on-the-spot repairs and we're still moving, but you can feel the damage in the way the whole chassis vibrates.

Stick your hand out and wave, says Dugz, I need to turn left here.

I wind the window down and signal while drivers speed past blowing their horns.

Corporate billboards, ghost factories and dilapidated farmhouses stud the still life of the Moravian countryside. The highway is eerily empty, maybe something already happened we don't know about – a pandemic, a declaration of martial law, a nuclear leak. The abandoned industrial estates of Bratislava fade into a ghostly nothingness as we arrive on the epic steppes of Hungary, an ambiguous desolation of brown sod where wisps of fog blow into a clear, heatless sunlight.

The temperature drops to zero as we descend the deep slump of Budapest, the sky roiling with cloud. We meet Laszlo, our promoter, at a gas station on the edge of town and crawl through heavy traffic to a venue in the cellars of an ancient castle moonlighting as a jazz club – plunging granite steps, vaulted medieval corridors, hewn grottos.

In the fetid underground laced with medieval bacteria and spores, I start sneezing uncontrollably. The fever rouses from its dormancy, a drowsy Dracula virus sprouting wings. I'm hypnotised by the situation, the job, unconscious of any other world except this dungeon – the bandstand, the illuminated blue bar, the boxes of records for sale, the tables of people waiting for the show.

Sweat soaks my jeans. The music is a release from trouble-shooting long-driving days. The concert accelerates to a sudden finish. The room swims in front of my eyes. I feel myself disintegrating. I've got to get out of here. It's a nightmare. I don't understand anything any more, and I don't really care either.

The taxis, says Laszlo, they are not answering. Very shit, but I will try again. Shittiest taxis in whole fucking Europe.

I slump at the bar. A girl asks me what I want to drink.

Laphroaig, I reply. I can't see her very well. I've got a temperature on. The whisky is good. I'm numb. She touches me and it feels like ice, her hand like ice on my icy hand. We burn like ice.

I'm a Sagittarius, she says. I like to ride. Racehorses, only bareback. The whip. I like the whip. I've never heard anything quite like the rasp in this girl's voice. Deadly irresistible. My eyes finally focus on her broad, tanned face. She's strong, fit, exploding with life and irony. My horses, she says, are some of the finest in Hungary. My husband and I own a stable, her face is close to mine but shadowed, hidden by the wave of her long honeyed hair. My husband likes you very much, she says, her eyes sparkling with decadent sarcasm. You want to bring your friends?

The band have dissolved into a psychedelic stew of strangers and strobe lights. Her face floats in and out of focus, her breath drying the sweat off my face. The promoter grabs my arm and I nearly tumble off the bar stool. Suddenly I'm aware of a massive wall of noise in the room, the late-night discotheque, the hundreds of people talking at high volume to hear themselves over the music.

C'mon, says Laszlo, we have shitty taxi now.

Do you want to dance? she says, and gets to her feet. Either I'm hallucinating or she's a superstar, a girl from outer space made flesh, all heels and Gore-Tex figure wrap. The sweat pours through me. The lights, the sound, the fever, and her.

I shiver in the back seat as the taxi threads through imperial masonry quiet as the tomb. Checking in to the hotel, dreaming long and strange. Now I'm bathed in sweat and the daylight hurls a thousand needles and I can't blink fast enough to shoot them all down. I think there's a woman in the bed with me but I don't want to look. The bathroom mirror doesn't lie. My eyes are sunken stones. When I come back, she's gone. There was never anybody here at all, I tell myself, and then I just stop asking questions, even to myself. Today is a seven-hour drive over the border into Slovenia and I need some pharmacy without a prescription.

Hughes is beating those fucking drums again. Every beat presses pain points deep in the base of my brain. He should know that I want to kill him now. The whole world should know. I'll do it on live radio. Take us to the station, point me at the mic. I will kill him then, on air.

You feeling alright? the promoter asks, a millisecond's lapse between the movement of her mouth and the sound of her words. A hundred years pass as I try to phrase an answer.

Not really. Feel like I'm going to die. I could use some painkillers.

She says – Aspirin?

Aspirin? I don't need fucking aspirin. I'm living one of my greatest fears, falling sick on tour. Every second is torture. I want painkillers and sedatives. I want a private room and a month off. I want to close the door and control who comes in or out. I want to see my kids. I don't want to sing to bloody strangers. Yet here I am again, nodding simplistically as the promoters say it's time to go on.

The drums stop and Hughes walks into the club backstage and looks at me and asks, You want some pseudoephedrine?

A single room, soaked in sweat, a straw Christ fixed over the bed. Through the curtains rolls a pearlescent haze of total fog. I don't know if it's day or night. I don't know anything. I can't think. The mobile has no network coverage. The phone in the room is dead. I have no idea where I am. Pulling on my jeans and overcoat, I stalk the anonymous corridors of an empty hotel. The reception is closed.

In the yard, the humid cold is thick and clinging. Vague shapes of buildings swallowed by fog gently suggest the end of time.

Across a space of little stones, I spy a cafe's lit windows, cakes and yoghurt on the buffet. I haven't eaten for days. A family are staring at me and I become uncomfortably aware that I may look somewhat scary so I force a little smile and the mother says something to the kids and they look away then quickly back again. I ask for tea and apple cake. The food feels gross dissolving into me. My clothes are hanging loose. Nothing is making sense. Dugz comes bustling in, all action.

We're in a hurry, got to get a move on for Ljubljana, we're shooting a movie today, remember? Then he double-takes quizzically – You alright?

The road disappears into silver-grey haze, a snaky trail signed by white pickets and cat's-eye reflectors. Handmade shrines for highway fatalities by the frozen roadside – some desiccated roses in a bottle, a portrait photo of a girl, tied to a picket with wire. Nimble deer dash through the headlights like the shooting pains in my brain leap from lobe to lobe, steel-edged detonations rippling through my nervous system.

You feeling alright? says Deadeye.

Getting worse.

Buck up, says Hughes, we'll get some antibiotics. You remember that finger infection I got in Braunschweig? The place with the crypt and the viruses that had hibernated there for like, several hundred years? Thought I was going to get the thing amputated. After twenty-four hours of antibiotics I was drumming again. Modern science for you.

I look at him blankly. The band themselves are becoming strangers to me.

Antibiotics are tricky to find on a Catholic Sunday in Ljubljana, but the film crew make-up girl has all kinds of painkillers in her bag. She explains that she broke her back dancing in the ballet. She's always in pain. When she says that, tears well in her black eyes and she swims through my blood shooting down viruses with vigilante bullets.

The dilapidated antique theatre is full of ghosts, echoes of emotion like a room's lingering perfume afterscent, long after the people have gone. I'm singing a sea shanty by the famous Slovenian entertainer Jezek, another dead man's song about dead men. Petra, the director, handles the situation with skill, moving quickly between takes. The cameras roll, needles of steel shoot through my head, my pineal gland squeezes out droplets of adrenaline like a sweating fruit; I see a ghostly chorus of sailors stalk the room, singing about life after death and curses from beyond the grave.

We nail the take and hit the bar, the boys cutting loose as it's the last date of our tour. I take pills with lovely Slavic names and feel high as the angels above, the respite from the fever a joy beyond description. Hours later I wake up in a densely furnished house surrounded by forest. It's raining. No one is awake. I make a coffee and take stock. The job isn't over yet – the band are driving back to Berlin and I'm due back in Italy for a recording session.

In the morning light, Petra's kitchen table is covered in money. I count it and recount it. The figures spin and glow and piggyback together, stacks of digits, columns of scrawl, asterisks and subtotals, piles of receipts, black coffee and cigarettes. Taking care of business. One by one, everybody takes a cut and we say goodbye until God knows when we all shall meet again. The van pulls out of the yard. The scene grows very quiet. Wind shakes the tall trees, the mulch on the muddy ground exhales digestive scents. It's time to go, I sense it in the light and the shifting leaves.

Pavel, a friend of Petra's, has kindly offered me a lift across the border to Trieste.

The road unravels at light speed, Pavel at the wheel. I'm dizzy, incorporeal. I wind down the window to get some air. The winter haze tastes metallic, like amalgam fillings. Tinariwen's desert rhythms are on the stereo but outside the trees are stripped winter-bare, the hills covered in snow; the air conditioning blows hot while I shiver.

Now I'm running, running through the concourse at Trieste Centrale, personal belongings trailing in my slipstream – money, documents, passport, notebooks. I scramble around the platform collecting pieces of an unravelling life, relics pulled from Berlin, things people gave me on the tour, sentimental things that I don't want to let go.

The train pulls out with me on board and soon the border slides by. Thank God I'm getting closer to home, back to Italy.

The other passengers watch me like I've got a device strapped to my body primed to blow. The intercity hurtles through the night into Padova. I change platforms, dragging my gear through stairwells and underpasses where the homeless beg for coins. The sweat is soaking me through. I need coffee. A bewildered businessman watches my bags while I work the automatic dispenser, drink three espressos in a row. I make my connection and find a seat.

A huge, bald, Shrek-like man walks down the carriage corridor grunting, looking for somewhere to sit down. The passengers turn away or put bags on adjacent seats to prevent him sitting down beside them. Instead, he sits down opposite me, a wound caked in dried blood slashed across his forehead, fraying bandages taped over the slashes on his arms, a bright-orange hospital band sealed around his wrist. He stares at me, grunting. I stare back at something in his eyes that looks like love. The eyelids swoon. He slowly falls asleep with a half-smile etched on his face.

At Bologna station I'm the last one out on the platform, the exit so far away I just rock back and forth on my heels, calculating the distance. Out of nowhere appears an African girl in a Trenitalia uniform. She pulls out a key and guides me into a steel service elevator, slowly ascending two levels onto the piazza.

Erik flashes his high beams, catches my eye and waves. We pull out of the parking lot with the NatSav barking directions in Dutch for the Ancona highway.

I made it here from Holland in twelve hours, he says, there was nobody around after Cologne.

Great, I reply. You get any sleep?

Not much. Did you? You look like hell!

We drive to a house high in the Romagnan hills. I'm on the third floor in a room with a bed. Several hours pass. Gradually I become aware that I'm not really breathing. Or no, I'm hyperventilating. Except it's very shallow and weak, like a cat with the feline flu. I call the Bomber at four in the morning. He tries to shake me off.

Can't you make it through 'til tomorrow morning?

You remember, I reply, you remember what happened to Hank Williams?

He hangs up and minutes later we're driving to the hospital in Faenza. Next thing I'm breathing through an oxygen mask, a catheter stuck in the back of my hand.

Don't you realise you could have died?

The *dottoressa* is young and scornful and speaks a precise English. You should have presented yourself days ago, she says, what have you been doing all this time? What was so important it was worth to die for? You have the *polmonite,* the acute pneumonia. You need to stay here for I don't know how long, under observation.

But the studio session starts tomorrow. I've got to keep moving, can't get laid up in this antiseptic, refrigerated desperation. Somehow, deep down, I still believe in the myth of my own indestructibility. I text the Bomber from my mobile and he drives over, waits in the car park, engine running. Slipping out a side exit, we make a getaway past the farms and poplar trees and wheels of straw onto the fog-cloaked Adriatic flatlands.

The studio villa stands in an open field behind a line of trees. The earth is a barren, pale lime-grey colour. Everything is shockingly quiet. There are no neighbours – Beat, the owner and in-house engineer, lives a kilometre away with his family. This old *caserna* is his studio, two floors of high-ceilinged rooms. The fog outside my window resembles the fairy-floss mould webbed across my lungs in the X-rays. I haven't washed for days; the thought of water touching my skin is intolerable. There's no showerhead, just a spout fixed in the ceiling offering a thin, tepid drizzle. I strip off, teeth chattering as the dark water swirls counterclockwise down the drain.

The big orange cat Milo stalks around the villa hunting for mice, then hides under the bed waiting for me to lower a foot down so he can gnaw my shin. Hypnotised by the moonlight spilling through open-shuttered windows, I feed him with pieces of stale croissant until he purrs. A slow pulse vibrates the walls, throbbing and arrhythmic like a helicopter overhead or a generator in the basement growing louder, boots marching up the stairs, paramilitaries poised to kick down the door. And then nothing – just the wind, the fog and fractured recollections of events from long ago, things that never happened, stray imaginings.

The pages of the book in my hands are fragile and obscure, the typeface mutates into illuminated medieval characters, the pages dissolve into sand spilling through my fingers and merge into drifting Saharan dunes and I become the book reading myself, the unknown letters branded on my skin, a desert wind howling through the spaces between my words. Assassins are tracking me; I read the beginning of a description of my murder at their hands tattooed in black ink on my black skin then my skin peels away and I lose the end of the story as my very bones reveal themselves, long and thin and white.

The slow pulse returns, my heart beating a hundred-decibel

refrain. But now the drum is different, external, not a part of me at all. Time passes incoherently until I remember where I am, the farmhouse in the flatland country outside Villafranca, the stripped poplars standing sentinel by the blackberry ditches, the recording session.

Big drums echo through the draughty corridors. Slowly, a song emerges from the background noise – I recognise it as one of mine. The band are starting work in the studio. Wrapped in a quilt and hugging the walls, I peer in through the little glass windows; they're all in there laying down the basic tracks – Erik, the Bomber, Diego, Beat. I crawl inside and slump on a couch. It's good to hear them talk and play, laughing and swearing in Italian; it's good to feel alive again, with friends. Three days pass in semiconscious states. The high temperature ebbs and flows and the strange dreams just keep on coming. Somehow through it all we make the basic recordings of an album, *Fatalists*.

With two days to recover before a show in London, I'm staying in a friend's apartment around the corner from the Clandestino club in Faenza. I dream a girl with long hair and callipers slowly limps into my room, her figure silhouetted against the light spilling in from the hall. She sits on my bed and talks to me, and as she does I realise I'm not dreaming and open my eyes to see her reaching over to touch my face in the uncertain way of the blind.

Are you there? she says in a broad American twang and I hear a shout that seems to belong to someone else, but is in fact my own.

I'm sorry, she says, I don't know where I am.

Neither do I, I reply.

A boy enters the room, apologising in a soft Tennessee drawl, and escorts the girl out of the room. Next morning, I meet the couple again by daylight and they invite me for a walk. Moving as carefully as a trio of octogenarians, we make our way through the town's historic centre. Charlie parks the wheelchair in a bird-flocked piazza.

It's so beautiful here, says Isabel, looking around with unseeing eyes, crying silent tears of joy. Thank you, she says, thank you so much for bringing me here. Italy. It's so beautiful. I will never forget this moment. The only thing making me sad is knowing I can never really thank you enough, Charlie. You're an angel. It's so perfect.

Charlie buys some gelato cones for the two of them, and taking me aside he says, More than anything she really wanted to come here and see Italy. We've seen Florence, Rome and tomorrow we're going on to Venice. It's been amazing, you know what I mean?

Yeah, I reply, I'm just wondering, how does Isabel see anything? I mean, she's blind, right?

Charlie smiles. I don't know, she just feels it, he says. Somehow, she's taking it all in, don't know how she does it. It's like she's incredibly sensitised, because of being blind, so she's developed other ways to perceive the world. Sometimes, she sees more than this world, other dimensions, I couldn't tell you what.

Is Isabel your girlfriend?

No, man, she's my sister, and the doctors all say she's going to die from this degenerative disease and there's nothing they can do about it.

That's terrible. I'm sorry.

Well, at least she's here in Italy now. Any day soon she could be taken away from us, you know? And this was her dream, coming back to Italy one more time. This was her dream and now it's real. What more can anyone ask for? We don't decide about our lives, but you know, we can choose within those limitations. Have a good trip, man, and I hope you get better soon. So long …

Charlie rolls Isabel away, the thin rubber wheels snagging in the rutted medieval flagstones.

That evening, I'm in Milan airport headed for London. Before boarding, I weigh myself at a *farmacia* on the concourse. I've lost ten kilos in the last month; I haven't been this light since I was thirteen years old.

Heathrow's rail connection drops me at Victoria station. A hurricane headwind blows through the tunnels to the underground. The tube is packed. I alight in the West End, desperate to get away from the crowds. I find Francis's apartment, the keys under the mat, make myself at home, wake up on a cotton couch cover soaked in sweat, pop more pills to get through the night.

A taxi drops me at the basement venue whose black walls are decorated with scenes from hell painted in blood red and chromium yellow – tortures of diabolic ingenuity, leaping flames, the anguished faces of the doomed. As the audience builds, so does the temperature. I sing into an inferno of red light and distorted, grinning faces. Tonight, I play in hell.

Anonymous London suburbs slide by on the road to Heathrow.

The taxi driver talks family – how they are everything, how much we need them, how he sends all his earnings home to Pakistan to look after his parents, then drops me at Terminal Five. Shakily I make my way to the departure gate for another flight between hemispheres. There are two of us left in the lounge, the last passengers boarding, and slowly I recognise Dan, another guitarist from Melbourne who's just finished a tour with his own band.

Man, you look terrible, he says.

So do you, I reply, what happened?

Came down with pneumonia on tour. I can hardly walk.

We laugh along the air bridge, silently dreading the long flight home.

Dirtmusic in BKO City | Bamako, 2009

Mohammed spots us clearing customs in the arrivals hall and I flashback to departing Mali one year ago, Mohammed following me through the departures hall, watching the cops warily out the corner of his eye. He tugs at the guitar case slung over my shoulder, grins with dazzling white teeth and parts the crowd flocking around the luggage carousel.

Man, I'll help you with your stuff! Welcome to Mali, man. You a musician? Yeah, I knew you were musician, man. I can tell, I'm a musician too. Musicians are like brothers, man. Is that your band? Where you from?

A burly, bald man in the arrival hall holds a handwritten sign: *Dirtmusic*. This must be Adama, the driver arranged to meet us. The five of us talk in sign language and broken French – Adama, Eckman and Brokaw and our manager, Peter – crossing the packed-dirt airport car park in the burning spice and diesel fumes of a humid Bamako night.

But Mohammed hasn't given up yet; he hustles us through the melee of battered Land Cruisers and tour guides and drivers and kids pitching at the incoming tourists and the African businessmen home from Europe flush with Western currency.

You like African music? he asks, you need a ride? To the city it's a long way, too far to walk! I can get a ride for you. You already got a ride? Oh, man … They're the wrong people! Don't you know? That's okay. Don't worry, come with me, we'll go to some good places. You like Mali music? That's why you're here? I know the places where the real Mali music is made, I can take you there, no problem. You want to go?

We throw the bags and guitars into the back of Adama's gutted Peugeot van, organising a quick getaway from this chaos into the further chaos of the city.

Listen, my friend, says Mohammed frowning, listen to my story. I'm a musician like you, but I got nothing. I need to send out my music to all Mali, to talk to the people, 'cause they be crying, man, it's the politics. What can we do? The people are crying. We look to you, my friend, you are the teacher. We will come to you, where are you staying? Ah, I know that place. I understand, very busy, you don't have time – my friend, we will come to you! Just for some advice to take our music to the world. You have a few minutes? Just a few minutes for my children, they have nothing to eat. But we can change all that, inshallah!

Two hours, says Eckman, that's all the time we got.

Ok, beams Mohammed, no one knows Bamako like me, my friend. We be there! The day after tomorrow!

Ten in the morning?

Anytime, we are there! Don't you worry! This will be good for you, and good for us, inshallah!

Adama eases out the clutch and edges the rusty transit van across the field, dodging vehicles from all angles. We cross the Saudi bridge over the glistening Niger into downtown Bamako – low concrete buildings, long straight roads, kids playing by the parallel open drains, itinerant SIM card vendors, cooking fires dotted over vacant lots, the savannah perfume of burning grass.

We're here to record a new Dirtmusic album in collaboration with Tamikrest.

After the the Festival au Désert, I had mailed roughly mastered cassette recordings of the desert jams from Berlin to a post box in the northern desert town of Kidal, hoping for Tamikrest's approval for a bootleg CD release. The band's percussionist and sometime rapper, Pino, diplomatically tried to avoid saying that the cassette recordings were too lo-fi for their taste, but after several distorted and intermittently truncated phone conversations between Melbourne and Mali, it was clear Tamikrest wouldn't consent to releasing the tent sessions.

Instead, the band proposed that we record together in a professional studio. Our manager, Peter, sourced some funds from an industrial sponsor towards the flights, and the record label helped with the basic costs. Working on a very tight budget, we organised a kind of recording session none of us had ever attempted before; but now, all the phone calls, paperwork, planning pitches, faxes and emails are behind us and we're ready to face the music.

Tomorrow, album rehearsals begin at the late Ali Farka Toure's Studio Bogolan: Dirtmusic and Tamikrest in an eight-piece formation.

They are fans of Western rock music as we are fans of Tuareg desert blues, and musically we have much to learn from each other. At the same time, there is another kind of exchange going on: Tamikrest songs will also be recorded for their debut album, to be released in Europe through the same record label as Dirtmusic. The band are looking for a way in to the international music scene and we are going to help them.

Tamikrest are a politically committed group – their words

and music form part of an ongoing mission to raise awareness of the oppression of Tuareg people. The Tamasheq desert culture's fraught relations with federal Mali, and the discovery of uranium and oil in the Sahara has created a lot of tension in the area. Armed rebellions keep flaring up.

When we met last year in the desert, we Westerners were protected, invited guests, dressed as international musicians, sharing music, the air, the skies and the stars as equals. Our Tuareg hosts walked tall in white and indigo robes, against a background of camels, capacious tents and the poetry of the dunes.

Here in Bamako, the situation is different.

Tamikrest arrive direct from the vast interior, a two-day journey by bus from their hometown of Kidal. Ousmane, Aghaly, Cheikh, Moussa and Pino, ragged from the trip, smile and brush the dust off their faded desert jeans and worn trainers and begin the ritual brewing of tea. After the dream of the desert, we're all amazed to see each other again here in the city's concrete chaos. We connect in lateral ways, swapping jokes and mixing up English and French and Tamasheq.

But our mutual language is really music. Brokaw breaks out a dobro, a metal-bodied steel-string guitar, Peter has an acoustic Martin dreadnought and Eckman has brought a Danelectro guitar that he presents to Ousmane, the band's leader, much to his delight. I've brought my battered Epiphone semi-acoustic and Moussa has a roadworn Japanese electric guitar of his own, so a ragged-ass guitar band manifests out of nowhere and the reunion becomes a jam session – traditional songs, Dirtmusic songs, Tamikrest songs, hybrids.

God knows what the staff here at the Hôtel Tamana are making of this ruckus.

Ousmane is charismatic and slightly built and speaks very, very quietly. Radiating tenacity, he draws people close for conversation, inside his personal space, employing silence as power.

Tamasheq music, he says, is really the sound of liberation.

When Ousmane makes comments like that, you listen.

Yet the situation is anything but clear. We receive a phone call from a woman claiming to be Tamikrest's manager. She sounds very urgent and demands we meet with her immediately, but in all our discussions with Tamikrest, they've never mentioned a manager.

A meeting on the *pension* verandah is swiftly convened. A conservatively dressed and scarved Tuareg girl walks in, all business and no play. Fatma speaks decent English and better French; she introduces herself as Ousmane's cousin from Dubai. There is an issue to address but we're not sure what it is yet.

Who made the deal? Fatma asks, who is organising this? You've been making agreements with the wrong person, with Pino, but Pino is not the real leader of the band. Ousmane writes the songs and sings them, he has the vision. Ousmane has to know about everything. Any agreement he doesn't know about doesn't exist.

Pino arrives awkwardly on the scene; he and Fatma exchange fire in Tamasheq. Turning to us, Pino explains that several of the band have been in refugee camps over the Algerian border since last year's hostilities turned into an uprising in the desert. In these circumstances, it wasn't always possible to include Ousmane in the discussion.

Clearly, much is lost in translation. Conversations including all of us take time to produce mutual understanding.

Ousmane listens slowly, carefully. Nodding his head when he agrees, holding up a hand to stop the flow of talk.

Tamikrest need Adama, our driver, to drive them as well as us. They are billeted on both sides of the river and Bamako is vast and slow. Slowly, we start to realise that the Tuaregs are very wary of the city. They don't really know it and, truth be told, don't feel welcome here. They are our guests. Hours pass. Everything will take as long as it takes until we understand each other. Maybe we will never understand each other. At sundown, after every last detail has been discussed, the tension eases and everybody starts smiling again while tiny mosquitoes materialise in livid swarms.

During the night, big malarial specimens hang from our mosquito nets, frozen in the early-morning hours as they wait for us to rise.

Electric guitars and basses worn smooth by the hands of all the players come and gone hang on the walls of the Studio Bogolan. Old Roland Jazz Chorus amps in various degrees of health are stacked up in a storage room; woven rugs cover the hardwood floor.

We fan out across the parquet of the main room. In a separated room of wood and glass Pino drums with his fists on a calabash, a demi-gourd laid flat on the ground that booms like a bass drum. In another booth, Brokaw tunes a drum kit, its snare skin broken and not a replacement head to be found anywhere. Aghaly has several djembes. Cheikh plays electric bass with a funky Arabic feel. Ousmane sings lead and lays down beautiful, unexpected guitar lines. Moussa chugs along on the backbeat with hypnotic, strummed bar chords.

We're not taping anything yet, just testing the songs and

starting to glimpse what kinds of progressions and shifts make sense, cutting out whole sections to create more space.

It's a big, powerful ensemble, four guitarists, three percussionists, and now we have to learn how it works, constantly stripping the songs down, shedding excess chord changes or extended arrangements in favour of more skeletal forms. In this way, the songs we brought with us are transformed by the collaboration into more essential, condensed versions, rhythmically mutating as new feels surface in the interplay between us. One-chord instrumentals stretch out over percussion grooves, creating space for the guitarists to improvise. The weird meshing of Western and Tuareg modalities generates unknown harmonies. Ousmane sings over a Dirtmusic riff in Tamacheq and a kind of fusion erupts between the bands. Ousmane gifts us the song, explaining its title, '*Imidiwan*', means 'friends'.

Eckman is back in the studio, recovered from the mystery bug that laid him up for several days, but now Brokaw has fallen into its feverish embrace. Studio assistants bring food for the afternoon *repas* to the shaded terrace in the Bogolan courtyard, kebabs, *pommes frites* and plastic containers of chicken or tripe, washed down with litres of sterilised water.

Tamikrest brew sugary shot glasses of gunpowder Tuareg tea, straining the tea back and forth then passing the glasses around one at a time. This stuff is like no other tea I know, a shot of raw adrenaline sweet as honey.

The engineer, Elie, and his assistant, Arouna, worriedly tweak the hardware in the control room. It's hard to get a straight answer about anything as Elie spends more and more time talking on his mobile. In between calls he says there's a lot of equipment that isn't working properly, that he needs to talk to the manager.

Test recordings on the control room speakers sound less than ordinary. It soon becomes clear that our engineer and his two assistants are struggling to pull a sound from the mixing console. Elie complains of having the flu but doesn't seem to have any symptoms. He walks distractedly through the big recording room, sometimes moving a microphone, usually talking on his phone at the same time.

The first takes are agonizingly slow. There are inexplicable delays. When we do record, the headphone mix is incredibly weird and the connections cut in and out. Take finished, we realise the engineer has already left the studio. The situation builds until Eckman confronts Elie.

I know you're a professional, he says, and that's how I know that you know that something isn't right! We paid the studio upfront before we even arrived, you promised us a fully functioning studio, but that's not what we've found here. And we promised Tamikrest that they'd record as well as us, we have a deal!

Suddenly, Elie smiles and relents and the atmosphere rapidly brightens into shouts and laughter. The effect is weird, like he's having a joke with us.

What the …? says Brokaw.

I have no idea, says Eckman, but let's roll with it!

Elie and Arouna and their third man gradually squeeze a hard, untreated sound out of the cranky digital recorders in the control room. It sounds very rough, but before we know it we're deep in a trance-like continuum of takes and more takes, three songs a day, seven or eight takes of each song, hours of music.

I've started smoking again, big flat packets of bootleg Dunhill Red bought from some kids out in the street. I share the cigarettes with Tamikrest, who in the tents last year at Essakane demonstrated a powerful command of chain-smoking. We chain-smoke our way through three days of intense recording until there's the basis of an album on the grungy studio PC.

Mohammed from the airport arrives at the Tamana for a meeting and he's brought along his friend, the rapper Crazy Man.

We have to talk man to man, he says to me, unsealing a large plastic ziplock bag on the table to remove an age-worn colour brochure entitled 'Sierra Leone'. Published in the late 1970s by 'AngloGold' as a spruiker presentation for investors and clients in a large diamond-mining operation, the brochure presents an overview of this small west African nation as a placid, stable, vacation-worthy arena for exploitation. The map is populated by Monopoly-board symbols representing the locations of gold, diamonds, oil.

The plastic bag also contains photos of Mohammed's family in Sierra Leone – his mother, wife and five children. Where Mohammed points to himself in these fading photos he's very hard to recognise; maybe these are photos of a different man, I can't tell and I'm not about to challenge him, but what's clear is that something really bad happened and this conversation is making him sweat.

He says – You know about the war in Sierra Leone, don't you, man? Very, very bad, all that fighting. I can't go back because all my family is gone in the fire. My kids died in the fire, and my wife. They were in the house. Bad people set fire to the house, everybody inside, some of us survived, but I don't know who or where. I got to stay here, you see, man? To make the music! For Farafina, for Africa. Rap music, Dirtmusic, Kabablu, Crazy Man!

Crazy Man, silent until now, wears a pale green kaftan, his shaven pate catching the light. He speaks a little of many languages, says he's got Kabablu waiting outside in the courtyard.

What is Kabablu?

Hustler Boyz! Crazy Man and Kabablu is Hustler Boyz!

Kabablu all live together in a room with no electricity near the airport, explains Mohammed. They got nothing, I want to help them.

I need money to buy batteries for their radio, says Crazy Man, how else can they study music? They must study to grow their music. They must study very hard! We have a message for all Mali, talking about justice and how the people have nothing to eat. We have to get the message out, for the children.

You make the music, says Mohammed, Dirtmusic!

We tell them to meet us at the studio in a week to work two hours getting their stuff down.

Why not? Mohammed says, why not? The boss is always right!

Inshallah! exclaims Crazy Man.

You are the teacher, Dirtmusic! says Mohammed, we listen to the teacher! We will make Hustler Boyz music, not just for Mali but all Africa, all the world.

It's the last day in the studio with Tamikrest. The control room is very hot and still. They are recording tracks for their album, songs that evoke a strong spiritual sense of the sacred Sahara, echoes of an ancient way of life predating Islam.

In the desert sometimes, says Pino, you hear music and singing when there's nobody there. Under the sand lie ancient cities buried long ago with names no one can remember. Sometimes at night you can hear them sing. And strange things happen in these wild, rough places, caused by men who roam like lone wolves, obeying no man and no god. An army patrol encountered such a man said to rustle sheep. Scared to approach, they observed him butcher, cook and eat an entire sheep – all of it! – during the course of a single night and come dawn, disappear. Afterwards, the patrol captain described the man as a monster, none of those tough guys would go near him! This man was an original Tuareg hunter!

Pino bites into a hunk of stewed goat, looks me in the eye and then at the falafel in my hand and says, salad is for camels!

Everybody laughs.

Have you ever, I reply, seen lights in the sky out in the desert?

Les lumières d'avion? Mais oui. Aircraft lights? Sure.

No, not normal aircraft, but lights in the sky that acted a bit strange?

Les étoiles? Stars?

No, more like strange machines moving faster than normal, or standing still. You know, like in the movies? Like, spaceships?

Les vaisseaux spatiaux?

Everybody goes silent.

Tu as jamais rencontre le diable, monsieur? asks Moussa with a grin – Have you ever met the devil?

The moment hangs in the air until somebody laughs uneasily, breaking the spell. Apparently, there's nothing extraterrestrial in the supernature of the desert. Instead, Ousmane, playing with the shrill Arabic ringtones on his mobile, flashes a publicity photo of

Mark Knopfler, guitar hero of Dire Straits, miniaturised on the Motorola screen.

You know him? asks Ousmane, what is he doing now, does he still play?

I really don't know, I reply, but I guess yes, he does.

Ousmane shakes his head disappointedly.

You don't hear about him any more but he's one of the greats.

And Hendrix?

Bien sûr.

Who else?

Santana, Ousmane says, laughing with his eyes, *le grand Santana!*

The Djembe Club is on fire. The bass churns through a blue pall of cigarette smoke, the cymbals shimmer and crash, people are dancing. I mean, really dancing.

Praise singers shout greetings to friends and relatives and bosses through a gloriously distorted sound system, backed up by casually rotating shifts of bass players, guitarists and percussionists. In this beautiful noise, the men's room is busted and waitresses navigate the crowd bearing trays of bottles high above their heads with expert ease.

Our time here is limited because we have to keep buying rounds of beer for a group of friendly locals following us around the club and we are running out of cash. There are few nightclubs in Bamako that serve alcohol and although it's free to enter, hardly anybody has money. But it's the kind of place you dream about, to hear and see live music, and that energy is a shot of love to the soul.

In the soft chill light of morning a concierge graces the terrace with white French-style bread and jam and nut-bitter African coffee in closed metal jugs. The concierges have turbans and delicately scarred cheeks and wary expressions, and they keep the house in immaculate order. A young Norwegian couple on their way home from the Festival au Désert tell us about the festival this year.

It was a downer in some ways, says Lars, it was a problem just getting in there near Timbuktu, there were roadblocks. A lot of international operators pulled out. Insurance issues. We were lucky, a lot of people never even arrived there from Bamako because the flights were cancelled.

Terrorist threats have been made to the organisers, says his girlfriend, and these threats circulated in the media and people got worried. But it was beautiful there and actually, there wasn't any trouble.

Yes, says Lars, but then there weren't any international artists at all. Exclusively African artists. Maybe it was like that because of those threats.

An Englishman breaks into the conversation from a nearby table. We never even made it out there, he says, they wouldn't take us! It was outrageous. But we did make it out to the festival at Ségou, me and my daughter, Isabel. Look at this stuff, some of my video footage.

Through the viewfinder of his camera I see performers, crowds.

Maybe I could shoot you guys too, he says, I overheard before that you're here recording, is that right?

Yes, says Peter warily, but we are making the video ourselves.

Well, these tapes are just for my collection, he says, then pauses – but you know, I've a friend at Channel Four and maybe, if he thinks it's good enough, we'll cut together a documentary on Malian music.

Did you give these performers release forms?

The Englishman seems offended. I'm a lawyer, he says, and these people are illiterate anyway, so what difference does it make?

Bored and dismayed by our turn of conversation, the lawyer's daughter asks, Hey, why can't we all just have fun?

Half an hour passes and the lawyer reappears in the courtyard with a local guitarist in tow. I'm going to tape this dude, he says, but could one of you please come and tune his guitar?

That guy doesn't need any help to tune a guitar, Brokaw says, he's been playing it all his life.

The internet is offline at both the *pension* office and the Studio Bogolan. Seeking out a Mali phone connection, I foray onto the street outside the K7 record store where a vendor organises matches for sale on a trestle table. Next to him, the tea man boils a bright red kettle on a tiny primus stove. Within a minute or so, a mindreading hawker waving bright Orange phone cards flags me down and sells me a SIM card.

I telephone my girlfriend in Melbourne. She's younger than me and possesses that aching, transient glow of youth I once found attractive. When she picks up she sounds like somebody I don't know. I get the strange feeling that this is a constructed conversation, her staged, phony voice distant and insubstantial as the wind howling on a wretched winter's day.

Yeah, she says. Hi! Where are you? Are you really in Africa? I never know where you are, you're never around! So ... I'm really tired. I'm hungry, too. I'm eating sushi tonight with some girls

I met in Brisbane. Hey, I tried to Skype you but, you know, it's always engaged. I just don't get how it works! Hey, I've dyed my hair … Did you know that? Remember when you saw me last, it was blonde? Well, it's not just blonde any more – it's ash blonde! Are you still there? I can't hear you, speak up … How's it going over there? Are you in Zimbabwe?

No, I say, as my head hits my hands and my mouth dries up. I'm in Mali. It's incredible, the music and the people. I think this album is going to be …

She interrupts the conversation to pour herself some wine and light a cigarette while she taps out something on her computer keyboard.

I'm going out tonight to a burlesque party, she says, clearing her throat. You should see what I'm wearing! Did you say you were making an album there?

I carefully lay the phone down, her voice flatlining across the airwaves. I hear the click of my phone credit disappearing along with her and know I won't be calling home again for a while.

I look around at the street, glad to be among strangers in the unquiet darkness of a place filled with so much soul, until I see a large group of people leaving the mosque and walking in this direction. Well-dressed, they glance at me contemptuously – an infidel, an unbeliever in their midst, pale-skinned and clutching a mobile phone like a spy reporting to his handlers. I slip the phone into my pocket and duck back into the K7 between the racks of Malian cassettes and CDs as Bamako dissolves into a twilight fug of petrol fumes and cooking-fire smoke.

In my room at the *pension*, a ruptured water pipe in the bathroom sprays a torrent of water at the ceiling all night long.

Sunday morning breaks chilly grey, the sun occluded by fog. News is circulating that a group of English and Swiss-German tourists have been kidnapped near the Niger border. In the studio courtyard, the muezzins draw breath before calling the faithful over the minaret loudspeakers. Elie's assistant unfurls a woven prayer mat and kneels facing Mecca, palms down and head bowed. Behind him, a slender wood awning shields a faded Mickey Mouse mural from the sun, two tough little motorbikes parked beside it.

Brutalist paintings of detainment camps – high walls and barbed-wire fences – hang in a gallery adjacent to the elegant Santoro restaurant. Drawn in a child's hand, stick-figure humans cower in jail cells or drift in the sea near a crash-landed airplane under fire from soldiers.

Meanwhile, a refined atmosphere reigns in the relative luxury of the dining room. Griots playing polyphonic koras pluck a river of sweet music from the air, interspersed with the quiet conversations of Europeans and wealthy Africans. The music turns sour as waves of nausea gather within me. I look at the fried goat's cheese, the tamarind juice, the capitaine fish and feel suddenly faint. The mystery bug was bound to come for me sooner or later. I decide to make a run for the *pension*.

As I walk along the Route de Koulikouro, the dust and fumes condense into the poisonous atmosphere of an inhospitable planet. Orange smog envelops the refugees in their dirt-floored cardboard homes, the beggars on the streets, the children leading blind adults, the couriers and cops in face masks, the girls carrying piles of fruit on their heads. Kids hawk second-hand Taiwanese toys and beg for cash as the gridlocked traffic radiates in a lugubrious haze.

It feels like I've either slipped back in time or been catapulted into the future.

In the empty reception lounge of the *pension*, Malian state television broadcasts a series of public service announcements – '*Mali contre l'excision!*' A short report on the cult of clitoridectomy follows, along with polemics regarding teenage prostitution, slavery and the legacies of rapacious foreign corporations. Then a focus piece on persecuted albino African kids taking refuge in the hills, like a species of white wild bunch. I drift off into strange dreams before being roused off the floor by a curious security guard – '*Ça va, monsieur? Ça va?*'

In the Bogolan studio, white-robed master musicians from the Symmetric Orchestra syncopate wildly on a big balafon, Brokaw playing along with a steel slide. I'm curled in a foetal position on the couch, hallucinating African masks detaching from the walls and floating in thin air. The music rambles on to no fixed destination until Elie receives a call from Peter, saying he's been robbed. The engineers panic and a distressed Adama speaks to us in Bambara, leading to inaccurate translations from the crew.

Peter has been ripped off by a woman! Money, passport, all is gone!

Never walk alone in Bamako at night! insists Elie. And do not show your cameras on the street, you will be mugged! This is a dangerous place for you!

Yes, somebody snatched my wallet from my room when I was down the hall, says Peter. I saw a woman running … It could have been anybody. It's only money, nothing more.

Later that night, within the rough concrete walls of the airport club, Baba Salah and his band mix blues and electric Afrobeat with searing energy. Brokaw is invited to the stage, shredding along on his plexiglass guitar while jubilant revellers stuff cash into his shirt. The club MC is yelling into the mic at a hundred decibels; the sweat burns under my collar when he singles me out of the crowd to play bass. Pretty soon Eckman joins us on guitar and we're all under the drummer's polyrhythmic thumb, even as the other musicians text and talk on their mobiles right there on the bandstand.

Mohammed, Crazy Man and the Hustler Boyz crew arrive at the studio ready to tape. The Boyz themselves are a wild crew, and the street energy they bring with them into the studio could be cut with a knife. Brokaw is on the drum kit, I'm playing bass, Eckman is producing in the control room and we've got no idea what to expect.

Toasting everybody present – Dirtmusic, the engineers, Kabablu and the year 2009 – Crazy Man incants in dialect before the Boyz take up a hyena chant and the drums kick in with a tough, repetitive beat. I search for a key with the old Fender bass, working off the tone of Brokaw's kick drum. The Hustler Boyz leap around the room, shouting out answer calls to Crazy Man's rap.

Bambara morphs into French punctuated by occasional English phrases – *Bamako remix two thousand and nine! This is the hustler Kabablu collection, check it check it out, ghetto melody, boom boom fire!* No one knows where or when to stop. Takes dilate to six minutes, even seven. None of the takes are the same.

An epic series of high fives later, Mohammed and Crazy Man

suddenly become serious and want to talk business. We offer to mix the takes and send them over but the guys have no postal address. We settle on sending the mixes by email and, against unrealistic expectations, underline the fact that we can't guarantee these recordings will be released.

Crazy Man looks bemused. Why not? he says incredulously, this is gold!

Out in the streets, a festive mood celebrates the inauguration of the president of the United States. Cries of 'O-bamako!' resound, two names morphing into one Afro-American sound bite. A sense of awe hangs in the air at the fact that an African brother will now assume the most powerful job in the world. Stencilled spray paintings of Obama's face appear on city walls overnight – *O-bamako* – the meme of the moment.

The presidential inauguration warps and flickers on a television screen parked on two mud-streaked Coke crates at a local street kiosk. A French translation runs over the audio obscuring the American voices, while the image is fuzzy and degraded, like a transmission from another world, which in so many ways it truly is.

You guys looking for something to eat? You know, something good?

Gotcha looks like a hard-times survivor. Something shifts and moves in his eyes when he talks, like he's simultaneously in conversation with somebody else.

I know the place you're looking for, he says, I'm going to take you there. This is my uncle. Say hi.

The uncle smiles an unreadable smile, the light flashing on his glasses. We try to shake them off, but Gotcha is insistent.

You guys musicians? I knew it. I'm a musician too. I worked for years in Switzerland. I played with Dee Dee Bridgewater, man. You know Dee Dee? Look, man, right here, this is the place. Best kitchen in the whole Hippodrome. Very tasty. You'll like this.

The Aqwaba has seen better days. We sit in a discotheque courtyard framed by palms near a stage piled with chairs and speaker boxes. Large orange bats casually defecate overhead, shaking the heavy foliage.

I shacked up with a chick in Geneva, says Gotcha, seven years. Funk jazz is my scene, they love that shit in Switzerland. I do percussion, bongos or whatever you got, man, it's okay. I can do the job. I'll get you my CD. C'mon, tell me where you're staying. We got to make plans.

The uncle keeps on smiling but Gotcha seems a little wounded when none of us offer an address.

I got to split, he says finishing the beer, important business. But we'll be in touch, right? I see you guys all the time out on the street. We'll be in touch real soon.

The taxi thumps along a pot-holed road between the concrete walls of chemical plants, tanning works, automobile graveyards. Families cluster around open fires, streetlamps far and few between.

Are we lost? says Eckman, I mean, look at this place. Where are we going?

Can we turn back?

The taxi driver headshakes a refusal and pretends to know his way around, becoming increasingly agitated until he's shaking almost epileptically. The four of us instinctively attempt to open the doors.

Not get out, he shouts, not get out taxi!

In a cul-de-sac he executes a three-point turn near a ramp over an open drain and stalls the engine. Steam gushes from the taxi's bonnet. Two armed security guards in camouflage gear approach us suspiciously then advise us with hand gestures not to hang about. Peter calls a private cab number. Twenty minutes later a battered brown Mercedes sedan pulls up.

Where you go? the driver says, I know a place, not far. Tourists, yes?

A long wooden bar runs the length of the room with about thirty white-skinned hostesses parked behind it. The owner is a smooth-talking Middle Eastern cat who explains that all the women working at the bar are Russian.

Fly in, fly out, he says, all around the world. It's a beautiful thing.

A handful of white men in states of advanced homesickness soak up the hometown atmosphere of illuminated advertisements for Foster's and Miller beer. Cheesy 1980s radio hits blare from the stereo, swimwear models pose on tropical beaches across multiple TV screens. A group of French tourists switch the channel to karaoke and sing along with Robbie Williams and for a brief illusory moment all is sweet nostalgia as the irrefutable otherness of Africa recedes into their alcoholic haze.

Bamako by night becomes yet stranger at the Byblos discotheque. A scattered Saturday-night crowd of Western business travellers and local hostesses mill on a black perspex dance floor under roving spot beams and a mirror ball, shuffling to the Jackson 5.

The scene is vaguely unreal, like a movie set populated with stock footage of hired extras. I shake a leg to 'Don't Stop 'Til

You Get Enough' until, surrounded by hostesses, I feel suddenly awkward and retreat to the tables to shoot pool with Brokaw and two unshaven Englishmen whose muttered conversation and hangdog expressions give little away.

Import, export, says the more talkative one, mostly software.

The other guy says he's a stringer but the vibe is MI5.

A working girl's eyes, sleepy like a cobra roused from hibernation, glare between mascara eyelids while a heavy-set white businessman strokes her lycra-clad thigh. Turning on a certain angle to the light, the foundation-masked sores on her face stand out in relief against her skin. From the Byblos toilet walls to the streets and billboards, AIDS warnings signs are everywhere.

Walking back to the *pension*, Gotcha coasts up beside me, talking up his cousin in the army, how that's where the hashish is since the military moved back into the desert, how great the quality is and how it's pure, direct from the source in Morocco. The uncle manifests from nowhere and walks us across a field of corrugated iron shacks, open fires and groups of men standing around or sitting on blankets and crates.

Or you want the ngoni? Gotcha asks. Come on, I'll show you, man. The real thing, the real good ngoni. You can take it home with you! What's the trouble, my friend? I look after you, man. I try to help you out.

Uncle and Gotcha hustle me inside a corrugated-iron shack suffused with the fumes of meat burning on a diesel grill in the corner. Six or seven guys stand around in faded T-shirts. Conversation stops as we enter. The head guy says something in Bambara. I don't like the tone of his voice. Show him your money, says Gotcha. I tell him I don't have any, and as the atmosphere shifts, a knot forms in my stomach. My phone starts ringing in my inside jacket pocket and I let it go. It stops then starts again, pulsing against my rib cage – the only person who knows this number is my girl in Australia. The thought prompts me to act: I push my way out of the shack, walking quickly across the packed dirt and small stones. Following at close range, Gotcha smells dangerous, gets in my face, talking about trust.

Don't you trust me, man? I played with Dee Dee Bridgewater! I'm your friend, I'm a player like you, we're brothers, man, so what's your problem? I'm just trying to help you out! Hey, listen to me, man, I'm your friend!

The clouds have dispersed over the dusty hills fringing the city. Adama is driving us to a wedding party. Elie arranged this for us as something to remember before we fly out. Several hundred women and girls of all ages wearing brightly coloured gowns and turbans gather under a huge marquee. The only males here are in the band. The wedding rolls on for a week but only females attend this special day.

A petite wedding singer holds the microphone, telling stories, exchanging greetings with the audience and singing about the bride and the bride's family, praising God and their children's children and the peace of the nation. A steady influx swells the gathering, spilling across the packed-dirt acre on an inexhaustible stream of folding chairs.

We're sitting with four percussionists, several ngoni players, electric guitarists, bass players and keyboardists, a band of interchanging musicians playing non-stop celebratory major modal mayhem. Here, music is created like bolts of cloth, only by the minute instead of the metre.

The wedding singer tells jokes and sings of love in the voice of wrath, makes a tender dedication sound like a threat of revenge, bobs and weaves, maintains an expression of astonished delight. She sings for three hours before losing her voice and passing on the microphone to one of her young acolytes.

Picking through the trash and weeds and motor parts looking for somewhere to pee, local kids surround me – *Monsieur! Monsieur, qu'est-ce que tu fais ici en Mali?* – What are you doing in Mali?

I look at their open faces and clear, bright eyes and realise I have no idea.

Blood and Chocolate | Brazil, 2010

Butcher and Alabama have been awake all night. Recognition ignites their faces when they see me and I return fire with a jet-lag stare. We've seen photos of each other online, although we look radically different in the fluorescent overkill of the arrivals hall. We couldn't be anybody else, and besides, that's how it started – an online exchange floating the idea of bringing me and my music to South America. Now here we are in São Paulo International GRU, shaking hands.

Green succulents swarm the surrounding hills. The humidity is high. The road residue slicks on my skin as we haul luggage across the car park under a sky laden with heavy grey clouds. Alabama, tall, dark and quiet, gets behind the wheel of a black sedan. A distorted Maltese cross logo on the steering wheel catches my eye. I ask what make of car this is, but Alabama isn't sure.

General Motors? he says quizzically, and pulls out onto a billboarded highway. Pepsi, Monsanto, Proctor and Gamble, Johnson and Johnson, Prada and other international trademarks of high fashion, megasized supermodels, television icons, sports goods, sex supermarkets. Slunk down in the backseat with a Panama hat pulled low over his brow, Butcher raps fluently in a southern American drawl.

The Gories, man, you know, Demolition Doll Rods? They're friends of mine and they do pretty well around here. You know

Oblivions? Wild shit … It's that Detroit sound, you know what I'm saying? It makes a lot of sense in a place like this.

Traffic intensifies as we enter São Paulo through peripheral districts of low-cost tower blocks, the petrosmog absorbing us into a grey fugue of iron and cement. Huge subtropical bushes and trees decorate the flow of rough concrete. The elevated highway called the Minhocão, meaning 'giant worm', slices through the city centre in a pall of carbon monoxide. We ramp off and cruise downtown along Paulista Avenue, a long, straight, boulevard of corporate skyscrapers. Squeezed between these modernistic monoliths of big-league capitalism lie the shopping malls, the São Paulo Museum of Modern Art and a legion of destitute Brazilians sleeping on cardboard groundsheets. The scale is vast, a déjà vu of the futuristic cities from 1950s comic-book art – except that the superheroes have been made redundant by surveillance, gated communities and private security.

Vendetta's house is overshadowed by a construction site. The projected thirty-floor tower block, eight or nine floors high and in steady progress, ascends skywards two metres away from my bedroom window. Work begins at seven every morning behind a walled perimeter fringed with the glittering razor wire of a maximum security prison.

Vendetta is my tour agent in South America; luminescent blue eyes, black hair falling over her pale, tattooed shoulders. She is quick and clever and her female energy makes me feel somewhat safe, the kindness of strangers surprising me yet again.

Those bastards, she says pointing at the worksite. It's just not fair, none of this is fair. Me and the neighbours, we're going to sue their ass. I'm not moving anywhere! Why should I? I like it here!

In the backyard, her dog, Elvis, is barking at a low-flying helicopter, and even after the copter is gone the manic spoodle barks on, mixing into the drone and thump of the pile drivers and earthmovers next door.

We drink thick, drip-filtered coffee in Vendetta's kitchen. My headache lifts as I listen to the boys talk, the low beat of their voices calming my nerves before we head out along a series of backstreets, boulevards and a piece of clotted highway arterial to reach the Caffeine rehearsal studio. Caffeine is rough and ready, but the guys have sorted a perfect backline for my sound – a Japanese 335 copy semi-acoustic guitar and a Peavey four-by-twelve vintage reverb guitar amp with a triggered overdrive channel. That overdrive channel – and the noise wall it delivers– is my key weapon in this three-piece set-up of bass, drums and electric guitar.

Butcher and Alabama are both guitarist-vocalists and front their own bands, or perform one-man shows playing drums, guitar and singing simultaneously, channelling mavericks like Joe Hill Louis or Juke Boy Bonner. They're from the garage trash rock scene where irony roams free and sure enough, they bite into my music at high speed, crackling with electric nervous energy.

Our first show is the next night at the Lions Club: varnished Brazilian-pine parquet floors, uniformed staff, wall-length mirrors and a second-rate sound system better suited to a disco than to rock and roll. I need to recalibrate my body clock because I'm already fading, and our concert starts around two in the morning.

The audience is riding high on cocktails, blow and beer as we begin the long, fast, syncopated ride into intensity, dissonance, oblivion – rock music essentialised as rhythm and chaos, aimed at the mind and at the hips. Waves of movement pass through the room and the walls start to sweat. Song requests and phone numbers written on flyers and random pieces of paper appear near the monitors as the crowd builds up. The speed of events and the jet lag swing me around in a vertigo clinch, and after ninety minutes we close the last encore and retire to the men's room for an after-show debriefing. Telltale snorts echo from the neighbouring cubicles; the ceramic lid of the cistern is crosshatched with thousands of fine blade marks.

As dawn breaks over the skyscrapers, I'm on the Lions Club terrace with a girl I feel I've known forever even if I can't remember her name. She describes her home state of Bahia, an untouched paradise three days' drive north where animals run free and nature reigns supreme.

São Paolo gets to everybody, she says. It can get to you too. Understand? Go to the northern beaches, go there for your soul. For your soul!

São Paulo – the summit of each hill reveals vistas of further high-rise suburbs dwindling into the smog-filtered silhouettes of even more distant skylines. A profusion of radio towers pump evangelical religion and schmaltz music into the atmosphere; an element of the phantasmagorical hovers in the patches of air and sunlight trapped between skyscrapers.

Detailed surrealist murals decorate the walls of the city. The spiky runes of a cryptic pictographic language – *pichu* – scrawl across homes and business and civil monuments from street level to miraculously unreachable locations. The tags and murals are as quickly covered over by the artists' rivals as they appear. Renate, a photographer who tracks the *pichu,* describes it as a mysterious, organic rogue algae sprouting on the cityscape.

The symbols of *pichu*, he explains, derive from the magical religions. The churches are everywhere, but maybe you don't recognise them as churches – these are African mystical traditions, and man, they are strange … The Portuguese traders sold African slaves into Brazil since hundreds of years, the slaves brought their mystery cults and mixed them up with our magical Catholicism, and the local indigenous traditions, to create these voodoo evangelical sects … Like the Candomblé, which itself is just one strain of the vast Orisha religion. I know this because my sister joined one of the cults, and she's alright, man, but I honestly don't think anyone understands the whole thing, it's just too big.

As the days go by I notice this mystic undercurrent animating local Brazilian street life – a broken bird arranged on a pile of crushed glass in the gutter; an icon spray-painted in white on the blindside of a black bathroom door in a small-town garage; colourful posters for evangelical meetings, faith healers, black Madonnas, indigenous saints. One morning I encounter an old guy sitting out on a step on the street, eating breakfast off a sheet of newspaper, his dark face roughly daubed vivid white, small feathers and twigs in his hair like he'd arrived there in the dizzy morning after some Dionysian ritual out in the jungle.

The walls of Carniceria, a former butchery, are hung with machetes and old advertisments for meat products. The sound system is clapped-out; Alabama maxes it into distortion for enough level to get over the background noise. I'm playing solo tonight and there's no stage, so I keep it short and to the point. The punters buy me drinks and request songs, face to face. Afterwards, we shoot pool in the green fluorescence of a snooker hall, devil's dandruff dusted across the shabby toilets, *cachaça* circulating in plastic cups. Upstairs on the street, crackheads fire up in a doorway while the girls gather around expensive European cars at the kerb, and the spruikers bark like chained Dobermans guarding the whorehouse doors of hell.

Favelas, slum cities, evolve in unexpected places – on a hill behind a local neighbourhood, on the flanks of an arterial road, behind an airport or in an industrial zone, on the edge of a lush private golf course, or climbing through the electrosmog to a summit crowned by São Paulo's myriad radio towers..

On the black-and-white screen of a kiosk television, live-eye reporters duck automatic weapons fire, interview street kids, stand aside when the tanks roll by. The army assault on Rio de Janeiro's favelas is only just beginning as the government, anxious to prove that they will act tough on crime, attack the tribal drug cartels with everything they've got, short of nuclear weapons. These elaborate crime syndicates constitute a pirate state complete with its own justice policed by heavily weaponed gangs, and there is no solution to this stand-off in sight while subsistence farmers and their families continue to migrate from the land into the megacities, swelling the millions-strong ranks of the dispossessed.

Rule of law is always tenuous where people are afraid of their own government and only money talks. Gated communities are patrolled by armed guards, while Nigerian pushers run crack houses in the upper reaches of a central city shopping mall. In this hypersexualised society, the female ass has acquired a semiotic divinity; sex has become a form of hypnotic diversion similar to the mass-media dumbing down in Berlusconi's Italy, distracting people's attention from complex issues of injustice and corruption.

People avoid the cops here, and maybe the cops avoid the people too because I see precious few of them on the streets. The favelas are run by a mafia-style 'secret' state maintained by the drug industry, while an impenetrably corrupt political class rorts the system from above. Although the economy is apparently booming, the scale of homelessness and poverty reveals that the dividends are enjoyed only by an elite minority.

In Berlin they might be bankrupt, but at least, as Berlin's gay mayor recently stated, they are sexy. Vendetta loves this statement and repeats it over and over again.

The Vegas Club on Augusta Street has a *Scarface* feel, red velvet curtains and muted brown floors and trimmings, carpeted stairways and split-level connecting corridors guarded by huge uniformed dudes with jailhouse eyes. The bandstand, a treacherous half-moon shape, pulses under the strobes and I shy away from the edge, wary of the plunge to the dance floor two metres below.

It seems to me a redhead is dancing across the opposite wall, waving her arms and shouting some unintelligible message, but the sweat's in my eyes and I can't read her.

Butcher is driving the tempo hard and fast. I surf his nervous energy by dropping words and phrases, making it up as I go along. The music is mutating under the sway of heat and pressure, hybridising desert blues and garage trash, forcing me to play in a whole new way – fast, heavy, laced with feedback. The guitar in my hands bucks like a sacrificial bird, I'm wringing its neck to squeeze out the last drops of adrenaline but it won't lay down and die and I feel its life force enter my blood and scream through my veins, taste it in my throat, feel it flood into my brain.

As the after-show DJ kicks in, Alabama pulls the gear off the stage and we breathe in the cocktail of exhaust, disinfectant and cheap perfume out on Augusta Street. Vendetta organises a fast getaway to the petrol station for the simple pleasure of cheese bread with doce de leite, a caramelised condensed milk with enough sugar in it to turn you diabetic. I lie awake in bed as the sun rises and the construction site springs back to life with its metal monster soundtrack jackhammering my dreams.

Sometimes we unconsciously invite people into our lives who end up wreaking havoc. No matter how far you might go to escape such predators, they still haunt our thoughts and reactions, sitting on our shoulders like smirking ghosts with the power of rejection propelling their rage. A stalker like this has been on my case since months, ranting at me through the internet, and although I block her out, she somehow has my number and her manic texts and unanswered calls keep coming thick and fast.

My girlfriend back in Australia has sent me an email saying she can't see me any more. I try to block it out, but this girl is under my skin with her fast talk, her strange past and her fragility, and I know I like her far too much to simply dismiss her distress. At the same time, I don't have the energy to fight, nor the determination needed to fix this right here, right now.

I doze off, dreaming about a gun: I'm in a shooting gallery at a carnival with this gun in my pocket. I fire bullets at the glass bottles but my bullets bounce off them as if they are made of steel. I fire into them again and again and yet not one bottle will crack, not one damn bottle will take the bullet …

It's just the crush, superstition. Don't want your love, indecision. It's just a crush, strip it down, planted seeds of paranoia. Don't want your heart …

We're recording a new song in the Caffeine studio – me, Alabama, Butcher and Renato. I'm singing the lyrics from the train wreck of my life as the band pulverises a crystalline blues riff into a pyramid of shiny white powder. *And so it blows, blow by blow. Strip it down …*

The road is addictive. Loved ones tire of your absence and drift away and you know that fact and yet you're still drawn to the risk and the fascination of the unknown.

It's a shot in the dark …

The music is my cure, blues that cut to the heart of things, looking for answers when there's none to be found.

Peak-hour traffic, humidity and rain, inching through the São Paulo traffic towards the highway for Bragança. Hours pass as the backdrop of unfinished concrete buildings covered in *pichu* roll by. Motorcyclists weave through the traffic tapping their horns. Trucks overheat and break down. Inside the car the air conditioning is feeble but the alternative, opening the windows to let in the noxious fumes of low-grade burning carburant, is worse. In a long tunnel I watch kids playing in a service shaft – around them, the torn cardboard boxes that serve as doss pads. It's hard to escape this city. By the time we do, night is falling and fat clouds are squatting on the lush green hills and valleys. Out here on the interstate, Brazil looks like a postcard from Vietnam.

Alabama takes a call, hangs up, says something to Butcher and they laugh that slow, heavy laugh I recognise from perverse

South American westerns where mean hombres laugh down life's cruel ironies in the void of a godless cosmos. Spotting his opportunity, Alabama U-turns through a break in the guard rail across a highway slick with brake oil and gasoline – Mari's car, carrying friends and equipment, has broken down a little way back and is pulled up behind the barriers of a roadwork site. In the drizzling twilight we remove our amps and band gear from their car into our own and sadly watch them dwindle into the fumes and headlights as we take the next bend, already running late for tonight's show.

In the Bragança club, television screens pump heavy-metal videos from the golden eighties into an empty room. There are no stage monitors for the band, and the promoter provides me with a twelve-watt guitar amp for a vocal wedge. Alabama, Butcher and I convene outside in the falling rain.

How does this work? I ask. How do we do this?

Just go with it, says Butcher. I mean, I know the situation is weird but that can be cool too, you know, like *Metallic K.O.*, you know what I'm saying?

Alabama just keeps loading in the guitars and backline shrugs, waiting for one of us to decide.

Look, says Butcher, with Mari and the friends stuck out on the highway, the least we can do is play the damn show.

Paradoxically, the sound is excellent. A strange crowd rapidly convenes. Butcher chills the tempos and the audience of bikers and jungle desperadoes groove on the extended psychedelic instrumental passages. It's easily the best show so far and afterwards we drink cachaça distilled with honey, a golden-brown liquor that tastes like the food of gods, while a petrolhead lays a monologue on me over the heavy metal music from the bar stereo – My bike is my girlfriend, my wife and my mother, man, my bike is everything. I'm nothing without my bike, because my bike is me, you know what I mean? She's my woman!

Back on the interstate, the night hurtles past. What do we call this band? I ask them. We need a name by now.

How about, like, The Moses? Butcher suggests.

The Moses Whip? Like God's big Old Testament stick?

No, the whip is too dark. What about Complex? As in, everything's really fucking complex, as in all the time?

Ok, the Moses Complex …

The glow of São Paulo fills the night sky as we streak back into town on the empty early-morning highways.

Southbound for Curitiba, tall rainforest palms and mountain pines rise out of the fog and the drizzle never stops. From a high curve we see the massive traffic jam below and Alabama starts his chuckle of doom, a reefer clenched in his jaws while he gently handbrakes our descent. One lane is closed, and the other is punctuated with huge holes and slick with mud and oil. The sugar-cane ethanol fumes snaking through the air-con merge with the *maconha* smoke and the windows fog up. Traffic stops altogether.

Vendors stroll barefoot between the lanes selling hot peanuts in paper cones, bananas and hard candies. Directly in front of us is a panel van, spray-painted black. Even the numberplates, taillights and windows are spray-painted black – a kind of do-it-yourself hearse. The door opens and a tall, balding man emerges and stares at us through the windscreen, then approaches and signals to Alabama to get out of the car. The man is wearing a leather pouch around his waist.

That's where he keeps the scalps and fingers, Butcher remarks, all kinds of people out here in the hills.

Alabama stays in the car, rolls the window down. In dialect the bounty hunter tells us, Three to four hours minimum, I got it on my radio.

Sure enough, we inch along the highway all afternoon until the skies suddenly open up on an exquisite indigo twilight and the city of Curitiba appears as a sprawl on the horizon.

The Wonka basement is packing out fast. Seventies punk bands cavort in nostalgic, grainy black-and-white on the video screens. Street hustlers strafe the crowd bumming change and cigarettes. Patrons chop stardust in the stalls while full bladders hammer on the doors. Halfway through the set, the promoter cuts through the sardined crowd with a tray of beers for us and wipes the sweat off my face with paper napkins.

After-show, with no backstage, I'm stuck in the crowd signing records. We've already sold out the merchandise and I'm in a hurry to leave. A brunette with chemical eyes bars my way and digs her nails into my palms hard enough to break the skin.

Alabama drops me at my hotel where the key card self-destructs in the slot and I reconstruct the room's power unit in total darkness listening to my own shallow breathing and the amped-up beating of my heart. After the noise and the rush and the press of things I feel the silence and the stillness envelop me in a cold, tingling embrace.

Waking up, it takes me a while to figure out where I am. These mornings are becoming progressively more disorientated. Feelings are becoming increasingly third person after months on the road as I struggle to keep my demons under lockdown.

Intense heat beats down on the inscrutable streets and the starving emptiness inside me overrides all other thought. I devour a deep-fried banana and drink a freshly juiced mango *vitamina*, purchase a toothbrush, buy a chip for the mobile phone, sort through email in a gloomy internet shack, reboot my mind and head into the gathering rain clouds.

Below Curitiba the landscape turns German – Hamburg Süd international freight terminal, Kraus machine repairs, signs to the Deutsche Ecke, Mercedes dealerships and billboards for *stollen,* a traditional German Christmas cake. The past travels with us. Emigrants carry it everywhere they go, their traces still visible in this pseudo-European landscape aglow from the summer rains. Meanwhile, the bootprint of the USA looms large – huge shopping malls and housing estates under construction sprawl along the highway, overseen by a giant green copy of the Statue of Liberty with the face of a man, the garish mascot of a supermarket chain.

You can always pick the tourists, says Butcher, like the backpackers at a roadstop greasy spoon, they wear the indigenous stuff, those damn beads and ponchos and cotton hippie pants. Brazilians would never wear that stuff. Not even real índios wear that stuff. Everyone prefers some Nike trainers and a tracksuit. If you offered the average Brazilian the choice of two identical products, one Brazilian and the other US-made, side by side, nine out of ten Brazilians will select the American option. Because people think that anything we can do, they can do better. And in reality, they make a lot of things that we're not able to make at all. But a lot of the raw materials, they source 'em here where the price is cheap.

The holiday apartments of Florianópolis rise above a bay framed by spanned bridges and we cross over to the island and cruise slowly through what could be a coastal resort in Sydney's northern beaches or the Gold Coast.

As night falls on the vacation island, so does my mood. The stalker won't give up and I won't give her the encouragement of a reply. Her madness invents baroque new forms of self-expression, running like teletype across the back of my brain. I press delete on Butcher's keyboard and cut all the internet connections; banshees howl in the distance. In the meantime, the man has been and gone and my teeth are frozen cold by pure blow.

On the bandstand at the John Bull in downtown Floripa the crowd groove and jostle, clustered around close enough to touch. The Moses backbeat loosens me up and I step over the monitors and play to the crowd. The music is very fast, even though these ninety minutes appear to unfold in slow motion. When the show is over, time slows down further to an eerie crawl. I look around the venue and the crowd and realise that I am trapped here.

I smoke a million cigarettes to fumigate the emptiness, but nothing really helps.

Four hours later, I wake up cold and confused, unsure of where I am. I pull on my jeans and checking my pockets, realise the money from last night is gone. I feel like an idiot, like I had it coming, like a loser – better shake these thoughts, get some air. On the path to a wild beach near the head of a blood-red river, a huge tarantula crosses in front of me, big as a rat and covered in black hair. The stalker revisits my thoughts and I see her pulling a gun on me in a backstage if I ever go back that way again, feel the metal tip penetrate my rib cage, hear them calling for the ambulance. The tarantula parts the grass with its forelimbs and disappears into the underbrush.

I climb the cliffs to feel how very close the edge is and contemplate the long drop to the rocks below.

Down at beautiful São Joaquim beach, the sand is hot and the water's cool and thick balls of cloud drift in a cobalt sky. At the bamboo-palisaded beach bar 'The Girl from Ipanema' oozes from the loudspeakers, big bowls of açai jelly are served with granola and yoghurt; fresh juice drips from the sugar-cane grinders, prawns doused in Tabasco, lime and pepper sizzle on the grill. Three bionic beach girls photograph each other rolling around in the sand in shiny wet bikinis. The one with the angel wings tattooed on her back keeps trying to catch my eye and when she does, quickly looks away and smiles. In the distance, a beach bum strums a nylon guitar and his friend bongos time on a plastic flagon. The perfume of *maconha* drifts through the air. This should be paradise, but I've brought all my baggage down to the beach, a mass of raw scar tissue, festering in the noonday sun.

In the roadhouse outside Joinville, a hard-luck-faced woman in a muddy car park chastises her kids as they fool around in the rain. The kids taunt her in return and she hurls maledictions at them, rocking a newborn in her arms. On the TV, a Latin country-music beauty pageant – showgirls with condor-feather headdresses and bareback rodeo riders in Stars and Stripes bandanas, followed by a competition for the best and biggest female ass in all Brazil, hosted by the infamous Watermelon Lady.

A newsbreak flashes images from the street fighting in Rio de Janeiro – burning cars, Black Hawk helicopters, the army in the slums with bulldozers razing illegal dwellings. Overhead, bunches of banana hang from the porch. We drive on south through the flatlands, garage rock blaring from the car stereo.

A suicided uncle haunts the house in Porto Alegre. Walls of Catholic iconography, statues of the Virgin Mary, family photos going back generations, everything faded from the entropy of a passing generation. I know I will not really find sleep in this sombre bedroom, vacated by an aged couple in such haste that they left all their personal effects where they were – the Portuguese bibles, the Cabbalistic symbols, the portraits of the saints, the Christian aphorisms sewn into the hems of yellowed doilies.

The night bus for Uruguay leaves at sunset. The blonde Germanic bus line hostesses speak in rapid-fire Spanish; they take our passports and we take our seats. After a few hours the lights go out – the unlit highway is scarcely trafficked and the bus is plunged into semi-darkness. A baby cries and Butcher falls asleep next to me. The phantoms smack their lips and come to visit; they know I have no way to escape them for the next twelve hours. I swallow some Temazepam and drift off to the rhythm of the wheels, against my will, because I know my dreams will be poisonous fantasies.

They were just waiting for me to leave town. But I'm back now with kamikaze calm and nothing to lose, fighting evil with ruthless glee now that life has revealed its core emptiness; the transition from pacifist to murderer is just a step in the dark, blood on my hands, blood in my eye. I look around the bus and notice the seat upholstery is covered in blood. Viscera trails down the corridor. Nobody seems to notice the carnage – the telltale bloody handprints on the windows, the hair stuck to the roof. I tie a rope to a fixture in the water closet to hang myself from. It will take them days to notice me because I am a black hole – no light gets in or out of me. I'm ready to drop when there's a knock on the door …

I wake up, coming to my senses at the Montevideo bus terminus. I order a coffee at the bar but the power suddenly fails, plunging the whole place into darkness. Outside, a car alarm is howling. People move in slow motion or stay stock still where they are.

I walk out into the blazing heat to be immediately vaporised by the light reflecting off the Silver River, big as an ocean, Argentina on the other side. I'm dematerialising into nothing, the molecules busting apart in a domino effect of tiny fissions and I think this just could be the perfect place to disappear without even really trying.

Montevideo high street – pick-up trucks, rusty utes and rococo cathedrals, twenty-five dollars for a cup of coffee. The dispossessed drift in from the hinterlands like water dripping slowly from a leak in the scheme of things. On foot or riding mule-drawn carriages laden with bundles wrapped in garbage bags and tied with string, they move among the skyscrapers and business travellers and fashion victims and rich kids like phantasms from a bygone era.

A teenage girl, heavily pregnant in a tight halter top exposing a long caesarean scar across her belly, lingers outside a hamburger joint with her mother and little brother and cadges a smoke from her mum's packet and lights up, exhales with relish. The mother resumes pushing her supermarket trolley.

There's a party going on near the water under a dark moon; a lot of local movers and shakers, musicians and filmmakers are there. The blow is all around and the people talk on automatic – animated, charming, repetitive, a little too friendly until it tires you out, smiling. Vodka sours, caparinhas, cocktails.

Are you alright, man? asks the retired rock singer with tombstone teeth and eyes like burning dark coals.

Yeah, I'm good, bud, I reply.

He squints and smiles again, You're sure?

Whatever ails me, his shit can't fix it.

Looking around at this crew, marooned on a remote colonial coastline similar to where I came from, I see an aura of collective isolation and realise we're all cousins of the southern hemisphere's lost worlds.

In the long shadows of morning the workers and the homeless drink gourds of *mate* tea through metal straws on the broad city streets while cleaners sweep the cracked pavements in slow motion. Classical music plays quietly from the loudspeakers in a city park. Blood sausage and dark chocolate sweat in a cafe window. Montevideo is slowly waking up to the low rumble of buses and ancient trucks. I crash at the hotel, and a few hours sleep later meet Alabama and Butcher in reception and we eat steaks to take the edge off the hangover. Freedom is hard work. Freedom can be lethal. We're light, loose, barely tethered, and still one more week of the road to go.

The silhouette of Argentina heaves into view across the vast silver estuary, punctuated by the high-rise towers of Buenos Aires. An hour to retrieve the luggage in a ferry terminal with dysfunctional air conditioning and I'm a borderline crack-up coming apart at the seams. I'm struggling to shake off this psychopathic mood swing, breathing deeply in the back of a taxi gridlocked in the downtown traffic. Juani, our Argentine promoter, sits in front, remarkably charming and hospitable. I watch the Bourbonic architecture and tree-lined boulevards pass and begin to sense magic here.

The Especial club is a series of large rooms with an expanded glassed-in mezzanine affording views of the stars and the city skyline. Only a limited number of patrons are allowed on any given night since the notorious nightclub fire in Buenos Aires several years ago. Downstairs, the club is filling up fast. Performance transpires in a blur of rhythm and electricity, a hell-raising live set in front of a riotous audience.

Departure is at 5 a.m., and we burn the night down to embers. The taxi driver has a gaucho ponytail and a biker beard and a taxi customised with CB radio fittings and a techno-pumping sound system and we're bulleting across Buenos Aires, airport-bound. The bubble of transient star reality bursts as we haul our gear across a rain-soaked footpath into departures and confront the iron-fist bureaucracy of uniformed, middle-aged civil servants in bulletproof glass booths. At the gate the ground crew examine our documents again while large brown cockroaches scatter around our feet in the direction of the air bridge.

In the arrivals hall at Porto Alegre a burly middle-aged man holds up a sign with my name handwritten on it. In the shower of a high-rise hotel, thoughts slip through my fingers and disappear down the drain. The venue is nearby, a huge glass greenhouse box in the museum of culture with a high, raised stage and a powerful, professional sound system. The local promoter pays us upfront in cash and we split the money three ways in the dressing room. Onstage, the room's abundance of light and air bounces through my emptiness unhindered, like photons in a particle accelerator. Several people are dancing in the seated crowd and the nervous promoter asks us to turn it down – but that's one thing we can't do, this beast operates on volume. The sweat is draining out poisons through my skin, scouring toxins from my soul. I love the music. It's the only thing keeping me together.

The tour's finished and we're chilling out on beautiful São Joaquim beach. Butcher and Alabama mix caipirinhas, watching the breakers roll in. I strip off and feel the ocean's power drag me out to where the Surfers for Jesus are riding the waves. The Surfers have come here from the drug scene and the jails and the gangs to find God and repudiate Satan here on the big Atlantic swell; they recruit souls and hold revivals on the beach, teaching the local kids about surfing and Zen and the Gospels.

Maybe there really is redemption in these waters. The breakers crash through me, shedding old skin, salt disinfecting the wounds. Big ocean birds hang suspended on high thermals, reefs of white cloud float across the sky; I'm superimposed on this scene, a last-stop beach poised on the lip of the world. I can feel my ego shrinking as my ambitions and pleasures become increasingly ludicrous. I let the ocean carry me along, my heart beating against the tide. My mind goes blank and my spirit starts slipping away until, out of nowhere, my girl's emerald eyes pierce the nothingness and I remember her words – Everything carries me to you, darling, and always will …

Slowly at first but with gathering speed I break into a stroke, headed back to shore.

The Bridge to Nowhere | Italy, 2012

The shop girl is very pale, very thin, dressed in nun-grey and somewhere between twenty-five and sixty years old, depending on the light and the angle. Another girl does invisible business behind a parallel counter, maybe her sister judging from the similar glare of Catholic disenchantment on their faces. Half tobacconist and half random items – cigar snippers, jalapeno good luck charms, *tarocchi* cards – this two-thirds empty shop is ready to fold beneath its own entropic weight, just like the entire city of which it is but one fading particle.

Posso aiutarla, she asks – Can I help you?

Shaving cream, I explain, and she unlocks a dusty glass cabinet where military-green canisters of Proraso line up on a shelf like landmines, shipped from the factory thirty years ago when a curious neighbourhood shop such as this was still a viable business. She shuffles the creams back and forth across the glass counter and says – Like these?

Exactly, I reply, except in a more compact size.

Well, we do have a smaller one, the other girl says nonchalantly, pulling another canister from a lower shelf. The difference is negligible, but it's the only shaving cream I've found so far on the Via Plebiscito and I need to sharpen up after a thirty-hour flight because tomorrow, here in Catania, it's the opening concert of a three-week solo tour. The last show is in Milano and in between there are fifteen other concerts throughout Italy, promoting my new album of both famous and obscure love songs from the distant, romanticised past.

The first girl carefully wraps a sheet of *La Sicilia* around the time-smudged canister of Proraso, as if it were another timeless classic of Italian design, like the Sistine Chapel or the Reggio–Salerno highway. Later, when I unwrap the package, the page reveals itself to be *cronache nere*, local reports of sordid happenings – crimes of passion, homicidal vendettas and violent family feuds. The scrub-bearded jailbird face of a guy in his sixties stares me down from a mugshot, an itinerant vendor of shoes arrested up on the volcano near Nicolosi for trafficking crack cocaine.

The dawn is grey and humid, eyes half-open; I miss my girlfriend, I miss my kids. I don't recognise the room, but that doesn't disturb me as much as the insults traded by two unseen rancorous crones in the narrow lane outside the *pensione* window. This is a *zona popolare*, its ghetto frustrations ossified in black volcanic stone. The Via Plebiscito dialect is harsh and nearly incomprehensible and the rising tension in the quarrel sounds like the prequel to murder. I pull on my jeans and boots and head for the street markets at La Fiera.

Trestle tables loaded with fish, octopuses, live lobsters, masses of prawns and molluscs; great shanks of horse meat swathed in flies; giant artichokes and purple cauliflowers; sportswear; boxes of shoes and shirts of uncertain provenance; piles of Romanian Prada, Chinese Armani; Africans selling bootleg designer sunglasses and pirated DVDs. I buy a strict black Sicilian suit and tie and a pair of beautiful brogues and a punnet of Siracusan strawberries and sit down at the Bar Mirella with a copy of *La Sicilia*.

La Sicilia has a very tight focus, publishing almost no news from the world outside Sicily, let alone beyond greater Italy. Gravitating to the *cronache nere*, I pick up on the story of a priest arrested for paedophilic practices; remanded for trial, he's been invited back to the parish priests' quarters in his diocese of Acireale for an Easter feast of pizza and doves. The community is outraged but the Church makes no comment.

It's in the warp of things here that wrongdoings and kindnesses are equally obfuscated by paradox and contradiction. Catania is an Ancient Greek city beneath a medieval city beneath a pseudo-modern city, folded over on itself like a *cartocciata*, one of those intricate savoury pastries that make up the high-calorie lexicon of the *tavola calda*. Repeated eruptions of Etna have buried the city's layers like tomatoes and bechamel over leaves of lasagna pasta.

Archaeological excavations in Catania inevitably produce relics and, if not done to procedure, the wrath of the national trust. A planned subway system to ease the extreme traffic congestion has been delayed since the 90's; digging beneath the beautiful rococo Via dei Crociferi, excavators recently found a dense cachet of baby bones in a tunnel under the street connecting a Benedictine monastery with a Carmelite nunnery, grim artefacts of the dialectic between repression and desire.

Massimo, Marcello, Cesare, Bepe and I are lounging around with drinks in the shadowy Lomax theatre after the first concert of the tour. Old friends, the guys guested with me tonight as they did on the recording of this new album; but the talk is of another old friend of ours who died very suddenly yesterday and was swiftly buried this evening high up on Mount Etna in the baroque village of Nicolosi.

Non ci posso credere, mutters Cesare – It's unbelievable.

Ehi, si! Sono incazzato nero! Bepe says with carnivorous relish – I'm fucking furious! *Minchia!* Shit priests with their incense and all that crap, he would've fucking hated it! It's the ultimate irony of his fucking life! But the mother and the family of course they insisted on a Catholic burial, even if they're not that religious anyway, insisted on all this religious bullshit to bury a man who didn't give a damn about any of it, I mean, his liver exploded before he'd even reached fifty years of age and he never even told anybody he was sick! A man who drank and snorted like hell to defy the moral dogma of an institutionalised hypocrisy he despised! Hymns and Latin catechisms! Like spitting on his grave!

Corrado is at the wheel of the car puffing on an electric cigarette, his cameras and lenses and battery packs strewn across the clothes and newspapers on the back seat. Marcello's cherry-red DeArmond semiacoustic is in the boot of the Yaris along with a spray canister of deoxidant cleaner, several large candles from the Catholic merchandiser on the Via Vittorio and a box filled with exotic pastries, *tavola calda*.

We drive south past the Catania city limits and the signs pointing to *la fiera dei morti*, the market of the dead. Every year on November 1st, All Saints' Day, kids are taken to the cemetery to lay flowers at the graves and then to the *fieri dei morti* to receive presents from their deceased grandparents or whoever else in their family no longer walks among them, keeping them close.

Corrado's pale blue eyes watch the chaotic traffic wearily, ready for any surprise the streets throw our way – rogue driver, police barricade, religious procession, a ball bouncing from a kids' soccer game, a donkey cart or a ghost-riding teenager on a stolen *motorino*. Corrado is an intense, politically motivated photographer, twenty years younger than me. Friends for several years, we've been on the road together before but this morning he seems different – his eyes are dazed and distracted, and lurking in their depths I sense something he wants to tell me but can't bring himself to express. Through my haze of exhaustion I start to wonder if both of us will be able to last the distance from here to faraway Lombardy.

The Ragusa road cuts inland past Iron Age cliffs ravaged by Ionic winds, meeting the coast again near the oil refinery at Priolo. The sixties-vintage petrochemical plant reeks of methane and belches fire from candy-cane smokestacks. Corrado winds the car windows shut.

The cancers, premature deaths and birth defects in this area are well documented, he says. My family is from Siracusa, and we, everybody really, we've known about it for years, decades even. There's a very scary video report on the subject but you won't see it on Italian television because, like everything else here, it's a political issue.

Managed for sixty years by successive Christian Democrat administrations and the Mafia, Sicily has about 10 per cent of the Italian population and 10 per cent of seats in Parliament. The collective vote has been reputedly manipulated since the Second World War. The petrochemical plant at Priolo, like its cousins at Barcelona and Gela, dates from the Fascist era and is now partly owned by Russian giant Lukoil. There are no plans to wind these installations down.

As twilight falls, Corrado pulls over at one end of a long bridge spanning a deep valley in the hills on the outskirts of Ragusa. Wind whistles through the quivering reeds; circus posters peel from concrete pylons.

Il ponte suicidio, he says – The suicide bridge; from here they jump to eternity.

At the cultural centre in Ragusa, copies of an anarchist newspaper are stacked neatly on the bar, the front page reporting new oil-drilling speculation in the Val di Noto and calling for civil disobedience campaigns. Aproned ladies prepare antipasto – cheese, pepperoni, *salsa piccante*, potato chips, tiny hunks of focaccia. In this cosy scene, random drop-ins talk through the sound check while I'm getting shocks off the microphone's frayed electrical wiring.

By nine, the club is so crowded latecomers can't get in. Afterwards, we smoke outside in the freezing wind while hungry-eyed local musicians ask me questions about the scene on the mainland, not far away but too expensive for them to visit.

È l'Australia? They ask me, *come è? Bellissima?* People with relatives there speak of it as a kind of Promised Land. I say nothing to undermine their dreams.

At three in the morning the promoter drives us to a magnificently decrepit villa exposed on a promontory of rock seven hundred metres high with a ravine plunging away to one side. A savage wind howls through the villa's porous joints, thrumming the windows like drumskins. It was built in the eighteenth century for a wealthy city family; time has stripped it skeletal. We switch on a couple of two-bar electric heaters and prepare black tea to bolster us against the shattering rain and the howling banshee wind.

In the morning, we stop for coffee and *cornetti* in a tiny hilltop town. There's a guy in the bar drinking a shot of grappa, a dead ringer for the actor Tony Curtis. This similarity might have been the bane of his existence because it's pretty early for a shot of the hard stuff and he looks annoyed with me for noticing him at all.

Tony Curtis? I whisper to Corrado.

Fonzie, he replies, you know, *Happy Days*.

But Corrado doesn't look happy; the rings under his eyes are broader and blacker this morning, a thin resin of cold sweat sparkling on his brow. I ask him what's wrong and he just winces and presses his hand against his side.

Are you okay, man?

Yes, he replies, washing some pills down with water. It'll pass. Where the hell are we, anyway?

I look around at this landscape that time forgot and reply – Deep in the Bronze Age. He laughs slightly and I say to him, Look, man, do you want me to drive? But he just looks away and shakes his head.

The GPS navigator loses satellite connection as the mountains wrap around us in a mix of abandoned highways and Greek ruins. Neolithic dolmens surface among the tall cacti and swaying reeds and stringy eucalypts fringing the roadside. On the far side of Caltanissetta we encounter last night's east wind again, the car shuddering in its icy, cyclonic blast. As we pass Palermo, sunbeams power down through the clouds, framing the psychotic ballet of Sicilian drivers jostling for position on a four-lane highway lit up like a Michelangelo masterpiece. The sun finally sets over the Trapani saltpans, windmills silhouetted iridescent orange on the island's far west coast.

Tonight in the club there are too many people and the sound system isn't powerful enough to drown out the chatter. My solo show is largely ballads, all of them in English. I like the sense of intimacy and vulnerability this allows me to project and the heartfelt connection these songs can establish with the audience. Every performance is different: some nights you can sweep the people along with you, and then there are nights like tonight where you can just quietly die alone on the bandstand.

After the show we follow the promoter to a *pensione* in another town twenty miles away. Light rain falls, smearing an oily film of streetlamps across the windshield. Corrado steers distractedly with one hand while arguing on the phone to his girlfriend who seems to be having a conversation with several other people at the same time. Meanwhile, the promoter's taillights recede, blurring into all the other anonymous red spots in the distance. Corrado suddenly pulls over on the highway shoulder. I can hear the girl shouting like a lunatic over the background noise of a party and see the distress in his eyes. When she hangs up, his mobile reignites as the promoter calls through, asking where the hell we've gone.

Ci siamo, says Corrado wearily, *no problema.*

We eventually find our man in the main street of a mysterious little town in the back hills of Trapani province. He hands us the keys and drives off into the night and we let ourselves in to a strange and musty *pensione*. The air is stale with neglect, fixtures dissolve in our hands, taps fall from sinks, light bulbs blow, curtains rip; we are destroying the place without even trying. Corrado accidentally locks his key in his own room. There's no one in the building but us. Outside, the alien town is utterly still.

C'mon, man, I say. There's got to be a way.

Corrado looks at me for a few seconds and then his eyes light up as he pulls a card from his wallet, walks down the hall and swiftly, silently, slips the lock of his door, *click!*

The hotel laundry ignites at seven-thirty, the waters rushing through wall tubes behind my head. Confused by lack of sleep and annoyed by the hotel's stark hostility, I wander out into a grid of sandstone buildings. Mountains of granite surround it on three sides and to the west sparkles the distant Mediterranean.

We drive out onto a plain where the concrete spans of a vast bridge dominate the landscape like a futurist Roman ruin. There is no way to get on or off this unfinished hunk of highway, the enigmatic product of a shady deal between the state and private contractors. Here below, the wind is fierce, the fields rustling with wildflowers and reeds. Corrado is shooting a video using the bridge as a background; I'm playing guitar and miming to a song from my new record blasting out of the car stereo, sunglasses on to keep the wind-whipped grit out of my eyes. Conceived in one continuous take, the video has to be right from start to finish. Occasionally a vehicle traverses this little unnamed byroad so we reset positions, return the CD to the head of the track and begin again.

Over my head towers the bridge to nowhere, suggesting a world where perverse dreams can be realised in plain view and no one asks questions. From Brussels to Rome money moves in mysterious ways. In the Italian electoral system, billions of dollars are unaccounted for. At the opposite end of the country, Treasury investigations into the right-wing Lega Nord and its campaign funding have sparked a major scandal.

Northern League leader and bellicose demagogue Umberto

Bossi created a political machine rooted in the dismay of Italy's industrial north, which over the space of a generation has been utterly transformed by immigration and neo-conservative politics. The Lega is agitating to break away from southern Italy to establish a semi-independent state free of Rome's control.

Bossi holds a charismatic grip on his supporters even after a stroke prematurely aged him nearly ten years ago. Bossi's two spoilt sons, groomed to succeed the tribal throne, are now at the heart of the scandal regarding public funds – money magically morphed into luxury cars, university credentials and second mortgages, even pipelined further afield into untraceable accounts in legal black holes like Tanzania. Photos of the Bossi boys go viral as the media feeds on the nation's political tragicomedy.

The Lega is a key ally in Berlusconi's ruling coalition. Now that the scandal is public knowledge the Lega is under pressure to sack fraudulent ministers, yet those implicated refuse to recognise any proof, manoeuvring to save themselves from demotion and criminal proceedings; the trick is to retain parliamentary immunity. Somewhere, not far away, legions of lawyers score stratospheric sums processing the litigation.

The club in Palermo is a high-class venue in the gentrified streets around the old port precinct. The room swims with light and perfume and mirrors and beautiful women with their high-rolling boyfriends – perfect for this session of romantic love ballads and sensual crescendos. I break down the distance between us by telling the audience little stories about love gone wrong and the tangled webs we weave, how sometimes we find ourselves becoming the kind of people we never wanted to be in order to keep love alive.

Endless glasses of expensive wine are ferried to the stage as the music hypnotises not just the audience but me also, and I play long over time.

The *pensione* is a massive nineteenth-century building with giant arches opening onto a courtyard worn smooth by the hooves of Bourbon cavalry. The scale is vast, but there's no elevator; a concierge winches our luggage fifty metres into the air on a length of iron chain. The chain jams, my precious Samsonite swings in the wind and it feels like my life is hanging in the balance; I imagine the fall, the contents shattering on the giant flagstones. Everything we need and care about can be snatched away from one moment to the next. We live at our own risk, no guarantees.

The chaotic all-night traffic on the Via Roma won't let me sleep. *Carabinieri* streak by, sirens blaring. I check my phone – no messages. I'm loose, swallowed whole into the great unknown.

Corrado pulls over to the side of the highway and rests his head against the steering wheel. Eyes glistening, he finally reveals to me that he's suffering from a case of kidney stones so painful he can barely think. But no, I can't drive the car. And yes, everything will be alright. I don't believe it but I admire him all the same because a lesser man would have pulled out of this trip before it even started.

We stop at the next gas station for more painkillers. There's a display of pirate CDs and we buy some for the road – a couple of greatest hits of the seventies that turn out to be low-class re-recordings of the original classics, and a couple of bootlegs – *Lou Reed Live 1972*, a Johnny Cash compilation. I loosely translate Lou's song 'Vicious' to distract Corrado from the pain as he drives.

When I explain what swallowing razor blades means, he slaps the wheel and tells me that's exactly how he feels right now and laughs until the tears glitter on his cheeks.

It's another intimate affair tonight in Brucoli, on the Golfo di Catania. No stage, no separation, and a tight circle of spectators. I ask the crowd – Has anyone here been betrayed by someone they loved? The girls with their glistening dark eyes and long black hair start whispering secrets to each other while the men up the back drinking lager softly jeer at the girls and the boys out in the street gun the engines of their *motorini* – everybody knows what this is about.

Later, I sit on the breakwater behind the club, opposite the beach where I took my kids to swim in the green waters sixteen years ago. Tonight these waters are a trapdoor into a more innocent time that somehow faded while I was travelling, dreaming and always busy – yet wondering why I was here and not there with them. You can't steal those years back again.

Above all else I'm worried about my girlfriend in Australia. She's going under the knife tomorrow and she's scared; I feel for her fear. We're in touch all the time by phone, net and text but nothing replaces being present. She insisted I go ahead with these concerts; when she breathes in the gas, I'll be playing a private last-minute show in Catania. I can feel my world ripping down the seams, splitting into parallel realities. In the process, I'm tearing too. I wonder stupidly what the point of all this could possibly be, then I recognise the club DJ's song drifting across the breakwater, a sentimental song that she loves. Hearing it out of the blue takes me back to a rave somewhere in the nineties – 'Don't say you're happy out there without me, I know you can't be'. Another life in a different time and place, rewinding before my eyes too fast to recognise.

An hour later on the road back to Catania, we're running out of petrol. I feed the machine twenty euro at a self-serve gas stop on the headlands over the bay of silence, 'Folsom Prison' booming out of the car's open doors. Across the dark turbulent waters, the scattered lights on the volcano's slopes vanish into a haze of erupting smoke and dust.

Emiliano looks every inch the criminal lawyer in his immaculate brown suit and pink shirt. Faceless, balding men in suits are running this country, he says. They call it a technical government, like it's some kind of science, but running a country should really be about human beings. We are flesh and blood, we laugh, we cry, we love. These politicians don't understand the heart of this country. Italy has been sold out to the European Bank, to a bunch of bureaucrats. To them, it's all just numbers. But when we bleed, we bleed blood, not numbers. When I cry, these are tears from my human eyes, not numbers. And yet, that's exactly what they want to do, turn us all into numbers!

How's business? I ask.

They are beating down the door! Never enough lawyers for all this crime. The life of crime is going good! That's the system. Technical government! Look at them on the daily terror of the *telegiornale*. They don't even look like politicians, they look like deep-sea dwellers caught in the *frutti del mare* nets and dragged into the spotlight blinking their blind, pale eyes.

It's unbelievable, I say.

No, replies Emiliano, it is very, very believable. A lawyer from Cagliari wants to sue this new government because there is a constitution that says the government must be elected by the people! But it's a scam! Just another trick! Listen – you know Lockheed Martin?

Sure, by reputation.

Well, they are selling their new jet fighters to Italia. Each one sixty-five million euro, paid for by the people's money. But if you lose your job, you get nothing. If you lose your house, nothing. Because your taxes go straight to Lockheed Martin, with, you know, a few big pieces going to Italian business. Private business. In Italia they make the money disappear! Emiliano dusts his palms together with a loud slap. Just like that, he says. Now you see it, now you don't. An ancient tradition.

Like everywhere, I say.

Emiliano's spectacles flash in the light as he shakes his head – No! Here in Italia is different. There is the mystery tradition … It is different. From Italia, they exported the trick of the money mystery all around the world, starting a long time ago. Since the *quattrocento*, he explains, waving his hand in a reverse gesture over his shoulder. How you say? Fourteenth century, *si*.

Then he stops and takes a deep breath before continuing – In the meantime, Berlusconi's coke dealer is finally repatriated from Honduras to bear witness at the trial for his underage escorts! I tell you, letting the Italians run Italy is like giving a spaceship to a tribe of Neanderthals!

On the high mezzanine stage overlooking the bar I'm beating time with my boot heel on a block of amplified wood and cycling riffs while the crowd, hearing the guitar from out in the street, pack into the long room below me, their loud whispers and laughter almost nailing me to the floor. I had thought that being alone was what I wanted, what I needed, and yet there is this emptiness inside me that I get lost in more often than I care to admit.

I can't stop thinking about my girl, Alannah, thousands of miles away, lying on a hospital bed in a doped-out haze, prepared for the laser knife. My thoughts fracture with uncertainty: What if she doesn't wake up? How will I live without her in the knowledge that I wasn't there at the end? I'm so distracted, I'm not even aware of finishing one song and moving on to another. It's like I'm watching the whole scene from a slight distance while the night dissolves into white rum and cigarette smoke.

Later, in my hotel room, I anxiously wait for her to call while I watch the shifting mass of headlights and streetlamps on the Viale XX Settembre disappear out of sight in either direction. Around four a.m. I hear the electronic pulse of the mobile phone as it auto-illuminates on the bedside table. A message lifts the long night's despair – my girl's home, she's safe.

Huge waves of relief flood through me like some unknown wonder drug. It's been a long time since I felt this way about a girl – I talk to complete strangers about her; I worry and fret that this might be love, something I never dared do again. Maybe we never had control, but we know enough to stagger on through our strange, demanding lives in circumstances she and I never would have imagined when we first met as kids in the ferment of the eighties, all those years ago. The decades unwind as I rest my head back on the damp pillow and wish she was here with me and that I could look after her, but the parallel life of working in Europe often leaves me depleted of what that really requires. I listen to the quiet streets below – a dog howls, an early waking baby screams – but nothing can hold me back as I drift off to sleep and into a recurring dream.

The city is the usual nameless labyrinth of skyscrapers and flyovers, simultaneously unknown and strangely familiar, but this time I'm on my way to meet my girl after a long time away. My taxi hits an apocalyptic traffic jam on the freeway to the airport and by the time I arrive, the flight has left without me. I tell the faceless driver to turn around and head to the railway station but the last train of the day is just pulling out as I reach the platform, all of its carriages empty. I walk down to the bus depot but somehow it's already midnight and the place is closed and locked and the streets around me are completely devoid of people and cars. Far, far away I hear a phone ringing and reaching for it in the early light of dawn, her voice comes down the line as the world starts to slowly spin again, one more time …

I butt the reefer out against a grommet. It's a dark moon and the stars are few and the wind whips across the decking like a knife. The Naples-bound ferry *Pantelope* plunges through the troughs and crests, the scattered lights of Mount Etna gradually fading as we enter the Strait of Messina.

I imagine in the skies overhead the ghostly span of Berlusconi's dream bridge linking Sicily with mainland Italy, designed as his eternal legacy to the nation even as every year the island tectonically slips a little further away, towards Africa.

Down in the bulkhead, Chet Baker croons 'Let's Get Lost' from Corrado's laptop. I sleep with the roll of the ship, waking in a fugue of grey marine dawn light to the Neapolitan-accented bullhorn announcements of arrival. Truck drivers congregate at the bar for early-morning espresso and freshly baked *cornetti* full of tongue-scalding Nutella. We buy cheap black-market Marlboros as the ferry shudders into dock and talk to some friends from the band Colapesce, travelling like us from Sicily by sea to avoid the Reggio–Salerno highway to hell.

Ciccio explains that Colapesce was a diver so famous that Swabian King Federico of Sicily demanded he dive below Sicily to discover what was there. Colapesce found three cracked columns supporting the island in imminent danger of disintegration and chose to remain there, holding the columns upright to keep Sicily from sinking.

In another version, Ciccio continues, Federico commanded Colapesce dive deep beneath Mount Etna to discover the world's interior. Colapesce reported back that below Etna there was only fire, feeding the volcano. When Federico demanded proof, Colapesce dived again with a staff of wood, but only the staff floated back to the surface, charred.

The port of Naples expels us into a grinding crush of traffic and roadworks. We orientate by Vesuvio's volcanic silhouette through a series of ambiguous double-backs and low-cost flyovers, picking up the A16 at the foot of the Apennine mountains to drive up into the hills. The Campania region is desolate and paradoxical, its slow-motion lifestyle an act of resistance against endemic bad luck. Yet unlike wild Calabria further south, Campania is a densely populated zone where savage topography meets low-cost urban infrastructure in a lose/lose situation, towns sprawling into one another in a maze of unnamed roads, garbage and minimal signage.

Rain falls on the scaffolded central piazza of Avellino. An earthquake razed this town thirty years ago and the scars are still visible. Surrounded by hills nearly a kilometre high, the city is a reconstruction work in slow progress.

Serge and his girlfriend Anna are serving lunch. My cousin Gianfranco, says Serge, was only released a few months ago from jail after a thirty-year sentence for conspiracy with the *Brigate Rosse*, the Red Brigades. The main leaders escaped to South America through the covert intervention of the secret services but the small fish in the ranks of the BR were exposed, tried and sentenced. In the 1970s, there was a darkness in everything; everybody knew, but nobody spoke of these things while they flooded the streets with heroin, just to keep the underclasses quiet.

Anna dresses the salad and delicately passes the plates around like a girl in a house of glass.

They built this high-tech jail up in Lombardia, she says quietly, near Voghera, to house hundreds of so-called terrorists, mostly Marxist students agitating for a utopian revolution. In jail they had no newspapers, no television, virtually no contact with anybody. Even the books their families sent them were rationed, five pages a day individually scissored out of the binding. The ideological wars are long over. Nobody cares about that shit any more.

And Gianfranco, continues Serge, just got out of jail at the age of fifty-three after serving a life sentence for treason or some bullshit like that. A changed man, you know, just like anybody you'd see in the street. Some say a new revolution against the banks and the Vatican will soon be necessary. I very much doubt this will happen. But if it does, my cousin Gianni won't be taking part. The poor guy is just trying to find his way in the changed reality of now after decades of isolation.

Corrado and I wait in Sarno's concrete piazza for another local promoter to answer his phone. Promoters never answer their phones; it's easier for them to keep you hanging on until you wonder why and when and how you're even here at all – then you're at their mercy. Time slows to a glacial crawl. We watch the inscrutable septuagenarians around us play *scopa* and sip Moretti beer. Children trade insults and play 'dodge the passing motorcyclist'.

Some ten years ago, Sarno was flooded, then buried by mudslides; the psychic aftershock still hangs in the air. Most of the old town is unsafe, barricaded off. A text comes through giving the address of tonight's *pensione* but the GPS navigator can't locate the street. Schoolkids tell us the way – down a long country road with dry-stone walls either side, finishing up in the shadow of an autostrada overpass. When we finally locate the street, it turns out that the number doesn't exist.

The holiday apartment is in the basement of a concrete palazzo, cold and dank with the earthy odours of underground. The feature wall of the *salotto* is a wallpaper vista of a tropical beach; in the middle of the room there's an exercise bike on a circular rug. I tell the proprietor, a tough bird in her sixties, that I don't want to sleep underground –could we can take a room upstairs, maybe one with a balcony?

The *signora* glares at me and raises her voice – But this isn't underground, she exclaims, it's a little bit of both! You have all the natural light you need!

Well, where is the window? I ask.

Right there, she snorts indignantly, right there in front of you! And points to a window high on the wall leading up to a grate in the courtyard where I can just make out a fingernail-coloured sliver of peeled sky.

The theatre is full of ghosts, and people too. There's a bottle of Oban whisky near to hand and I nip into it, relishing the reassuring warmth it feeds into my blood.

'In the Pines', the first song, flows easily enough and after it, greeting the audience with the words 'Welcome to your town', people start to laugh while my mind fishes for gags like a stand-up comedian. I try different approaches in my strangely accented Italian, checking to see if I'm understood, searching for the joke, something ironic to close the gap between us. I speak of love and how it changes in the hands of different songwriters, how it means different things to everyone, how it messes with our lives, how we're lost without it, we're lost with it and in the end we're all lost anyway.

The human voice draws people in, channels universal emotions, more than the guitar and lyrics and electronics. Love needs no translation, it's veined through the sound. A song like 'Love Me Tender' has already travelled the world, like 'A Thousand Kisses Deep', or Suicide's 'Cheree'; there's a surprise factor in dropping these well-known songs into the set, a kind of jukebox shock effect. I put my own spin on these tunes, using my real life as a key to unlock them and transform their meanings.

Cops stop us on our way home after the show, bored, trigger-happy cops on a lonely road in the badlands of the Camorra. Corrado can't resist it, he's giving cheek and a whole lot of attitude to spare while they stare him down with their seen-it-all black-hole eyes. The cops repeatedly check all our documents, keeping us baled up into the small hours, sauntering backwards and forwards from their patrol car, talking on the radio with HQ. They seem determined to find a reason to detain us but in the end they lose interest and just ignore us as we drive away.

Back in the jailhouse holiday apartment, we smoke until dawn. Corrado talks about his mother; how she's in hospital fighting for her life. Meanwhile, my girl and I are arguing by text message. At this distance, the disconnect of time and life can start with nothing then escalate into a drama at lightning speed. Post-op drugs confuse the emotions, it doesn't take much to spark an explosion. When the birds start to sing, I'm still awake, scrolling through her long texts of doom and disappointment, the ground sinking beneath my feet.

The landlady's daughter makes strangely tasteless coffee in a breakfast room full of gaudy flowers while a girl and her boyfriend on the TV argue about their relationship in front of a studio audience. Rain patters against the windows, a symphony of autostrada traffic buzzing on the wind. The wi-fi doesn't work, of course. Cut off from my other world I step outside to catch a signal so that I can call my girl back. A Fiat sedan barrels into the cul-de-sac at excessive speed, missing me by inches. For a brief second I'm confused as to whether this is a reality talk show or a cop drama. Then the driver leaps out, spoiling for a fight, followed by a barking white terrier. Stickybeak neighbours watch from the apartment towers. Everything is under surveillance.

Minchia, says Corrado, *sono tutti pazzi* – They're all crazy.

There's a cafe down the road, large, dark and empty. The bar girl, her eyes glued to the screen, sings along with some excruciating Italian pop hit blasting out of MTV. We drink strong black espresso in silence.

Out on the *Nazionale,* signs for the archaeological site of Pompeii send us cross-country around the jagged summit of Vesuvio. After the earthquake city of Avellino and the flooded squalor of Sarno, we wander the Roman ruins where an entire population died in minutes flat inhaling noxious volcanic gasses. The energy there is palpable, the undead tending to their pools and gardens while tourists take snaps with their mobile phones.

Overshadowed by Vesuvio's smoking crater, Naples appears in the Mediterranean sunset like a futurist collision of centuries past. Graffiti-tagged baroque palaces sulk resplendent behind barriers of uncollected trash and explosive palm trees. Battered little cars shoot by at hallucinatory speeds between the exquisite statues and the architectural marvels, disregarding pedestrians, traffic lights and any common sense. The city howls with energy, writhes with eroticism.

An elderly *parcheggiatore,* speaking through a throat box, charges one shiny euro to leave our car unmolested while we search for our wayward promoter. You can never find your promoter; it's easier for them to remain unavailable until you start to wonder who you're working with, and for, and why – and by that point, once again, you're at their mercy. Carlo has not been answering his cell phone for a week and the hotel he booked for us no longer exists. We walk the narrow streets around the Spaccanapoli down to the club. Carlo is sitting in the cool dark of his bar, hungover after a fight with his girlfriend.

You know how it goes, he says, opening some cold bottles of Nastro Azzurro.

Yes I do, I reply, I know how this goes, man. It tears me up at night until I can't sleep, just laying there in a straitjacket of nervous tension.

Ah, you too? Carlo laughs. The thing is, I can never understand what it is that I do wrong! There's always something for her to get pissed about. None of it's under my control anyway. You see the city, the people here? You know what I mean? It's some kind of jungle, man. And the women get pissed with the situation, but what am I meant to do about it?

It's always the same, I reply, the whole damn thing – man, woman, breaking apart, coming together, it's normal.

There is no normal, Carlo says – *L'anomale e normale!*

He's right – the abnormal *is* normal. The idea of normality never made sense to me, particularly when you look below its surface at the mass of contradictions in everything we do, say, and pretend to be. After midnight the audience finally appears and time accelerates, the primal energy in the room heightening reality in a blur of raised voices, teased hair and flashing eyes. The show wraps at three in the morning; by the time we reach the Hotel Schilizzi, dawn is breaking again and I'm still totally wired.

We're at the central station. Naples grinds away in second gear – the sound of car horns, punctured mufflers, underground worksites; the smell of the sea, the humidity and chaos enveloping us in a slow-motion Old World embrace. I'm scribbling figures on the back of an envelope while Corrado and I divide the money into three piles. Junkies and panhandlers cruise the parking lot, peering hungrily through the windows of our car at the loose cash scattered across the dashboard.

I'm going to miss you, brother, I say, what'll I do without you?

I want to come north too, he says. It's been a long time since I saw friends in Bologna. But Mama's sick. I've got to go back, she needs more antibiotics. Maybe I can fly up to meet you in a few days and we'll just keep on driving. I feel better when I'm driving with you, man.

I stare solemnly at him, my throat squeezed tight with sadness – for him, for her, for all of us. I tell him I'm always here if he needs anything at all. He fades into the frenzied traffic blowing the klaxon goodbye. I look around the station piazza at the gypsies and tourists and students and cops, then start lugging my heavy bags through the terminal crush to the platform for an express train north.

Taking a seat on the *freccia rossa,* I thumb open a newspaper on the empty seat next to me: a grainy black-and-white photo of a sheeted body on a Rome street, cops and reporters surrounding it. This dead Mafioso, according to the text, had been in hiding since the nineties heyday of his gang, and was shot down last night heisting a local jeweller:

The gang only enjoyed a few years of absolute dominance after a lightning ascent that blew away all rivals, achieved through a network of deviant intelligence officers, rampant neo-fascists, bogus freemasons and corrupt bureaucrats. A river of drugs that changed the physiognomy of the streets, consolidated ties with the Mafia and the Camorra, bought and sold property, a giddy vortex of big money.

Then, they began to squabble between themselves, maybe because in this fast-changing world, their ferocity was no longer useful and hence their protection counted for less ...

The silver Fiat Punto, upholstered in pungent fake leather, glides out of the hire-car lot at Forlì airport, gearstick throbbing in my hand. Seven shows to go over eight days with two black suits, a credit card, a GPS system and a carton of Gauloises, cruising down the old Roman Via Emilia under a cloudy sky en route to the next show on the Adriatic coast.

Rimini is a quantum shift from the haunting paradox of Campania or Sicily. The streets of the elegant historic centre are full of fashion stores, girls out shopping and business types knocking back Campari and white wine at the end of another working day.

At the Neon Bar, the DJ is playing Dirtmusic's *BKO*, the lighting is low and the tipsy crowd spill into the street. There's nowhere to hide and I'm tired of being questioned or photographed, tired of new faces so similar to so many others already seen; with no back up and no backstage, my mind is elsewhere, focused on what I'm doing. The girls' obscure shy glances reflect my own exhausted stare. Look at me, but don't look at me. Listen but don't speak. Look at me all night long. Now leave me alone.

Nights on the road slip by, leaving in their wake a numbing psychic fog. Conversations and introductions blur into one another, names fade, city streets acquire new identities after midnight. Working alone, you have to keep double-checking little details like where and who you are and what happens next.

Another strange apartment, empty but for a queen-sized bed, the weight of history pressing down, the millions who already lived and died here, walked these streets, slept in these anonymous rooms. Waking in the pitch dark, I grope the walls searching for a door, a light switch, a clue to where I am, then stumble into the hall unsure if I'm dreaming or awake.

Music surrounds me, the sound of choral hymns. Slowly, my eyes adjust to the grey seepage of dawn light through window shutters, an adjacent Catholic church just metres away, the mass in full swing. As I splash cold water over my face a feeling of detachment overwhelms me, like I'm floating on the ocean in a life jacket, distant choirs warping on a sea breeze, the Christmas tree lights of a cruise liner receding into the waves.

I throw back the shutters on a clear, blue-sky spring day, a mountainous spine of the Appennini marching towards the horizon. Out on the autostrada, I open the throttle and the Fiat hits a relaxed cruising speed at 140 kilometres per hour, grapevine-studded fields stretching away towards the craggy silhouettes of Romagnan hills. I'm struck by a sense of being alone and answering to no one, a kind of total freedom.

Hours later, rain hits the flatlands. Traffic slows and condenses into clumps of big container rigs and erratic small cars randomly merging lanes, interspersed with the occasional high-end intercity cruiser, a Porsche or Maserati parting the steel curtain like a shark cutting through schooling fish.

This is the north, and after the rural desolation of the southern highways, its massed intensity reminds me of the world I come from – modernity, metal, carbon monoxide. Chain-smoking, I turn up the volume on *Time Out of Mind* and count down the kilometres through long, curving twin-carriage tunnels, then taking the exit on a Ligurian mountain top overlooking the seaside town of Spotorno, I descend the knotted road in third gear, mist wreathing the escarpments, the sea a turbulent slate grey, down into the maze of one-way streets blocked off for today's Labour Day holiday.

Along the *lungomare*, red banners of worker solidarity flutter in a chilly sea breeze like ghosts of the socialist *internazionale* – Italy is the only country in Europe where you might still see the hammer and sickle fly. The theatre foyer is crowded with glass display cases – handwritten notes, typed letters, fragments of maps, photos creased and worn, tattered medals, binoculars, a ribbon, an envelope, a poem in a child's hand, relics of the *partigiani*, the partisans who waged guerilla war under Nazi occupation.

From the windows in the backstage, I watch railway lights stretching into the distance quiver in the sea breeze. Simone, a young local songwriter with sleepless eyes, is getting ready to go onstage and open the night as the audience arrives.

The big question is to sing in English or Italian, he says. My heart tells me one thing, my brain another. My English isn't great, but it's the language of the music I love.

Onstage, Simone rants and moans, stalks the audience with his eyes, slashes at his guitar. I can't understand a word he sings, not that it really matters; his whole style is inexplicable. Afterwards he says – You know, this kind of music I do will never be popular in Italia. People don't want it. But it's what I love to do. So I can't stop. I will never stop, no matter what.

Good for you, I reply. I don't know how to stop making music myself. After a long while it's second nature, it becomes life, the illusion of life.

Yes, he says, everything is illusion, the glass at your feet, the guitar in your hands, the microphone and the people watching you in silence. It's a ritual that no one exactly remembers the meaning of any more.

But that doesn't matter, I reply. We're in the business of manufacturing memories, just an emotional illusion, here today, gone tomorrow. It's only music – but it means something real to people.

It's only music? he quizzes, unwrapping the cap on a bottle of grappa. I give him the wink and dust off the shot glasses.

The morning after, a downpour lashes the hotel parking lot and a migraine assails me as I struggle with the fractured remembering of last night – talking with people after the show, photos and autographs, the urgency of not leaving anything behind, the pervasive uncertainty of everything.

I keep glancing at the passenger seat, checking that the black briefcase is still there. Everything relevant to my survival is inside it – money, documents, pharmacy, electronics. I can't trust myself, can't trust anyone else in this hard concrete world, fragile as glass, where the grey sea heaves and the heavens spew forth lightning and sluices of cold spring rain. Dodging the holiday campervans through the mountains, I struggle to decipher the road in a shit fight of white lines and mirrors, Johnny Cash on the stereo in rhythm with the windscreen wipers.

The Autogrill is packed with slow-motion senior citizens wonderstruck at the corporate banality of the twenty-first century, strangers in a strange land. Over another espresso I scope this morning's *La Repubblica*: high-profile ex-showgirl Lega Nord parliamentarian Monica Rizzi resigns her membership of the Knights Templar, denying any conflict of interest between the clandestine society and her official duties. Rizzi has an insider connection with Umberto Bossi's *cerchio magico* – the 'magic circle' of the Lega Nord – where secret decisions are made by both decree and divination.

At first glance, the so-called magic circle refers to Bossi's inner sanctum of political strategists and crooked financiers, but in the pre-Alpine flatlands of Padania, medieval superstitions flourish in the blood-and-bone soil of a fascism 'lite' where Manuela Marrone, wife of Umberto and supernatural seer to the entire family, has guided the party's fortunes with grimoires of astral magick and tarot card readings.

Violent storms strike after the Piacenza highway exit, veins of fork lightning splitting a bruise-purple sky. I'm heading into the deep Italian north, a gathering at Maria's house in the provinces of Brescia for the extended Labour Day weekend. A group of old friends and relatives congregate at the kitchen table around excellent bottles of wine and trays of oven-roasted meats and vegetables.

My mother is a full-time job, says Danilo, a truck driver with a huge appetite and a dodgy liver. She's dying and needs, you know, a lot of attention. I swear, it never stops! It's like she's trying to torment me with her constant demands! What does she want from me that I'm not already doing?

Some people are just misunderstood, says Ivano, no one gets us! Like that Murdoch, he continues with a ready smile but no trace of irony – this phone hacking scandal was a set-up. He's got rivals in the media world, and they've got a big bag of dirty tricks.

You know that he's Australian? I ask.

That Murdoch is really Australian? Ivano replies – I mean, really? I had no idea. I thought he was an American.

Well, he's an American citizen now.

Such a great guy, it's terrible what they're doing to him. The destiny of giants, to be brought down by pygmies!

In broad Bresciano, an accent that bears a relationship to Italian like Scottish does to English, Danilo interrupts Ivano's bizarre locutions to offer a round of grappa shots before taking a tangent on Lombard wines.

All the varieties of grape in Italy, Danilo explains, like Brugnola, Barbera, Grignolino and so on, originally came from France after a mystery disease decimated Italian vineyards in the seventeenth century. They had to start all over again.

But this Nebbiolo, he says uncorking a bottle of white wine, the grapes were harvested by night, wreathed in fog, the drops of condensation still quivering on their taut blue skins. You like to drink? Danilo indicates a pantry behind the kitchen stacked floor to ceiling with elite vintages. In Italia, everybody drinks, he exclaims proudly – People know how to enjoy life!

Exactly, confirms Ivano. And Italians respect people who appreciate the best life has to offer. Take Berlusconi, for example. Decadent, yes, but so what if he buys his sex? These orgies are unreal – they have MDMA, PMDA, ecstasy, crack and what they call *brivido*, a mix of Ritalin and injectable viagra. The girls are all fourteen, and they're all given castles. And Gaddafi is picking up the bill! *Jesu Christo!* Berlusconi already has a penis enlargement and Bettino Craxi's kidney installed in his flank. Slush fund, trust fund, they're all in it together, just for the money. And hell, we can all understand that!

And sex, says Danilo. Sex and money, the good things of life. Anybody who says otherwise is just a damn hypocrite. Am I right or am I right?

You're crazy, says Maria giving him a slap over the ear. You talk a lot of shit. Now serve the polenta!

Later that afternoon, Davide and I weave our way down the *strada statale* to Brescia, both of us with one eye closed to better follow the white lines.

Police control? says Davide, squinting into the night. Don't you worry about it – they're all drunker than we are …

The Lio club is a dilapidated wooden saloon nestled between two intersecting railway lines on the outskirts of town. A Wild West feeling pervades the air. Trains thunder past in the twilight, feral dogs scrap by the boom gates. People arrive on motorbikes, in cars and on foot as the mountains fade into the night. By showtime the place is getting crowded and I find a sweet spot on the stage and expand the music using a grappa shot glass for a guitar slide. Davide steps up with his Jazzmaster and adds some ethereal guitar lines. The crowd howl for encores.

The band Sepiatone have arrived in the backstage, thick with smoke and hilarity, chewing over old times while the bar staff sweep out the venue. The four of us have been playing and writing together for twelve years and we share a history. It's good to see them; old friends are, like family, our only true reference in the unravelling map we trace through space and time.

The white noise of this Italian space odyssey is humming behind my eyes – the singularity of the road, the moments of intense meaning lost in long stretches of the absurd and the incommunicable. I sense myself rapidly ageing like Kubrick's sole surviving astronaut, staring into the enchanted mirror of a baroque, Italianate nowhere. Random thoughts arise as the subconscious slips its leash, like how easy it would be to fall through the cracks in this silver Fiat, drive it to Macedonia or Bulgaria and sell it, change my name, start a new life. Nobody knows where I am except the eavesdropping spooks that monitor my credit card and my mobile phone, just another ghost on the highway sweating in the raw sunlight until the temperature suddenly drops – an electrical storm is brewing up over Verona, lightning splitting the Alpine sky.

The city centre is jammed with people dressed in green and waving Lega Nord banners from some faux-medieval pageant. There is hysteria in the air, as if lynch-mob violence could randomly erupt at any second. Demagogues are inciting the crowd with militant rhetoric steeped in the brogue of the deep north, the accent making it hard to grasp, something about the thieves of Rome, traitors to the cause, hypocrisy.

Recognising I'm in the wrong place at the wrong time, I back out the way I came, following the GPS to the industrial zone. The club is big and the audience small and very enthusiastic. The performance spirits me away into a completely different mental space. Music is the medicine keeping me sane. Maybe it's the same for the audience queuing up to buy records after the show.

An early-morning jackhammer symphony rips me out of my sleep, disorientated, irate. All around, sunshine-bathed Alps and the blinding colours of spring. I'm up, down, happy, sad – everything is gut-wrenchingly emotional. I tell myself to embrace the strangeness without becoming desensitised – it's a long drive to the Lago Maggiore for tonight's private show in a country *osteria.*

Clouds gather overhead and traffic intensifies on the A4. Semitrailers dominate the roadscape, three lanes crowded in either direction.

I break at an Autogrill, park and walk inside, drink an espresso and some juice. The Lega Nord scandal and the Bossi boys are spread across the TV screens in the bar. The secretary of the Lega has resigned; black luxury sedans prowl through the streets of the Quirinale in Rome, ferrying the powerful *disgraziati* to their penthouses and private jets.

When I return to the *parcheggio*, my car has gone, disappeared, completely vanished! White-hot panic burns a laser trail through my blood – everything is in the car! It must be here … I pan around the asphalt lot – generic automobiles, corporate Autogrill logos, closed-circuit cameras. Check my pockets – keys, black tablet, receipts, aspirin, Gauloises. Then slowly I turn to look behind me. It takes a while to grasp the image – the silver Punto, stranded on a nature strip adjacent to the highway itself, and no crash barrier to prevent it rolling onto the carriageway.

Jesu Christo!

My briefcase is still on the seat – passport, money stuffed into an envelope, a stash of painkillers, antibiotics and eye drops, keys in a zip compartment. Two black suits hang from the roof over a guitar case coming apart at the hinges. A mess of magazines, newspapers and oddball gifts from strangers – discs, letters, stale pieces of cake – litter the backseat. On the floor are boots, discarded electronics, empty water bottles.

Butting out a half-smoked Gauloises, I grip the wheel with both hands as a sheet of spring rain hits the windshield and the autostrada pixilates into fractals of steel and tarmac. Near

Malpensa airport, the navigator loses satellite contact in these thick, pristine forests, lakes and mountains shimmering in the distance along the French frontier. Schoolkids describe the way to the *osteria* in the hills, an elite restaurant in beautiful nowhere, perfect for an illicit assignation or a wedding reception.

In the *osteria*, five guys in their sixties camouflaged for the hunt are necking a bottle of prosecco at the next table. With their macho *Boys from Brazil* vibe, they seem like retirees enjoying a holiday away from their wives after successful careers spent stepping on other people.

The Mediaset *telegiornale* plays on a TV over the bar, Lega Nord leader Umberto Bossi's minders attempting to shield him from intrusive journalists and cameras not far from where we're enjoying the springtime sunshine.

One man in a peaked Tyrolean hat says, I don't know why they bother the guy. You know, even if the allegations of the Bossi family's corruption are true, it doesn't change the way people feel about the Lega. It's a religious thing, a sense of faith in the party itself. Blood is thicker than water!

Another guy in aviator mirror shades and a Western hat says, Yeah, look at Berlusconi. Even after all the communist lies about tax fraud and cocaine and orgies with beautiful women and collusion with the Mafia …

Dio cane! says the third man, you can trust a man who knows how to properly enjoy life – look at them communist judges with their faces like dogs' assholes …

Well, yes, says Aviator Shades, but the point is none of this changes the way the faithful feel about their heroes. The people of freedom elected Berlusconi because he's a good businessman, not because he's a saint! Even if the commies take him down, the *cavaliere* will stay at the centre of power in Italy because that's what the people want, and this is a democracy!.

The guy in the Tirolean hat laughs and slaps the table with open palms.

The Bossi clan, he says, have simply done what anybody else would have done in their position – rip off the system! Because you'd be a fool if you didn't. Taking advantage of a situation is free enterprise, and free enterprise takes balls!

Next day, I walk through the village on streets of smooth round stones and out into the fields. Last night I might have got stuck into the grappa, too many people and not enough distance between us. Fragments of conversations under the influence, out-of-character recalls, non sequiturs. My nervous system is shot, and there's no one to pick up the slack. It really hit me this morning, but it's too late to turn back – I'm at the end of the run, out of reach, over the edge, beyond the pale.

The venue is a *centro sociale* on the outskirts of Cuneo, an underground concrete bunker, home to the local outsiders and artists and aspiring musicians. The show is incredibly hot and shatteringly loud and after it's finished hours pass talking to old friends from the zone until it gets late and people leave for distant towns to relieve their babysitters.

I load the Fiat and drive through the small hours to the Hotel Nettuno on the Strada Statale in a nearby town. They're cleaning up after some huge reception in the restaurant. I ask a uniformed waiter for the wi-fi code so I can get online and talk to my girl by satellite.

You got to talk to the boss, he says, and points down a faux-rococo corridor leading to a separate bar where the owner of the hotel and a few of his cronies sit around drinking whisky and smoking cigars. Donatello statuary loosely copied in plaster is dotted around the room, da Vinci prints framed on walls, all very sombre, like a scene out of *The Godfather*.

The owner, a tough, corpulent man in his sixties, beckons me over through a pall of smoke with one aggressively twitching crooked finger.

Are you the musician man? he inquires.

Yes sir, I am a musician.

Ah, the musician man! What's your name, maybe I've heard of you?

I tell him and he writes it on a piece of paper, folding it away in his wallet.

You played here in town tonight?

I did.

You did, did you? And where you going tomorrow?

Milano.

Ah, Milano, the big city, he says, searching me with his eyes, weighing me up. You do this all the time? Travel around, playing in nightclubs all over Italy?

All over the world, I reply.

So this is your job? You put on the pretty face, make *la bella figura*? You like our Italian women? Maybe you know a woman in Milano, huh? You got yourself a girlfriend?

Yes I do, sir, I reply. I want to call her right now. Can you give me the wi-fi password?

He waves my question away with a sweep of his cigar, exhaling a thick cloud of smoke. You like our Italian women a lot? he demands, his penetrating stare daring me to slip up in this cat-and-mouse game of empty innuendo.

With much respect, I do appreciate your Italian women, I reply. Now, the password, can I have it?

He holds my gaze for a long silence before writing the password down on a card.

Ospite, he says, you are our guest. *Capisce?*

Downstairs next morning, there's a huge buffet – *cornetto di marmelata, torta di limone, caffè americano, succo di arancia.* Absurdly handsome waiters drift uselessly through the breakfast room. The only guest here, I stare at a flawed fountain of Apollo, examining my psyche for cracks. Three weeks out on the road playing every night is drawing to a close. I've had enough; at the same time, there's another part of me that never wants to stop, not for long.

I pack my bags in the dim morning light, staring out over a saleyard dotted with more faux-Renaissance concrete statues of Roman goddesses and heroes. A life-size statue of Berlusconi glistens among them; he appears to be staring off into some brave vision of the future that only he can see, tabloids tucked under his arm. Modern Italy recycles its own history, each successive incarnation a more distant version of the original until they fade into our sunset era of reproductions.

I'm running late for the album release press conference in Milano's high-street Fnac media store. Leaving Saluzzo the navigator makes an error, sends me back south-west towards Genova and instantly I've lost a couple of hours. I pull over to the side, some kind of Paganini Caprice screeching across the wasteland from the car stereo. The sun slips its cloud cover, beams down upon me like a cosmic searchlight. I strip off and change into a black suit and a white shirt, then trim and shave in the side mirror of the Fiat. Trucks rocket past, trash blows across the fields, I feel the solar rays on my skin and the gravel beneath my feet, my heart beating slow and steady.

Milan's one-way warren of narrow streets draws me into a pedestrian zone. I follow the blinking icon on my mobile screen with anxious glances while cameras track my number plates through the swarms of tourists and shoppers. It occurs to me that I may have already run up a million euro in traffic fines.

In the meeting room everything is clean and bright. I feel rough, like I've just wandered in from the desert with sand in my eyes and blood on the soles of my shoes. Pretty people lounge around in elegantly understated clothing. A radio DJ interviews me in front of a few hundred people in the halogen light of this marketplace of pop culture.

How do you feel about Italy? he says. You have been here many, many times. Some have said you must be part Italian yourself. What do you think of our country and its music?

I look around at the expectant faces, young people, older people, all kinds of different people waiting for an answer.

Italy, I say hesitantly, is to me incredibly inspiring. The time I've spent here changed my life and the way I see the world. This is a country of great extremes and contradictions, and the best and the worst of human beings is on display. There is a sense of classical drama being played out around us, and it seems to me we all have walk-on roles …

I'm strangely free at last, weightless, relieved. I wander down the Via Torino, debriefing, letting the memories wash through my mind on random recall. A purple and gold twilight gleams through reefs of sculpted cloud over the A5 highway for Varese, clouds assume mythical shapes, a flock of birds move as one giant organism, geometrical contortions against a biblical sky.

Italy, a place so devastatingly, indescribably beautiful, is blurring into the night, losing shape, swimming out of focus. I wipe my eyes clear with the back of my sleeve, press down on the accelerator and glance at the cell phone screen, punching in the next destination.

The Storm Breaking | Mali, 2012

An enigmatic space on the map that up until recent days has rarely made global headlines, the landlocked African state of Mali spreads out below us in a Saharan haze. Three of us – producer Chris Eckman, videographer John Bosch and I – are flying in blind to record a new Dirtmusic album with Malian musicians. We've brought no complete songs, just a few pages of notes and fragments and a plan to create something out of whatever comes our way. And we've got backup.

Ben Zabo and Sidibe meet us in the arrivals hall. Ben, a rising star of the Malian music scene, is our main man on this mission. He was assistant engineer when we recorded the *BKO* album here three years ago, and his raging band will be our main musical rhythm section during the first week of sessions.

Sidibe, our driver and wingman, we know from previous visits. Sidibe has spent years as a specialised tour guide to desert towns such as Gao and Ségou; built like a middle-weight boxer, he speaks a little bit of many languages and wears a chunky silver bracelet inscribed with 'Boss'.

Business is not good, he says, there's no work, nobody's been coming here since the beginning of the year, since the troubles began. But it will change, inshallah!

But if the situation does change, it won't be in a hurry. Reports from Timbuktu and elsewhere in the north detail sharia law executions, amputations, rapes, mutilations and murders.

Music, dancing and smoking have been banned, and the Islamic shrines of Timbuktu declared idolatrous, their cultural treasures desecrated and destroyed. Since January, nearly half a million Tuareg civilians have exited Mali for neighbouring states, their homes transformed into strategic bases by Islamist jihadi. The refugees live in tent camps with minimal NGO support. Azawad, the Tuareg name for the self-declared independent state of North Mali, is now the cover for an emerging terrorist base nurtured by al-Qaeda and equipped with heavy weaponry looted from the Libyan civil war. The abyss is wide open.

Outside in the twilight the airport car park is nearly empty and the currency changers and bag handlers and hustlers are noticeable by their absence. A hundred metres away the new airport terminal is frozen in construction, a lean silhouette of girders and concrete against the darkening sky. We load our guitars and bags of electronics into the boot of Sidibe's maroon Mercedes and join the stream of motorbikes and trucks flowing over the Martyr's bridge into the raw humidity and concrete of Bamako city.

We check in to the Tamana, a split-level old colonial compound with a lovely terrace of mudbrick rooms wreathed in magnolia and mosquitoes. We are the only guests. The exotic aroma of the city is keen as ever, but the background buzz of distant motorbikes and street life is strangely low-key, reinforcing the impression of a city holding its breath before an oncoming storm.

Ali, a guy from the Dogon country whom I know from previous visits, greets me. He is dressed in a Disney-bright safari suit, his bald pate perfectly shaved.

How did you know I was here? I ask.

Everybody knows, he beams, welcome back to Mali!

Great to be here, I reply, but what about the troubles? How is the situation here in Bamako, with the fighting in the north?

Ali bares perfect white teeth and starts firing an imaginary Kalashnikov from the hip.

Everything okay, he says, this is my answer to the troubles!

Ali's sidekick joins in the charade, mimes a grenade launcher perched on his shoulder blowing out shells and they both crack up laughing as if they've not a care in the world.

Around us, a soft, spectral light dances on the lush subtropical trees, and jungle vines rustle in the breeze. Unpacking back in my room, I burn down a roll-up and stare at the ceiling fan, getting my bearings; just then I hear the muezzin's distant night call from the mosque. The mournful wail evokes visions of heavily armed desert warriors in four-wheel drives, cruising the streets for hostages and flying the black jihadi flag. A shiver passes through me – we are so vulnerable here. There are still in the order of twenty-five Western hostages out in the desert, people whose names and situations have long since disappeared from the international media. They are kept in reserve as bargaining assets or as human shields for when the counter-jihadi blowback comes.

If it comes … Crashing into jet-lag sleep, for a brief moment I cease to care.

Chris comes down to the terrace for breakfast, his expression tense. Have you heard the news? he asks. Take a look …

We read the grim reports over a painfully slow internet connection: sixteen Islamist preachers shot dead yesterday a couple of hundred miles away at an army roadblock near Ségou, on their way from the north to an Islamist symposium in Bamako.

The atmosphere ratchets up a leap of notches. This kind of massacre could be the tipping point for a terrorist counterstrike here in the capital. Speculating on a Plan B, we browse the outbound flight schedules – a single flight out to Europe every day. But in the event of a martial-law airport closure, we develop a plan to drive south to the Guinean border, paying bribes to cops and customs as we go. Sidibe watches us with faint amusement; he doesn't consider an alternative plan to be really necessary.

Nothing can happen here, he says confidently. They will not dare attack the city because there's no way they could win. Out in the desert, ayeee – he wrings his hands – that was a different situation. The Malian soldiers were from the south, the desert was not their home. The government gave them old rifles to shoot with, but the rifles grew so hot in the desert that the soldiers stripped off and wrapped the rifles in their shirts, not to burn their hands. They couldn't see what they were shooting at, and when they could see, their bullets passed right through the enemy – You can't shoot them, they said, they're phantoms! They don't die! Bambara fighters fear the power of the *diable*! *Gris-gris*, they said, Juju! And they ran. But then, an army patrol was captured, hands tied behind their backs – bang, bang, bang! The terrorists made pictures, put them on the net.

Sidibe cups a hand beneath his chin and splays his fingers, making a code sign – the sign of the beard – and shakes his head, laughs.

Here in Bamako, he explains, the real concern is Islamist sleeper cells, suicide bombers, kamikazes, the enemy within.

Chris and I continue picking through the few news reports available on the web:

> *Iyad Ag Ghaly, ringleader of the rebel Malian Ansar al-Din jihadist insurgency, has just declared war on the infidel in response to the massacre of the clerics. Previously known for exploits in drug-trafficking and hostage abduction and negotiation, more recently for authorising the destruction of Muslim shrines in Timbuktu, Iyad has been cited by those in the know for his apparent collusion with the notorious Algerian secret service.* (AFP/Reuters)

In an extended rant published on the net, Iyad boasts of sweeping away the rest of Mali and victoriously crusading on to take Paris, and then London, New York and the rest of the world to satisfy the one bloodthirsty god whom he claims to serve. Previously, Iyad failed to persuade Mali's religious elite of the merit of his plans.

> *Some 100 Malian religious leaders announced their rejection of the Touareg Islamist group's strategy at a June 18th–20th conference in Kidal attended by Ansar al-Din leader Iyad Ag Ghaly. 'They refused to accept Ansar al-Din's application of Islamic Sharia, such as flogging and torturing people, and have categorically rejected Iyad Ag Ghaly's call for jihad,' Ag Mohamed (a participant in the event) explained. 'Clerics have agreed that many criteria have to be first available before jihad can be declared,' he added.* (Quoted from AllAfrica.com)

Philippe wanders into the courtyard in his dusty dungarees and field cap. A French émigré living in Bamako for nearly a decade and a passionate supporter of Malian music, Phil has been corresponding with us in recent months about life, music and the reality on the ground in Bamako city. Phil was never in any doubt – You guys have got to come! We've got to keep the music and the communications flowing!

The problem, Phil says, is just people. Mali is made up of many different tribes and for years they've lived in peaceful cooperation, until now. The situation can only be resolved through goodwill and dialogue, and the music is a way to bring everyone back together. Make a great record, and send out a message to the world about the tragedy unfolding here and how it could be averted with support from outside.

Samba Touré, formerly guitarist with Ali Farka Touré, and a rising star in his own right, has accompanied Philippe to meet us. Tall and powerfully built, in black jeans and a bright purple shirt, Samba carries himself with a natural sense of authority. He is not optimistic about the situation – his home village, near Timboctou, has already been overrun by the Islamists.

The music, says Samba, is very, very important. Right now that's all we have.

We're talking in an empty Vietnamese restaurant on the desolate Hippodrome tourist strip. Disorientated tropical fish swim in a tank of discoloured glass. Ben and Chris order beer, while I order a bottle of French wine from a lonely shelf behind the cash register. The waiter makes quite a to-do of serving the wine, dusting off the bottle and tying a serviette around its neck in the shape of a bow.

Nobody wants the mercenaries here in Mali except the president of the Côte d'Ivoire, says Ben. This is what the people say. He used the soldiers to get into power and now he wants to send them away so he doesn't have to pay them any longer. But the neighbouring countries won't send the weapons we need without their mercenaries because they don't trust the Malian army after the March coup. That's why nothing is happening, why the beards are running loose all over the north. The guns and bullets the army needs are just sitting down on the docks in Guinea.

In the background, the TV plays a Malian news broadcast – grainy cell-phone footage of Kalashnikov-packing jihadists patrolling the deserted streets of Timbuktu, then footage of Malian army militias training in a barren field, belly-crawling, somersaulting, practising manoeuvres with faux-wooden machine guns. After last week's mutiny, the regular army is still confined to barracks a mile away from where we are drinking soup served by an elderly Vietnamese exile with distant eyes drawing you back down the Ho Chi Minh trail.

Sidibe guns the Mercedes through hot streets, windows open to catch some breeze. We drive past fruit and vegetable markets packed with yams, pineapples, plantains and other unidentifiable fruits; past the Libya Hotel, the national museum and a giant statue of Mao Tse-tung in a large rotunda; past the rampant hippopotamus of civic pride from which the city takes its name; past shacks hammered together from scrap metal and oil-stained wooden planks, occupied by artisans, random machine-parts dealers and rotisseries; past hair salons in kiosks the size of a call box, and street kids selling cigarettes and phone cards and, short of that, anything else they've got – toy Chinese tennis rackets with a gimmick cricket sound, used sets of Scrabble and Monopoly, a toy ball, batteries, cell-phone covers, or just plain begging; past the blind and the old, led by children, palms for alms through the windows of our car – Blind man, a little girl says to me, blind man give something to God, and she gestures at the old man beside her, his blank, glazed eyeballs staring off into the torpid African sky.

Traffic weaves around a sharply dressed girl picking herself up off the ground after a high-speed spill on the back of her boyfriend's motorcycle, neither of them wearing helmets, she smoothing her immaculate hairdo as if nothing really happened. Buses loaded with hard-muscled itinerant workers shoot past, their rusted frames stencilled with faded images of Che Guevara, hammers and sickles, stars of Islam. Near the river, in a field by an overpass, a man in tattered denims vomits on the ground; beneath the concrete flyover, women and children wait patiently for a lift, an assignation, a sign.

A demonstration is exploding at a key roundabout in the city centre. Mobilisation! Now! Sidibe steers away from the shouting and confusion, a taste of what the collapse of the rule of law might entail.

These are the so-called patriots, Sidibe explains, maybe the same people who stormed the palace and beat up the President, the same nationalists who looted Tuareg merchants and sent them packing back to the desert in fear of their lives!

Minutes later, a police patrol pulls us over – the only white faces in circulation – demanding documents. The cops are tense and their agenda opaque but our passports and visas are in order, and with Sidibe's interlocution they soon let us go.

We drive up a broad, red-dirt street flanked by acrid drainage ditches, eventually pulling up at Salif Keïta's Studio Moffou. Barefoot kids run about playing games with bottle tops and stones. *Toubab!* – White man!, they shout at us, *coulibaly!* – everything's okay! We grin and wave as they cluster around in bare feet and thrift-store T-shirts, parting ranks to allow a herd of skinny African cattle passage along Rue 747.

The studio's magnolia-wreathed mudbrick verandah opens onto a small control room with a dusty analogue recording desk. In the tracking room, a fluorescent tube hangs askew beside a painting of a roaring buffalo; several microphone stands lean against another wall beside a vocal booth, beyond which lie two other storage rooms that could be used as isolation booths. With a heart-thumping handshake we are introduced to Abou Cisse, our engineer, young and skinny, black dreads and pale jeans.

Ça va? he asks us, indicating the recording space. Chris and I exchange looks, realising that the space is a little too Spartan and claustrophobic for our project. But Ben can read us and he proposes that Abou show us Salif Keïta's club next door, a night-haunt concert hall with a tiled cement dance floor and a mezzanine balcony panelled in beautiful red wood. The acoustics are excellent. Tracking the sessions as live performances with no headphones and all this space surrounding us would be ideal.

Oui! Ça va bien! we reply. *C'est possible?*

Abou confers with Le Vieux, the studio guardian, and both smile, obviously digging the idea as much as we do.

Oui, c'est très possible!

A boy, trailing a few cousins and little brothers, offers me a tiny shot glass of thick, sweet tea on a painted tray. Just then, flanked by an entourage of immaculately suited minders and assistants, Salif Keïta himself strides through the atrium with a natural authority you can sense even at a distance. He welcomes us to Mali and to the studio – Everything here is open for you, he says in a friendly way, shaking hands before vanishing into the compound.

The music is about to commence.

Ben's band are tuning up. Tall and lean, Jonathon is on electric bass, with a steady smile and keen, intelligent eyes. Jean is on drums, a driving force used to playing for hours at all-night sessions. Kassim comes from a traditional *griot* family and plays balafon, a tuned percussion instrument, something like a marimba or giant wooden xylophone.

The musicians are from the region of Bwatun, half in Mali and half in Burkina Faso. Ben describes the Bwa half-jokingly as the Germans of Mali: industrious, high-minded, beer-drinking and hard-working. And pretty much straight off they connect with the Krautrock tangent in our music – long, monotonic, atmospheric jams will form the basis of our collaboration, giving us space to discover common ground.

John is up on the mezzanine coaxing the lighting desk back to life. After a series of electric shocks and rich American expletives, a revolving discotheque gobo pulses out a looping random colour pattern across the dance floor. In the club's shadowy dark the effect is psychedelic, a play of shifting tones washing over our skins and instruments. Two weather-beaten, early-eighties Peavey solid-state guitar amplifiers hiss behind their improvised sonic baffles. I plug a beat-up Japanese guitar into one of the amps and it sounds distorted, reverberant, knife-edge sharp, with a backwash of atmospheric, solid-state white noise.

Invisible tensions are driving us, and the stress is good for the music. Each recording stems from a simple, spontaneous riff, an electronic pulse seeking that vanishing point where we all sync together and the music makes sense. The songs take time to reveal themselves; everything is a process of discovery. We don't talk much about what we're doing, just allow it to happen.

The band quickly get used to Chris and I changing instruments or experimenting with tablet synths and effects chains while they nail a groove and just sit on it. Ideas slowly form during long, twenty-five-minute takes rising and falling in speed and intensity, occasionally peaking and crystallising as the serpentine rhythms roll on, morphing into new beasts, into the unknown.

Clouds gather across the sun and the sludge in the open drains shimmers in the shifting light. Kids queuing up for free sachets of soap powder turn to point and stare at us; we smile and wave back before older kids usher them away.

In Bamako there are kids everywhere – half of Mali's population is under the age of fifteen. Most girls have babies strapped to their backs while they work, walk and talk. This is a generation of millions of children growing up without formal education, in a country invaded by fundamentalists who want to close down all the schools and lock the girls up at home. There is no infrastructure for these kids, and no money – Mali is one of the poorest countries on the planet. At night they cluster around old TVs placed in the street, craning to look over each other's shoulders at images of a world that doesn't know they exist.

The low-pressure system over Bamako promises rain but the storm is slow to break and the smog and humidity rapidly make the air unbreathable. Driving back from the studio we pass the *grande marché*, the great open-air market in the city centre. Along these streets, every window is broken from the coup riots. A chaos of pedestrians and motorbikes swarm through the slow-moving traffic. Boys scramble blithely in front of the Mercedes as if it isn't even there, Sidibe waving them off the bonnet, Lobi Traoré's high-octane Afro-rock blasting from the car stereo, everybody shouting, hustling, in motion.

Back in my room, a large black spider hangs suspended from the bathroom ceiling. Keeping a wary eye on it, I scrub myself down under the slow, cold trickle from the showerhead. Outside, bats shriek in the trees.

In the middle of the night I wake up with vicious, stabbing stomach pains. The torment is relentless with machete stabs of fierce pain which allow no sleep or rest. Codeine eases me through the small paranoid hours into the hazy morning.

I crawl out from under the mosquito net half-awake, and checking my cell phone realise I'm running late, pull on my jeans and stumble downstairs. Chris, John and Philippe look grim, faces buried in the websites of the BBC and *The New York Times*. The bad news just keeps on coming.

It's the anniversary of 9/11 and the US Embassy in Benghazi, Libya, is ablaze. The US ambassador has been lynched. Simultaneous assaults on other Western embassies in Africa mean this is no coincidence. I skol some coffee, fire up another Dunhill Red and scan the online news. In Paris, cartoons coincidentally published today satirising Wahabi Islam have created an international media furore, while in the USA, an obnoxious video on YouTube caricaturing the Prophet has gone viral.

Across the planet, people are riled and angry, but North Africa is particularly hot. The Benghazi assault is obviously an organised paramilitary mission, heavy weaponry employed to blow holes through security walls. The US ambassador's mutilated corpse is paraded through the streets to the apparent delight of exuberant crowds burning the Stars and Stripes. Philippe recommends I don't watch the gruesome footage on the web.

You don't need it, man, he says. Focus on the music!

It's our last day with Ben's ace rhythm trio. Ben notices the delirious sweat shimmering on my skin and laughs gently.

Mon ami, mon ami, don't you like the food?

Later, Ben and his band are playing in a club out on the city's edge. The audience dance a slow, sexy shuffle that grows in numbers, speed and intensity, eventually becoming a circle embracing the entire courtyard. Ben works the stage like a natural, passing the mic to his wingman, merging his presence with the collective. The music is wild, exuberant and fearless. I plug a guitar in to one of the three amps and follow the D major drone down into the maelstrom of cascading Bwa rhythms. Beers are passed around, guitarists take turns on the lead, drummers swap – it's mayhem. Before it gets too late we leave while everybody's still having fun, driving backstreets to avoid police controls because not all of us are carrying ID papers.

Our third, silent Dirtmusic member, Peter, has just flown in from Germany with a Spanish tan and enough hard currency to keep the project running. Driving from the airport to the studio, we're flagged down by a police control within minutes; Peter has pointed a camera out of the window on a crowded street and the two motorcycle cops are irate.

Where's your licence to film the streets? They demand to know. You need a permit to take photos here. Did you photograph us? Did you make pictures of our faces? Well, did you? Give us your camera, we will destroy your film!

Downtown at the central police station, Peter waits in custody. Chris and I are not allowed in; we sit and bake in the car park, frustrated because the money isn't changing hands fast enough. Opposite us is a simple warning painted in big letters on the car park wall – *Forbidden to piss here, 500 CFR instant fine.*

Several hours pass until an infuriated Sidibe returns to the car with a smiling Peter. It cost twenty thousand to get me out of the interrogation room, he explains, unfazed. Boys, let's get back to work!

We have ten hours of music recorded so far, spread over some thirty-seven recordings. Chris and I are seeking to create a collaborative album or series of albums where we and our friends and guests create the words and music together, drawing on the current crisis for content.

Philippe visits the studio with Aminata Traoré, a high-energy girl wearing bright robes and glittering jewellery. Aminata is flying out to Paris tomorrow to sing at a concert for Peace in Mali along with expatriate Malian stars living in France. We play her a music track just once and she steps up to the microphone and sings in Songhai:

God save us from the current crisis in our country
We do not understand the war
We do not like betrayal
We only know hospitality, brotherhood and sharing
Why do terrorists come and spoil our country?

You cannot destroy our country
God forbid

Then at everyone's insistence Zoumana takes the microphone, the *soku* (one-string violin) slung over his back wrapped up in a dusty cloth. I'm not a singer, he protests, but as the track begins his voice erupts like a force of nature and he improvises these words:

God is a mystery
He has made some people rich and others miserable
He made fatherless children and motherless children
Worshipping God is not easy
And everyone will die in the end …

Next morning I wake up to another power failure at the Tamana – no wi-fi, no internet, no information from the outside world, again.

How you feeling, brother? Chris asks me.

I'm better, I reply. How you doing?

Good, he says, but John isn't feeling great. He wants to stay in his room today, backing up data, so he won't be coming along.

I knock on John's door but he doesn't answer. Sidibe blows the horn from the street. We pile in to the back seat for another long trip through the increasingly nervous city.

Musicians are waiting for us in the atrium of the Moffou wearing long desert robes, their faces shadowed by elaborate white turbans, ngonis and calabash gourds at their feet.

They are the Super 11, living masters of Takamba, a traditional musical form from the Saharan fringe that sounds like a portal into shamanic reality – complex, repetitive beats and drones delivered with shattering, primal intensity. Their manager introduces himself and we run down the details just to be sure everybody's on the same page. But I'm not only the manager, he says busting a move, I dance too!

Yehia, the main man of the band, gestures for me to come closer to him. We need travel money, he says in French, the bus fare is expensive all the way from Gao.

Gao is controlled by the jihadi. Music is banned, as are dancing, smoking and singing. Super 11 had survived there by playing at weddings, harvest festivals and social occasions, but now everything has changed.

How was it, I ask Yehia, crossing the front line in the north?

Very hot, he replies, making the sign of the beard.

And with the instruments?

Yehia gestures hiding the ngoni under his voluminous robes with a wry, knowing grin.

In the desert, everything is negotiable. Stories change, interpretations vary – there are few solid references and decisions are based on abstract reasons and mutable truths.

How are things going there for you in Gao, for your music?

Mauvais, replies Yehia. There is no work, no money. Again, he makes the sign of the beard and says, *Nous ne pouvons pas retourner* – We can't go back.

Hard negotiations follow. Like a shell game, we move the figures around until everybody is satisfied and pride has been respected. At which point the atmosphere suddenly lightens up, palms slap together and we all grin triumphantly, entering the studio to get out of the day's extreme heat.

Super 11 spread a carpet on the studio floor and sit cross-legged with their instruments. The dancing manager assists Yehia to set up his ngoni amplifier, an ancient valve device in a dirty bronze casing that gives the Super 11 their mind-bending distorted ngoni sound. And then they launch into raw Takamba – a combination of ancient rhythmic patterns and arcane melodies that more than anything else resemble mystic mathematics, sacred geometry. Chris and I improvise with them for nearly an hour, wild and frenetic, unheard of …

Suddenly the grid goes down again, plunging the studio into utter darkness.

Merde! Abou cries out. The hard disk crashed, we lost it all!

It's hot inside the studio, searing without, and the fates have shut us down. Super 11 gun a couple of scooters into action and take off in a cloud of dust waving goodbye, two to a bike, robes flapping in the slipstream.

I sit in the street, fire up a Dunhill Red. Girls in brightly coloured robes and processed hair drift by with trays of fruit balanced on their heads, trailed by groups of straggling children. Up on the corner, giant trucks filled with desert sand rumble past, headed for the roadworks and concrete mixers. An elderly imam with a short, groomed beard sways down the Rue 747 draped in white linen, orthodox to a fault and indignant to encounter my white face in his city. I avoid eye contact.

The drive back that evening is another suspension-thumping ride along potholed dirt roads packed with motorbikes and buses and trucks belching ethanol smoke. The fumes are inescapable. Sidibe observes that electric light is nowhere to be seen. Sure enough, entire districts of the city are blacked out.

The grid might be down, but the sky is erupting with sheet lightning. The storm is growing closer.

Down by the Chinese bridge it's time for the Friday sacrifice. Roosters ruffle their feathers in bamboo cages. The shaman draws his knife across a rooster's throat and the blood flows down the muddy bank into the heaving Niger River while the Toyotas and Mercedes thrum across the asphalt. The gods are placated for a little while longer; we will eat yet, and breathe. But first, something has to die.

The whole neighbourhood is dark and still, like the pause before impact. A few drops fall, then suddenly comes the rain in a violent deluge. We drive along the flash-flooded streets before the storm renders them impassable; Sidibe cranes out of the driver's-side window to see something of the road ahead, keeping his hand on the horn to let people know he's coming through.

Water swirls around our ankles as we stop at a chemist to buy some disinfectant salve for the strange rash that came up this morning across John's throat.

I don't know what it is, he says, I don't want to think.

The road back to our *pension* is a streaming river of mud. At the Tamana the power is still out, no electricity and no internet, rain pouring down in sheets. Around midnight, the rain eases; we sit on the terrace, wreathed in mist. An exotic bird, hanging upside down from a bough of the mighty succulent towering overhead, chimes bell-like percussion in the quiet after the storm.

It's no good, says Sidibe, the tourists have to come back. What else am I going to do? There's no money in Bamako – I can't even take a girl out and show her a good time. Is it easy to travel to Australia and live there? How much does it cost?

Without a visa, between ten and fifteen thousand dollars, I reply, but you can't trust the people traffickers. Some people drown in the Indian Ocean before they ever arrive, and even if they do make it across the wild seas they're locked up in detention centres on remote islands and left there for years.

Ayeeee! The world is a dangerous place, says Sidibe.

The warlords are demanding a ransom, Ben remarks, forty billion for northern Mali, but at the same time they've sent envoys to Bamako requesting technical help to run the electricity! And the water! These bastards don't know how to do anything useful. It really makes you laugh, but the people are suffering and that's not funny.

Yes, and a hotline to phone in details about impostor cops has just been created, says Sidibe.

Impostor cops?

There's a warning out for criminals in stolen uniforms carjacking and mugging civilians; and motorcyclists have been warned to be aware of steel wires strung at head height across roads by criminal gangs. You hit that wire fast enough and you're instantly decapitated, whether you're wearing a helmet or not!

The grid fires up and the lights come back on. Bats wheel overhead, clouds of mosquitoes swarm past like schooling fish. Whatever it is that ails me flows through my system in waves of nausea. I haven't eaten for days. I check my pharmacy bag – Nurofen, codeine, malaria pills, antibiotics, rehydration satchels and Xanax – and take a little bit of pretty much everything there. In the distance I can hear drumming from the Hippodrome high street and deep pulsing disco bass from the nearby Starlight Club. The neighbourhood is waking up after the rain.

I lie on the floor of my room watching the roof tremble in the gale. Far away on the other side of the world I hear my girlfriend's voice through a fragile Skype link on my mobile.

Are you alright? she says.

I don't know, I think so. I miss you, doll.

I miss you too, and I'm worried. What's going on there? I saw something on the news – are you safe?

There's a pause on the line and then she says something I can't quite understand, her voice fading in a satellite ocean of clicks, echoes and white noise. I try to call her back but can't get a connection.

Excitement is building for Salif Keïta's Mali Independence Day concert at Club Moffou. Back-up generators thrum behind the dance hall while workmen finish covering the street drainage ditches and technicians do a sound check in the *grande salle*. Salif's band arrive for the rehearsals on motorcycles and in cars, high-fiving and cracking jokes in different languages. Locusts leap and zoom around the atrium while the band slowly fire up some long reggae-style pieces, raw and flawless. Musically, these are giants, some of the best in the country – in the world, for that matter.

Come show time, the audience arrive in taxis and cars and four-wheel drives, glamorous women, handsome men and lots of kids greeting each other with jokes and boisterous enthusiasm. There is both jubilation and anxiety in the air. A girl in a gold glomesh sheath dress, hair sprayed high, is busy helping old people find a seat. A bar is open downstairs, but almost nobody is drinking alcohol.

This Independence Day is charged with meaning. With the

Malian state in crisis, the north overrun, half a million Tuareg refugees, and the war approaching, these people are scared for the future of their country. The excitement of the concert is tempered by a profound anxiety, and when Salif appears and takes the microphone the house stands up and applauds.

Several songs into the first set, his band pumping bass and beats and Salif's mighty voice in full flight backed by two phenomenal female singers, a series of huge electrical glitches rocket through the cables, startling not just the musicians but the audience too. Abou and Le Vieux struggle to solve the technical situation, frantically replugging the patch bay on the big mixing desk high up on the mezzanine. Cables crackle with huge surges of bass frequency, the whole system popping voltage demons and diabolic sparks. Then the stage lights flicker and suddenly the grid goes down again, plunging the *grand salle* into darkest silence.

Salif speaks to the house without a microphone, but in the hush everybody hears him clearly. We all know there are big problems at this time, he says, but we will find a solution with the peace in our hearts. We will never surrender our country, we are proud, and this place is the land of our people.

Everyone applauds.

We will be back, my friends, says Salif, be calm, a few minutes …

The crowd wait out on the street, as the air conditioning has shut down and the hall is humid and warm.

I see Abou streaking past me and shout out to him, *Ça va?*

Pas du problème, he replies and grins, giving me the thumbs up.

On the way home we are stopped at a police control on the Chinese bridge. They suspiciously check our documents and ask a few questions and when we explain that we are musicians they smile and say – Welcome to Mali!

Driving out to the airport for the flight back to Europe, past the dirt roads and ditches and packs of kids, the half-finished shopping malls, the half-abandoned housing developments and industrial complexes, we seem to be witnessing an apocalyptic Western future rather than an old society in transformation. Everything is frozen, derailed, nipped in the bud. It seems like we're getting out just in time, that it's going to blow wide open. The weapons are packed and ready, the soldiers eager to deploy, the financiers calculating their investments.

The struggle is escalating as the globalised world shrinks before our eyes. Every action, every event, has repercussions far and wide. The storm is breaking in Mali, but the rolling thunder can be heard in the distance, no matter where you are.

Acknowledgements

Earlier versions of *The Crystal Blitz*, *Matellico Moods* (originally published as *3 Scenes with Mario Merola*), *Return to the Source*, *Blood and Chocolate* and *The Storm Breaking* were published in *Overland* magazine.

With thanks to Anne Algar (Ruling Energy), M. Del Conte (Breaking the Ice), J. Kempelmann (Valley of the Moon), Chris Eckman (Return to the Source), Corrado Vasquez (Bridge to Nowhere), Peter Weber (Dirtmusic in BKO City) and Federico Sponza (Discography) for their photographs.

Discography

Hugo Race Discography

1982	Plays With Marionettes
1984	Plays With Marionettes
1985	The Wreckery
1986	The Wreckery
1987	The Wreckery
1987	The Wreckery
1987	The Wreckery
1988	The Wreckery
1988	The Wreckery
1989	Hugo Race & The True Spirit
1990	Hugo Race & The True Spirit
1992	Hugo Race & The True Spirit
1993	Hugo Race & The True Spirit
1994	Hugo Race
1996	Hugo Race & The True Spirit
1996	Hugo Race & The True Spirit
1998	Hugo Race & The True Spirit
1999	Hugo Race & The True Spirit
2001	Hugo Race & The True Spirit
2001	Sepiatone
2003	Hugo Race & The True Spirit
2003	Transfargo
2004	Hugo Race & The True Spirit
2004	Hugo Race
2004	Hugo Race & The True Spirit
2005	Sepiatone

Witchen Kopf (7")	Au-Go-Go
Hellbelly (compilation track)	White/Hot
I Think This Town Is Nervous (EP)	White/Hot
Yeh My People (EP)	Rampant
I Think This Town Is Nervous (EP)	Rampant
Here At Pain's Insistence	Rampant
Ruling Energy (EP)	Rampant
The Collection	Rampant
Laying Down Law	Citadel – Normal
Rue Morgue Blues	Rampant – Normal
Earls World	Normal
Second Revelator	Normal
Spiritual Thirst	Normal
Stations of the Cross	Normal/RTS – Flying
Valley of Light	Roadshow –Glitterhouse
Wet Dream	Glitterhouse
Chemical Wedding	Glitterhouse
Last Frontier	Glitterhouse
Long Time Ago	Glitterhouse
In Sepiatone	Milano2000
Goldstreet Sessions	Glitterhouse – Spooky
Mil Transit	RecRec
Ambuscado	Glitterhouse
The Merola Matrix	Desvelos
Live in Monaco	Helixed/Gusstaff
Darksummer	Desvelos

2006	Hugo Race & The True Spirit
2007	Dirtmusic
2008	Hugo Race & The True Spirit
2008	The Wreckery
2008	Rogall & The Electric Circus Sideshow
2008	Dirtmusic
2009	Hugo Race & The True Spirit
2009	Hugo Race
2010	Hugo Race
2010	Lilium
2010	Dirtmusic
2012	Hugo Race
2012	Hugo Race Fatalists
2013	Sepiatone
2013	Dirtmusic
2014	Dirtmusic
2014	Hugo Race Fatalists
2015	Hugo Race & The True Spirit

Taoist Priests	Glitterhouse – Spooky
Dirtmusic	Glitterhouse
53rd State	Glitterhouse – Spooky – Bang!
Past Imperfect	Memorandum
Perfect Toy	
In The Desert	Glitterhouse
Live In Wołów Jail	Helixed/Gusstaff
Between Hemispheres	Gusstaff
Fatalists	Gusstaff – Interbang – Other Tongues
Felt	Glitterhouse
BKO	Glitterhouse
No, But It's True	Rough Velvet – ViceVersa
We Never Had Control	Gusstaff – Interbang
Echoes On	Interbang
Troubles	Glitterbeat
Lion City	Glitterbeat
Orphans (EP)	Rough Velvet
The Spirit	Glitterhouse